D0250038

About the Author

MIKE FREEMAN is an award-winning sportswriter
and the author of *ESPN: The Uncensored History*.
He is married and lives in New Jersey.

MIKE FREEMAN

BLOODY SUNDAYS

INSIDE THE
ROUGH-AND-TUMBLE
WORLD OF THE NFL

Perennial Currents

An Imprint of HarperCollins*Publishers*

To my mother, Alice, the greatest inspiration

To my wife, Kelly, the kindest heart

To George Young ... the Hall of Fame beckons

A hardcover edition of this book was published in 2003 by William Morrow, an imprint of HarperCollins Publishers.

HarperCollins books may be purchased for educational, business, or sales promotional use. For information please write: Special Markets Department, HarperCollins Publishers Inc., 10 East 53rd Street, New York, NY 10022.

FIRST PERENNIAL CURRENTS EDITION PUBLISHED 2004.

Designed by Jeffrey Pennington

The Library of Congress has catalogued the hardcover edition as follows:

Freeman, Michael.
    Bloody Sundays : inside the dazzling, rough-and-tumble world of the NFL / by Mike Freeman.— 1st ed.
        p.   cm.
    ISBN 0-06-008919-9
        1. National Football League.   2. Football—United States.
    I. Title.

GV955.5.N35F74 2003
796.332'64—dc21

2003053951

ISBN 0-06-073931-2 (pbk.)

04 05 06 07 08 ❖/RRD 10 9 8 7 6 5 4 3 2 1

CONTENTS

Introduction

CONDOLEEZZA'S STORY

A snapshot. America's terror war rages on, which explains the agitation around the sunny West Wing office of Condoleezza Rice, President George W. Bush's national security adviser. Aides scurry in and out of the room, creating a frenzied buzz. When her office finally empties, Rice welcomes me with a pleasant smile and firm handshake and expresses relief that, at least for a few minutes this afternoon, she will not be asked to discuss the latest world crisis or suicide bombing. No, Rice is going to talk football.

Rice is a former Stanford University provost and political scientist. She is one of the president's most trusted advisers. If she were to leave government service tomorrow, she would easily command a seven-figure job at a top think tank. She could go to Wall Street. She could go into law. Hell, she would make a pretty good president herself.

Once the football chat begins, however, it is clear she has few such aspirations. Rice is asked about her future, and her answer would raise a few eyebrows. Her dream job is on Park Avenue in New York, as commissioner of the National Football League. She is totally serious. "That's absolutely right," she says, "though not immediately, and not before Paul Tagliabue is ready to step down. I want to say that for the record. I think it would be a very interesting job because I actually think football, with all due respect to baseball, is a kind of national pastime that brings people together across social lines, across racial lines. And I think it's an important American institution."

Rice is not the only person in the U.S. government who appreciates the importance of football and what it means to millions of people. Knowing that a World Trade Center–like terrorist attack on an NFL stadium filled with 70,000 fans would be devastating, in terms of both the potential loss of human life and the damage it would cause to the American psyche, the military was ordered to take unprecedented security steps after the September 11, 2001 attack. Some of these maneuvers never became known to the public, but Lieutenant Colonel William E. Glover, head of the Air Warning Center at the Air Force's Cheyenne Mountain Operations Center, says that the military put up combat air patrols over every NFL game during the 2001 season. Glover explains that F-15 and F-16 fighter jets would monitor the airspace around the stadium during the national anthem, stay for a short while, and then fly on to the next stadium. Since the aircraft can fly at two times the speed of sound, or around 1,500 mph, and cover large distances, groups of stadiums—for example, Washington, Philadelphia, and New York—could be covered by one swift patrol in a matter of minutes.

Now *that* is a prevent defense, one that may even have been ordered by the national security adviser herself.

Rice does not, of course, fit the stereotype of a pro football fan. She speaks four languages, plays piano so superbly that she once hung with Yo-Yo Ma to perform a Brahms duet, was a professional-caliber figure skater, and has written three books, including one on German unification. She is also a woman. While the NFL estimates that an increasing number of its fans, some 20 to 30 percent, are women, the sport remains mostly the territory of men, an arena for a sort of crude bonding, complete with tests of manhood and rituals that border on the grotesque. How many women attend a New York Jets game shirtless in 20-degree weather, beer guts flapping in the January wind, yelling that the Miami Dolphins suck, while simultaneously spitting beer on fans five rows down?

No, Rice does not fit neatly into any of the football-addict categories, yet her passion for the sport, her love of it, is as powerful as any-one's, man or woman. When we meet at the White House, Rice is moni-toring the latest series of violent outbursts in the Israeli-Palestinian conflict. But as we continue to speak, it becomes clear that between secu-rity briefings she sneaks away to check television or Internet reports on the latest NFL gossip. Rice regularly watches the ESPN television net-work's *NFL Countdown,* a testosterone-suffused Sunday pregame foot-ball feast that is two hours long—only hard-core fans need apply. I have covered the sport for a living, and even I can't watch that much analysis. Rice eats it up. How much of a football-head is she? Rice will tape a game and, despite knowing the final score, watch the entire contest upon arriving home from meetings or overseas trips. "I would have written several more books if it had not been for the NFL," she says, only half-joking.

Rice's passion for football stems from her study of the history of warfare. She is attracted to two fundamental similarities between foot-ball and combat: the use of strategy and the goal of taking territory. "I really consider myself a student of the game," she says. "I find the strat-egy and tactics absolutely fascinating. I find the evolution of the game really interesting—again, as it relates to military history. Military his-tory has swung back and forth between advantage to the offense and advantage to the defense. When the offense has the advantage, then a new technology will come along that will temporarily give the defense the advantage, and vice versa. Football has that kind of pattern too."

Though the pure, naked violence of the sport is what attracts most to football, the strategies coaches employ to thwart or trick the opposing team are a close second. It is why head coaches like Bill Walsh and Joe Gibbs, already in the Hall of Fame, and others like Bill Belichick, on his way there, or Super Bowl champion Jon Gruden almost become cult heroes, some as popular as movie stars. They are seen as geniuses by fans and the news media, as innovators in their football kingdom, devising schemes and tactics that outwit and outplay. Head coaches are raking in franchise cash because owners recognize their importance; their salaries are approaching the stratospheric levels, closing in on the $7 million or more a year salaries of star players.

The capitalistic sport of professional football has become a reflection of America in all its glory and foibles: it's bloodthirsty and profit-driven, it's egalitarian and discriminatory, it's scandalous and heroic. But above all, the NFL is the country's supreme entertainment. Daily sports pages can't tell the full story of the nation's ultimate franchise, the NFL. This book slips inside the sport to reveal the NFL's underground societies, the ravaged health of players, the unheralded talent, the thug life, the true leaders, and the possible future. That Condoleezza Rice—an educated, Republican, multitalented black woman—thrives inside the widening circle of American football fans is a testament to how far the sport has evolved. But despite her knowledge of football and her intense passion for it, Rice says men often underestimate what she knows because she is a woman.

As the Stanford provost, Rice oversaw the university's athletic budget and was ultimately responsible for hiring the football coach. Some of the candidates she interviewed were surprised by her football knowledge. "We'd go through the interview process," she said, "and inevitably I would ask some question of a coach, say, who came from an option team. 'You're not going to be able to run the option at Stanford. We don't have enough bodies to give up to run the option. What do you plan to do?' It always surprised people."

Her father, John, who was a high school football coach in Birmingham, Alabama, where the family lived, introduced Rice to football. "I was supposed to be his all-American linebacker," says Rice, who is an only child. "He had already bought the football, so when I was born a girl, he decided he had to teach me about football instead."

Rice's desire to become NFL commissioner is sincere, and she would be an excellent candidate. But would a group of mostly extremely conservative NFL owners elect a woman as commissioner? The NFL has struggled to hire black coaches; would it put a black woman at its most visible and important position?

If it did happen, Rice would discover that getting owners to agree on anything might be more difficult than achieving world peace. To the latter point she says confidently, "Listen, I've been the provost of a university, and I have the job of coordinating the U.S. government. I think I would be okay."

Paul Tagliabue, the current commissioner, has heard of Rice's desires. One day he sent her a football with the inscription: "To a true Pro Bowl player, be careful what you wish for."

II

A snapshot. Head south on Route 235, past the Midwest's vast bean and corn fields, past the American flags flapping on front porches and the tractors parked beside farmhouses, and eventually you'll hit the football capital of the world: Ada, Ohio. When Daniel Riegle, the plant manager of the Wilson Football Factory here in Ada, about an hourlong trip from Toledo, drives from his nearby home to the office, he doesn't hit one traffic light.

Ada is such a sleepy town it snores. The last exciting jolt to hit here happened back in 1978 when the city put in a new sewer line. How's that little tidbit to get the coffee shop gossip machine going?

A quiet town, yes. An irrelevant one? Far from it. Ada is the NFL. By extension, it is America.

The sport of football, with its labor harmony and television appeal, has replaced the mismanaged game of baseball as the national pastime, but the instrument that makes football go—the actual football itself—is increasingly made outside of America. That's right. A number of the footballs used by high schools and colleges have accents. What's next? Apple pie baked in Mexico?

Over half of all footballs made are foreign footballs, except the NFL's footballs, which are made at this Wilson factory in Ada, population 4,500, not China, population 1 billion. Every ball used by the NFL on game day is made here. About 130 workers, stitching, pushing, and sweating from 5:00 A.M. to 3:30 P.M., Monday through Thursday, produce 200,000 NFL footballs a year. Constructing the footballs is as intricate as stitching a quilt: it requires fifty steps and eight hours to produce one NFL ball. And there is no automated system. No whirring of soulless machines doing all the work. The footballs are handmade by people named Peggy, Charlie, and Aunt Maudie, and the workers hold titles like lacer and bladder-inserter. It has been this way for six decades. The factory's track record is impeccable: no NFL football made here has ever deflated during a game.

The process of making a ball that can withstand the pressure of a collapsing 350-pound lineman is complicated. The first thing you learn is that footballs have a bad rap. They're called "pigskins" for a reason no one really knows, but are actually made from cowhide. "Footballs have never been made from pigs," says Riegle. "You just can't throw a good spiral with a pig."

That's good for the pigs but bad for the cows. A 23-square-foot hide produces only about a dozen balls, with Wilson paying some $5 per square feet for the material.

The saying here is that a football comes in quarters, like the game itself. One of the initial processes in the making of a ball is the pattern. The outline of a football is pressed into the hide, and then logos are steamed on, using 500 degrees of heat.

An NFL football must weigh between 14 and 15 ounces, so the next step is weighing it. If the ball is too heavy, pieces of the leather are delicately shaved off until it meets professional standards. Then comes the insertion of a three-ply cloth lining. That gives the football its shape. Stripes are added next, and the sections are put together like Frankenstein's bum, using 140 stitches. Still, even as it takes shape, the football does not look like a football until it is flipped from inside out to outside out, a process called turning. While many of the stitchers and lacers are women, their hands taped, battling with large sewing machines and lengthy needles that resemble torture devices, turners are usually men, as it takes a great deal of strength to muscle the football into its proper form. The hands of a turner are cracked and coarse, as if they wrestle alligators for a living.

After bladders are inserted into the footballs, teams of inspectors poke and prod for defects like discoloration or wimpy inflation.

The plant has an old-school feel to it. Walk into Ada, walk onto the football processing floor, and it is like stepping back in time, decades ago, before the Internet and stock options, when production was simply craftsmen and their tools, except instead of cranking out Chryslers, they make footballs. They make dreams.

Many of the workers are die-hard NFL fans and feel no shame in admitting that on occasion they get emotional when seeing one of their footballs getting tossed around by the pros. "You can't help but say,

'They're playing because of our hard work,' " says Riegle. "I've actually seen workers while watching a game on Sunday point to the TV and say, 'Hey, there's my ball!' "

II

A snapshot. He has run this hill for over five years now, in the NFL off-season, usually twice a week, and actually, calling it a hill does not do it justice. Calling it a hill is like saying Michael Jackson is a trifle strange. The hill is more like the side of a mountain. When he first trotted up this slab of steep, winding rock and forest, he vomited twice before making it halfway through the three-mile trek. On his third run he slipped on some rocks, tumbled backwards like a bundle of clothes in a dryer, and came close to banging his head on a dagger of granite.

He always runs it alone, except for this one, humid day, and upon getting to the top, where the view of the green terrain below is almost worth the pain of getting up that high, he discusses his tumultuous life as a closeted gay man in the hyper-macho world of professional football.

"Steven Thompson"—he declines to use his real name for fear of being ostracized by his football peers—is the first active NFL player to admit and discuss being gay. No one close to him knows of his sexual orientation. Not his position coach, whom Thompson says calls soft players "faggots." Not his teammates, a small group of whom, thinking another player on the team was homosexual, gave him a nickname behind his back—GB, for "gay boy." Not even the women Thompson has dated, doing so for appearance's sake, so no one will realize the truth. "I would hate myself after each of those dates," he says, "because I was being a complete phony."

Thompson spends a lot of time in that world of self-hate. He claims that hiding the truth has taken a physical and mental toll, sending him to twice-monthly therapy sessions (he does not use the team's psychologist for fear of word leaking to management) and causing health problems, like severe bouts of insomnia. Thompson says that on occasion he has taken antidepressant medication.

Sometimes, when Thompson has reached the summit of this hill, standing there, taking it all in, he grows angry. Often his next thought is of calling a press conference so he could announce to the team and to fans that he is gay. This is the 21st century, he says to himself. Isn't football ready for somebody like me? Several times he has gathered the courage to go forward with his plan. On those days Thompson marched down the mountain after his workout, returned home, stomped into his living room, picked up the telephone, and started dialing the team's head coach, rehearsing how he would deliver the news, only to hang up before he even finished punching in the area code, the bravado suddenly seeping out of his body. The ugliness he has heard, the gay-bashing he claims has become commonplace in football, would roll before his eyes like he was watching a movie. This fantasy of telling the truth publicly, only to rethink, and then reject, the idea, has played itself out on this hill, over and over, for years and years.

"In our sport you don't make jokes about black people in the locker room because so many players are black," he says. "You don't really make a lot of jokes about women because now there are a lot of women reporters and if one overhears some sexist shit, it's trouble. But berating the shit out of gay people is okay in football. Some players and coaches use it as a sort of rallying cry. 'Don't act like a bunch of fags! Play hard!' "

Dave Kopay played running back in the NFL from 1964 to 1972 and declared he was gay following his career. He heard similar language many times as a player for five different teams. "People use the f-word [fag] like you're some subhuman, not capable of anything," he has been quoted as saying. "We're terrified of the stereotype of being silly, ineffectual people. Well, you try to pick up a blitz by Dick Butkus. He certainly didn't know who I was sleeping with."

Thompson has become resigned to this fact: he will never come out while still playing and risk losing everything—the handsome paychecks, the fun, the fans—so in his mind he has sold out. Thompson says he has become comfortable with this unflattering assessment of himself, though surely reconciling pride with that set of ugly facts is partly what causes the sleeplessness and bouts of depression, or so his therapist informs him.

But if he cannot make the admission in front of a pack of hungry cameras and flapping notepads and inquisitive eyes, Thompson figures he has done the next best thing. He will talk about being a gay player for this book while protected by a cloak of anonymity.

Thompson makes claims, lots of claims, about gay life and the NFL. Some come off as dead-on, some seem thoroughly unrealistic, while others carry the taint of bitterness. Two of these claims are indeed striking. First, Thompson maintains there is a large number of gay and bisexual NFL players, numbering between 100 and 200, some of whom know each other as gay, and some of whom even have relationships with each other.

Those numbers seem thoroughly unrealistic. He maintains that my skepticism is rooted in the fact that most heterosexuals instinctively do not think there is a significant gay population, especially in sports. Actually, my disbelief is based on pure, uncorrupted, journalistic arrogance. As someone who has written about the NFL extensively for more than fifteen years, covering five different football beats for four newspapers, my belief is that I would have heard of the subculture Thompson describes, especially if it were composed of hundreds of players. Until I met Thompson, I had not. And if Thompson's figures are accurate, that means, of the approximately 1,700 players in the NFL, 5 to 10 percent of them are gay. That number, to me, seems too high. (During an initial interview Thompson had claimed there were two to three dozen gays in football, but he later increased those figures to at least 100, he said, because, upon further reflection, he thought he had seriously underestimated the numbers.)

Debates are raging about the percentage of the general American population that is homosexual, with the Kinsey Report pointing to 10 percent, and the Family Research Institute estimating closer to 3 to 5 percent. Even using the lowest estimates, there are probably one or two gay players on each team.

It is remotely possible that hundreds of players could be leading Thompson's cloak-and-dagger lifestyle and going to extremes to hide their true sexuality, but word of gay liaisons between dozens of these men likely would have leaked out to some news organization, even if it was a raunchy tabloid such as the *National Enquirer*. Yet in the eight-decade history of the NFL, only four players who made regular-season rosters—Roy Simmons, a former New York Giants and Redskins guard; Kopay; just recently Esera Tuaolo, who played on five NFL teams and retired after the 1999 season and came out in 2002; and now Thompson—have freely volunteered their sexual proclivity for men. Simmons admitted he was gay during a 1992 television appearance on *The Phil Donahue Show* following his retirement from the sport. Kopay did it, also after he retired, in a 1975 interview with the now-defunct *Washington Star* and in a book published in 1977. Tuaolo acknowledged he was gay also after his playing career concluded, and Thompson has discussed the topic with me while under a pseudonym. Are the small numbers of NFL players who have come out a result of how taboo it is to discuss being a gay man in football—"definite career suicide" is how Thompson describes it—or are the numbers simply much smaller than people like Thompson believe? I feel it is a combination of both. If the numbers were truly in the hundreds, then certainly there would be more than four brave men like Kopay, Simmons, Tuaolo, and Thompson to come forward.

Yet while I dispute Thompson's statistics, in reporting for this book as well as while spending almost a year verifying aspects of his story, I visited gay bars and clubs across the country and attended several gay house parties. Indeed, at several of these gatherings I did see groups of two or three NFL players I instantly recognized. (I will not identify them.) I was admittedly, I am embarrassed to say, somewhat shocked, since I did not expect to see even one gay NFL player in the course of my research. (That must be the heterosexual bias Thompson describes, flaring like a sunspot.)

There is also precedent for the culture Thompson talks of. Two of Kopay's Redskins teammates, Pro Bowl tight end Jerry Smith and fullback Ray McDonald, were both gay. Kopay claims that he and Smith were lovers. McDonald, a first-round Redskins draft choice out of the University of Idaho, was arrested in 1968 for having sex with another man in a public park. He was later released from the team.

So, in the late 1960s, there were three gay men on one team. Would it not be reasonable to assume, Thompson says when told this information, that other teams had more than one or two gay players? And would it not be reasonable to believe, he says, that the same scenario would exist today? Maybe. And without question I am no longer so supercilious in my assumption that it is impossible that there could be hundreds of gay NFL players; still, I remain firm in my conviction that those numbers are exaggerated. Thompson maintains that by his speaking about the so-called hidden culture for this book it has indeed leaked out. Around and around we go.

Thompson says he has had a sexual relationship with one NFL player and, despite his passion for secrecy, has partied in gay bars and attended gay house parties. I tell him I find this to be a strange contradiction. Doesn't he worry about his secret becoming public? His responses make sense, and he rattles them off quickly and forcefully: he is not a superstar player whom most non-NFL fans would recognize; he limits his chance of exposure by not going to gay bars or parties in the NFL town in which he plays; and the gay players he knows would never reveal his identity publicly because they might risk Thompson exposing them. That last point, Thompson says, is akin to nuclear détente: any player who would dare name names would himself be identified and kamikaze his own career.

Thompson's second claim is that one of his close friends, a bisexual NFL player, left football because two years ago he discovered he was infected with the HIV virus. Thompson claims that the man said he caught the virus after dozens of sexual encounters with both men—several of whom were in the NFL, Thompson claims the player told him—and women. Thompson would not give the name of the player.

This claim rings true; for some time now NFL officials have worried privately about the promiscuity of their athletes. Officials have focused on convincing players that having large numbers of children out of wedlock can be harmful to the kids and ruin a player's finances. The NFL continues to warn players that promiscuity can lead to sexually transmitted diseases, including HIV. This is the NFL's next big battleground, according to therapists, team doctors, and trainers in the sport, because it is only a matter of time before an NFL player is forced to leave the game because he has contracted the deadly virus, just as former

Los Angeles Lakers star Magic Johnson was forced out of basketball more than a decade ago. If Thompson is to be believed, this scenario has already happened.

Indeed, Smith, the player with whom Kopay claims to have had a liaison thirty years ago, died of AIDS without fanfare in 1987.

"I believe one of the biggest challenges in the NFL is the multiple paternity situations," says Kevin Elko, a sports psychologist who has worked with NFL teams. "But football players and HIV is a potential problem as well. I'm surprised, with all of the young men in the NFL, there have not been more cases." Then Elko admits: "Actually, few people would know if someone was HIV-positive in the NFL. It would be kept very private."

Thompson cites what he calls the "backwardness of professional sports when it comes to gays" as a compelling reason for not coming out. Such a notion comes off as a weak excuse, he is told. His response is always—always—you do not know what it is like. He speaks it in the same tone a black person uses with a white one when the subject of racism comes up—you just wouldn't understand. Then Thompson recites the litany of ugliness by football types regarding gay people, doing so like a prosecutor making an opening statement to the court. Here is the time I stopped a group of college teammates from beating up two men holding hands while walking in public, here is when one of my pro teammates said he would rather commit suicide than be gay. Oh, and this exhibit is a beauty, he says, bolstering his claim that professional sports is not okay with gay, as he likes to rhyme, and that is the odd case of baseball player Mike Piazza.

In New York gossip about sports figures is as commonplace as a good slice of pepperoni pizza. Yet what happened to Piazza in May 2002 after an item showed up on the gossip pages of the *New York Post* resulted in one of the all-time bizarre moments in sports history.

It began with what the *Post* referred to as "a persistent rumor around town" about a gay star player for the Mets. The article did everything but name Piazza, and thus the All-Star catcher for the New York Mets felt compelled, just minutes before one of his games, to hold an impromptu news conference on the field to discuss his sexuality.

"The rumor's been brought to my attention," said Piazza. "First off,

I'm not gay. I'm heterosexual. That's pretty much it. That's pretty much all I can say. I don't see the need to address the issue further."

"I can't control what people think," he said. "That's obvious. And I can't convince people what to think. I can only say what I know and what the truth is, and that is, I'm heterosexual and I date women. That's it. End of story."

Piazza had done something no male professional athlete had ever done before. He made a public statement that he liked women. It was such a disturbing and strange scene that both tabloid New York newspapers led with the story on their respective front pages, despite news that on that same day federal law enforcement officials warned of possible terrorist plots to blow up the Brooklyn Bridge and the Statue of Liberty. Talk about not letting the terrorists win. The threat of gayness breaking out in baseball had knocked Osama bin Laden and his band of thugs off the front pages in a city still reeling from the destruction of the World Trade Center.

Piazza's manager, Bobby Valentine, says baseball is ready for an openly gay player, but Piazza's absurd announcement, and the subsequent fallout, proves to Thompson that it is not. Thompson is not alone. Says Philadelphia Phillies manager Larry Bowa, when asked if a gay baseball player could come out of the closet without serious repercussions: "If it was me, I'd probably wait until my career was over."

In football, calling a player gay is far worse than calling him weak or even gutless. Indeed, for an NFL player, there is no worse insult. That is why in 1999, with speculation swirling that Pittsburgh Steelers quarterback Kordell Stewart was gay, he called a players-only meeting to refute the rumors. Stewart ended his two-minute speech, according to two players who were present, by saying, "Remember, it's Adam and Eve, not Adam and Steve."

The rumors with Stewart became so prominent among opponents and fans—and not just in Pittsburgh but across the NFL landscape—that Stewart was verbally accosted during several games by a small number of opposing players attempting to use the issue, or non-issue actually, to rattle Stewart, according to current and former Pittsburgh players. One Steelers offensive player recalls a disturbing incident in a game during the 1999 season. He says that after an opposing linebacker had tackled Stewart, the defender told the quarterback, "Hey, Kordell, did you suck dick last night?" The Steelers offensive player, on the next play and out of sight of officials, said he punched the linebacker in the ribs as retaliation for the remark to Stewart.

During the August 1997 training camp practice of the Washington Redskins, running back Stephen Davis made a series of remarks to teammate Michael Westbrook insinuating that Westbrook was gay. Davis concluded his diatribe by stating that everyone on the team knew Westbrook "liked dudes." Westbrook was so angry about being called gay that he waited until Davis had his guard down and then sucker punched him, knocking him to the ground, and though Davis simply lay there, almost unconscious, Westbrook continued to pummel him, giving him a savage beating. Westbrook was fined $50,000 by the team, and Davis's face was so badly battered he was forced to miss the team's season-opening game.

How tough can it be for a gay athlete? Ed Gallagher, an offensive lineman for the University of Pittsburgh from 1977 to 1979, jumped from a dam twelve days after his first sexual encounter with another man. He survived but was left a paraplegic. Gallagher says that before his suicide attempt he had become unable to reconcile his image of himself as an athlete with gay urges. He admits that the incident forced him to come to grips with his sexuality: "I was more emotionally paralyzed then than I am physically now."

Michael Strahan, the veteran defensive end for the football Giants, explains, "It would be hard, if not impossible, for an openly gay man to exist in football. I personally could care less. I can't tell anyone how to live his or her life. I think there are a small number of people in our game who feel the way I do. A very small number. If a gay man came out, he would be ostracized. Few guys on the team would speak to him because they would be afraid they would be called gay just by associating with him, and the head coach would look for the first excuse to cut him."

There are heterosexual NFL players like Strahan—smart, open-minded, and generous—who would accept an openly gay player. In all likelihood, however, the vast majority would not. Strahan also raises another interesting point. The reaction the gay player received from team personnel and fans would depend on which NFL city, and thus geographic locale, he lived in. "I'm in New York, so I'm around all different kinds of people and lifestyles and cultures," Strahan says. "So I think there would be other guys on my team and on the Jets or in cities like San Francisco and Oakland that are also exposed to the same thing I am, that would be fine with it. But a gay player on the Tennessee team? A gay player trying to exist in Philly or Dallas? I just couldn't see that."

But would an NFL player in a city like San Francisco, which has a large homosexual population, be okay with a gay teammate? Not if you believe 49ers running back Garrison Hearst. Hearst was asked for his stance on gay football players in an October 2002 interview with the *Fresno Bee*, and his response proves Thompson's point.

"Aww, hell no! I don't want any faggots on my team," said Hearst. "I know this might not be what people want to hear, but that's a punk. I don't want any faggots in this locker room." Hearst later apologized for his remarks, but only after they had created a national firestorm.

Thompson, like Strahan and others, says an openly gay football player would have a much more difficult time in his sport than in baseball or any other sport. That is because football has more of a militaristic approach. Players are asked to conform for the greater mission, and though NFL players are increasingly becoming more independent and willing to break from various rigid football traditions, they are still supposed to be tough, even brutal—two qualities that are stereotypically not associated with being gay.

"It's that and more," Thompson explains. "Say I came out tomorrow. One of the first things that would happen is there would be Christian teammates who will say I am evil and going to hell. They would not want to play with me." Before you say that is nonsensical hyperbole, consider this. I have had conversations with a half-dozen NFL players of strong religious conviction who have said as much. In fact, the former Philadelphia and Green Bay Pro Bowl defensive lineman Reggie White is on record as saying that being gay goes against the wishes of God and he would not have played with a gay teammate.

Thompson continues: "There are going to be immature players who will be wondering if I am going to watch them in the showers. The head coach will be annoyed with me because I would be a distraction, and coaches hate distractions. There would be the fans yelling, 'Faggot,' at me. Some of the sponsors I have would drop me. It would be all of these things."

The fear of a gay player showering with heterosexual ones exacerbates the ugly stereotype that gays are predators. Tight end Jeremy Shockey, Strahan's Giants teammate, made several comments in 2002 that showed just how ignorant some people can be when it comes to gays, and why people like Thompson stay securely closeted. When asked on the Howard Stern radio show if he thought there were any gays in the NFL, Shockey responded, "I don't like to think about that. I hope not." Then, when asked if he had any gay teammates in college, Shockey, not exactly the smartest pup in the litter, replied, "No. I mean, if I knew there was a gay guy on my college football team, I probably wouldn't, you know, stand for it. You know, I think, you know, they're going to be in the shower with us and stuff, so I don't think that's gonna work. That's not gonna work, you know?" Shockey later apologized and said his comments were said in jest, but after listening to the interview, I didn't think he sounded like he was kidding. Former Packers wide receiver Sterling Sharpe says Tuaolo, who was a teammate, would have been seriously injured by his Packers teammates if he had come out while still playing.

Football is America, macho America, and being gay in the NFL may be seen as being un-American. Perhaps Thompson and Condoleezza Rice are part of that idealized world that Ada, Ohio, exemplifies. Perhaps they can be integrated into the gangsta-infested, zealot-coached world of the NFL. But this is the league the NFL has become, not just red, white and blue, but perhaps more colorful. More like a rainbow.

Thompson's emotions regarding his predicament alternate between agitation, confusion, and anger, and there are moments when he seems to experience all of those feelings at once, but like many coaches and players in the sport, as well as people around it, he has a passionate love and respect for football despite its flaws. He dedicates his life to it, working out and studying year-round. His mostly positive feelings toward the NFL, despite its feelings toward him, are not inspired solely by the money he earns, though he admits that is some of it. No, it has more to do with the emotional quiver Thompson gets in his stomach before every game. He describes it as the kind of giddiness he felt playing catch with his father as a child, a rite of passage many young American men have gone through for decades.

He envisions a life in the sport beyond his playing days, and that is another reason why he will stay closeted, he says, not just for the extent of his playing career, but probably forever, or at least until it is clear that not only his NFL playing but his hypothetical coaching and executive careers are over. "First, my sexuality is no one's business," Thompson says. "Second, I want to coach one day. Then I want to move into the front office of a team and become a personnel director or general manager. I might even want to work in the league office in New York. If I announced I was gay, I would never be able to do any of those things. The doors would shut in my face."

||

Snapshots of three completely different universes. There is the gifted former educator and possibly the most powerful woman in the world. There is the blue-collar collection of Midwest football manufacturers who feel an intense pride in the product they make for the sport they adore. And there is the player grappling with his gay identity amid his life in football.

The unifying chord between them is the NFL. The sport has that effect, sucking in hundreds of millions of fans from all walks of life who are drawn by the strategy of the game, the athleticism of its players, and, in many cases, the raw, angry aggression on the field. Comedian George Carlin deduced years ago that football is perfect for today's voyeuristic and violent American society. "Baseball is a 19th-century pastoral game," Carlin joked in one of his famous stand-up routines.

> *Football is a 20th-century technological struggle. In football you wear a helmet. In baseball you wear a cap. Baseball has the seventh-inning stretch. Football has the two-minute warning. In football the object is for the quarterback, also known as the field general, to be on target with his aerial assault, riddling the defense by hitting his receivers with deadly accurate*

missiles in spite of the blitz, even if he has to use a shotgun. With short bullet passes and long bombs, he marches his troops into enemy territory, balancing this aerial assault with a sustained ground attack that punches holes in the forward wall of the enemy.

"In baseball," Carlin finished, "the object is to go home. And be safe."

Or as director Oliver Stone told me when I once interviewed him about his movie *Any Given Sunday*, which paid homage to NFL players as gladiators, "You watch football for the potential of *gross* violence."

This book, more than anything, is an appreciation of the NFL and its players, a sport that has eclipsed—easily—the stumbling, mumbling, bumbling game of baseball as America's national distraction. What I have tried to do is present a portrait of the NFL that goes beyond day-to-day newspaper journalism and ESPN highlights and present it in its most complete form.

While many sports have continued to struggle for ratings and fans, and American companies have ridden the stock market like surfers dodging sharks, with Enronic scandals leading the nightly news, the NFL enjoys steady prosperity, not by producing computers or cars or long-distance telephone service, but by manufacturing and marketing real, rules-oriented aggression. Football allows intense and casual fans alike an escape from an even more violent world in which wars, terrorist acts, dirty bombs, and smallpox threats seem to produce hourly scares. One of many indications of the health of the sport came in December 2002 when DirecTV forked over $400 million per year over five years for the rights to broadcast NFL games, a 210 percent increase over its previous deal with the NFL.

The NFL hits the trifecta when it comes to American cravings. The game has more action than a Tom Clancy novel, thanks to the athletic prowess of players like Green Bay quarterback Brett Favre and linebacker Ray Lewis; it possesses dramatic flair with its salary-cap-induced, competitively balanced bloodline; and the NFL is, by far, better run than many major corporations. This feat is accomplished, in part, because of the leadership of a brilliant, action-oriented commissioner who values common sense over politics; owners who, for the most part, put aside their personal animosities and self-interests to legislate rules for the overall good of the game; and a street-wise union boss. Lastly, the sport is armed with a public relations shield that fiercely guards the image of the sport, crushing any foe—especially some of those prickly members of the fourth estate (nicknamed "Communists" by Hall of Fame–coach-to-be Bill Parcells)—seeking to tarnish its highly polished gloss. Oppose the NFL and you can expect an intense bombing campaign in return.

The NFL is not perfect, of course. Though the league has strengthened its rules in recent years when it comes to punishing players who commit violent crimes, especially against women, teams are still too eager to forgive such trespasses, in particular those committed by a player with ability. A sport that prides itself on always trying to do the right thing—and many times it does—needs to have a no-tolerance policy when it comes to violent criminal acts. If a player is convicted of serious assault, the NFL needs to ensure that more stringent repercussions are in place.

The NFL's lack of black head coaches in a league where six out of every ten players is African American is an utter disgrace. Since 1920, the league has hired more than 400 head coaches, and as of the end of 2002, seven of them, or some 1.7 percent, have been black. Former commissioner Pete Rozelle once said that "choosing a head coach is like choosing a wife. It's a very personal thing." One of the problems has been that the head coach selection process often begins and ends with the level of ease an owner and general manager have with a coaching candidate, and frankly, in my opinion, *some* of the NFL's owners and team executives, almost all of whom are white, are simply unwilling to hand over the reins of a team to a black man. They refuse to make someone who is culturally different from them their "wife."

A United Press International news item illustrates the tortoiselike pace of the hiring of black NFL coaches. The article began: "Rep. Augustus Hawkins, D-Calif., didn't issue a 'warning' Tuesday, but encouraged NFL Commissioner Pete Rozelle to talk to a citizens committee looking into charges of institutional racial discrimination in pro football. At a Capitol news conference, Hawkins and other subcommittee members chastised Rozelle for not responding positively to a study by Dr. Jomills Braddock of Johns Hopkins University documenting 'serious discrimination and employment exclusion problems in the NFL in the selection of assistant and head coaches.' " Braddock would later state in a *New York Times* article that owners found it difficult to hire blacks for management positions because owners did not want to be too close to "the help."

The UPI piece continued:

> *The committee asked for a Congressional investigation into the fact that the NFL has had no black head coaches. Hawkins did not agree to call the House Subcommittee on Education and Labor, which he chairs, for such an investigation. "Evidence on one side of this issue has been presented to this committee," Hawkins said. "I think the proper thing would be for Mr. Rozelle to present the owner's side. I think the matter should be settled in a peaceful, non-Congressional way. The issue is broad enough to bring an obligation to settle it. The worst possible thing would be to just let it stir around. I'm not issuing a warning. But before the snow falls in the Sierras, before the next football season, and hopefully this summer, I would hope this issue would either be settled or be in Congress."*

Little did Hawkins know that the snow in the Sierras would fall many times over before the issue of the dearth of black NFL head coaches was settled. *That story was written in 1981.* That year, there were no black head coaches. By the winter of 2003 there were only Herman Edwards from the New York Jets, Tony Dungy from the Indianapolis Colts, and Marvin Lewis from the Cincinnati Bengals. Thus, twenty years later the NFL was still grappling with this predicament, working on an average of hiring about one black head coach per decade.

There is hope, however, that the situation is finally changing. In November 2002, Baltimore Ravens owner Art Modell made Ozzie Newsome, perhaps football's most respected personnel man, the NFL's first black general manager. The Arizona Cardinals' naming of Rod Graves as vice president of football operations and the Jacksonville Jaguars' insertion of James Harris as vice president of player personnel soon followed. Both of those men are black as well. In 2003 there will be a record 14 black coordinators in the NFL. And Tagliabue, who has long been committed to diversifying the coaching ranks, established in 2002 a committee on workplace diversity, which recommended that any team seeking to hire a head coach interview one or more black applicants, a rule that, at best, has been loosely applied so far, but it is a start. Ownership agreed with the committee. Whether this is simple window dressing by the league to protect itself from a threatened discrimination lawsuit by Johnny Cochran on behalf of black coaches remains to be seen.

The NFL has other problems, such as the fact that gambling by fans and others on professional football remains a critical part of the sport. This should scare the hell out of its executives. A 1999 survey by sports agent Ralph Cindrich of 75 draft-rated college football players found that 56 percent of the respondents believed that there were college athletes who had bet on the outcome of a game in which they participated, while 11 percent said they were aware of at least one incident in which a college football player bet against his own team on the outcome of a game in which he participated. We can only hope the gambling players who reached the NFL level were disinclined to do so again.

A small but increasing number of reckless and nasty owners are entering the sport, like Washington's Daniel Snyder, who at five feet four inches is the Mini-Me of NFL owners. Maybe there is hope for Snyder, who has fired hundreds of employees, since he did hire the talented former Florida coach Steve Spurrier. My fear remains that Snyder's arrogant and impulsive nature will lead to the ruin of the Redskins, the franchise that was once my heartfelt favorite.

Sometimes the NFL is overly anal in its rule enforcement. When former quarterback great John Unitas died in September 2002, modern-day quarterback great Peyton Manning wanted to pay a tribute to the fallen star by wearing black high-top shoes during a game, the way Unitas did. The NFL said no, since it would violate uniform codes, and threatened Manning with a massive fine of up to $25,000. The league's fixation on what color socks its players wear ties into an overall over-the-top obsession with image. A ridiculous by-product of this obsession is the case of game official Sanford Rivers, a highly respected head linesman who worked a Super Bowl: in the summer of 2002 he became the first NFL game official in history to be fired because he was overweight. The league recently began enforcing strict weight requirements for its officials, some of whom believe the league is attempting to create a slimmer, more appealing officiating force more pleasing to the television eye; they say Rivers was a scapegoat. The league strongly denies this and claims that the new weight rules were put in play simply to protect the health of officials. Rivers eventually appealed the decision to fire him, and it was reduced to a season-long suspension pending his being able to make the new weight requirements.

An indication of the distrust some officials feel for the league office was palpable in a stinging e-mail one high-ranking official sent to Tagliabue in January 2003. A copy was also sent to me [some names have been deleted for legal reasons]:

> *I would like to call your attention to the double standard that has come into existence under the present leadership of the officiating department. I hope you will understand why I did not sign my name. However, if you take the time to investigate, I assure you my information is correct!*

> 1 *Since the tragedy of 9/11, if we took a family member to a game on the van, we were prohibited from bringing them inside the stadium area for security reasons. 118 of the current 119 officials understood and abided by this rule. Unfortunately, one of our members violated these guidelines and our ability to take family members on the van was suspended. However, during that suspension period a member of the officiating department . . . not only took his wife on the van but also took her into the officials' locker room in Texas Stadium on Thanksgiving Day, where she walked in on our [back judge] who was naked. Then, as [the woman] was leaving to go to her seat, she really showed her "class" by saying to the crew, "Don't fuck it up out there."*

2 *On the final weekend of the regular season [a department official] violated [the department's] rules by taking his wife into Giants Stadium and into the officials' locker room. Why are officiating department people any different than game officials? What gives them the right to ignore security directives and bring their spouse into the stadium and officials' locker room?*

3 *Finally, but perhaps most importantly as far as you are concerned, why were two second-year officials assigned to the Giants @ San Francisco playoff game, in direct contradiction to the agreement negotiated between Bill Carollo and Mike Pereira last summer? One of those officials was looking directly at the defensive pass interference foul, reached for his flag, but then signaled incomplete. Enclosed is an excerpt of the executive director's report as e-mailed to all officials after our clinic last July for your information.*

Is this the way you want the officiating department to be operated? Morale is lower now than at any time during the contract problems of last year. There is no leadership, no organization, and no understanding of how to evaluate an official's performance on the field. Officials are not being graded on any reasonable standard! Confusion reigns supreme! Simply ask any downfield official the definition of a catch. No one can tell you what is a catch and what is not, because the definition was changed so often this season.

The letter was signed: "One of 119 unhappy officials!"

If Tagliabue didn't get the point that his officials were extremely angry at what they felt had been unfair treatment from the officiating department after reading that letter, he certainly understood after another official mailed a second anonymous letter to him, dated March 29, 2003, following the league's decision to fire eight officials for alleged poor performance. This official claimed that one member of the officiating department was having an affair with a female sports television journalist and that another member of the department had been suspended for sexually harassing a female employee. The relationship between the league and some of its officials is shaky, at best, and if not corrected soon, the strain will begin to have an impact on what happens on the field.

II

The biggest problem professional football faces is a threat that players face alone, and one that is difficult for the NFL's leadership to control: the effect of years of participation in legislated violence. The vicious hits and repetitive blows, coming game after game, season after season, as well as the sometimes tragic effects of pain-killing medications and other remedies taken to ease the physical grief, slowly and excruciatingly break down the human body. As a result, the sport has created a legion of crippled and demoralized former players whose physical and emotional traumas post-NFL, some psychologists believe, resemble those of soldiers returning from combat.

Recently a study conducted by the players' union found that 61 percent of former NFL players had experienced concussions during their playing days, with a vast majority of them having been knocked unconscious at least once. The study also found that 49 percent of the former players, because of various brain injuries suffered during their careers, still experienced numbness or tingling years after retirement; in addition, 28 percent had neck or cervical spine arthritis, 31 percent had memory trouble, 16 percent were unable to dress themselves, and 11 percent were unable to feed themselves. Eight were diagnosed with Alzheimer's disease, and though the degenerative disease has yet to be linked directly to head injuries, scientists strongly suspect the two are connected.

The *New England Journal of Medicine* reported that, because of their large size, NFL players are five times more likely than other males their age to suffer from sleep apnea, a disorder that causes gaps in the breathing process while sleeping. The problem has been linked to hypertension, heart disease, and strokes, and one of the study's authors said he was shocked that so many NFL men in their twenties and in excellent health suffered from it.

While a mortality study of NFL players by the National Institute for Occupational Safety and Health found that football players do not have an increased risk of death overall compared with the general population, it did find that offensive and defensive linemen had a 52 percent greater risk of dying from heart disease than the general population, and three times the risk of dying from heart disease as players at other positions. Some former players refuse to believe those who had lengthy football careers have normal life spans, as the study states. According to former NFL great Mean Joe Greene, three of his Pittsburgh Steelers teammates died in their forties or fifties.

One of the best comments I have ever heard regarding what it is like to be an NFL player comes from Greg Lloyd, the former Pittsburgh Pro Bowl linebacker. He suffered severe complications following a pain-killing shot given to ease the discomfort of an injured ankle. It took Lloyd six months to recover, and the Steelers eventually let him go. He signed with another team, but his career would never be the same again. He says it was at the moment he got the shot he truly realized how cruel the sport could be.

"I guess it would be easy if you had a football injury to end your career, but this wasn't a football injury," Lloyd says. "I got shot with a needle, got a staph infection, and almost died. It was something I had no control over. Somebody injected me with a needle. Now it's caused me to switch teams and all that shit I had to go through."

"It leaves a bitter taste in your mouth," he says. "But what do you do? You can walk around and be angry the rest of your life, or you can get over it. I got over it. This is a meat business. We're no more than cattle. When you come into this business, you have to realize, 'I'm just a piece of meat. As long as I get the job done, I'm here.' It doesn't matter if you've put in ten, eleven, or twelve years. There's nobody to pat you on the back and say, 'Good job.' It's like, 'Hey, we can't use you anymore. Good-bye.' "

The main attribute of a player like Ray Lewis, whom I consider to be the most talented and ferocious middle linebacker of all time, is an almost superhuman ability to endure enormous pain, while simultaneously delivering it. "I don't hit people to hurt them physically," he says. "I hit people to take their souls."

However, if the statistics are to be believed, the same pain-conquering attribute that helps Lewis be the best now will cost him a healthy future once his career ends. That is one of the true conundrums of this sport.

All of these factors—the risk of serious injury or even death, the specter of permanent disability—have led a number of players to seek more control of their lives, especially when it comes to on-field safety and off-field finances. Football players know they will never make the kind of money that baseball's Alex Rodriguez did when he signed a $252 million contract, all of which is guaranteed. But more players are holding out for more cash when negotiating contracts, knowing that a sudden injury could make their next contract their last. Indeed, football players possess a sort of disdain for baseball players, who make monstrous salaries but take a fraction of the bodily risk that NFL players do.

"I'm not saying they don't work hard," says San Francisco wide receiver Terrell Owens. "But our training camp is two-a-days; theirs is scooping up groundballs."

Despite problems, some critical, professional football remains the most complete and most satisfying of all professional games, the sport most ingrained in our culture. The Super Bowl has averaged almost 90 million viewers in this country alone over the past six years—compare that to the NCAA basketball championship's 27 million, and it is easy to see why advertisers flock to football's championship game like a gallery to Tiger Woods. The 2002 World Series, despite being an exciting seven-game contest between the Anaheim Angels and San Francisco Giants, was the worst-rated baseball championship in history. One factor in the low ratings was the labor strife between baseball owners and players, who nearly went on strike, something that is a distant part of the NFL's past. Fox Sports chairman David Hill said, "Once again, baseball managed to turn off its loyal fans." And football is drastically far ahead of professional hockey, in terms of both its health and its popularity. When the Ottawa Senators filed for bankruptcy in 2003, they joined the NHL's Pittsburgh Penguins, who filed for federal protection from creditors twice, in 1974 and 1998, as the only two franchises in the four American professional sports to file for federal protection from creditors. It is difficult to imagine an NFL team in that position while so much advertising and television money is pumped into the sport.

When nine men were trapped in a Pennsylvania coal mine two summers ago, a story that received national attention, rescue workers compared the dire situation to a "fourth-and-1." Another spoke of the rescue operation as a dicey race against time—"like Joe Montana in the two-minute drill." When the men were finally rescued, the families exploded in applause that Governor Mark Schweiker said sounded like "their team had just won the Super Bowl."

The NFL's greatest attribute is that it pursues excellence, from the players who spill blood on the field while chasing fame, money, and respect, to the union, which wisely recognized that no sport in the 21st century can survive without a hard salary cap and relented on those points to help create a labor peace that has enabled the NFL to escape any type of work stoppage in decades. While football salaries still pale compared with baseball's, in 2003 NFL teams are expected to spend about $90 million each on player salaries and benefits, an increase of over 100 percent from 1994. The NFL and the players' union are such partners that when I once wrote a story suggesting that baseball's pension plan was better than football's—which it clearly is—union leader Gene Upshaw and his NFL counterpart, executive Harold Henderson, wrote a joint letter of complaint to my newspaper. Can you see baseball commissioner Bud Selig and union leader Donald Fehr doing that?

There is little in sports more exhilarating than a Favre comeback or the glittery moves of Atlanta's Michael Vick or the almost heroic toughness of Steve McNair, the Tennessee quarterback. Strahan's tactical use of hands, power, and gravity to toss an offensive lineman 50 pounds heavier is majestic, and Tampa Bay cornerback Ronde Barber's elegant cover skills are enjoyable to watch. Marshall Faulk sidestepping through a hole barely a foot wide can leave you dumbfounded. No professional athlete has approached Jerry Rice's combined level of talent and professionalism. The tremendous skill and work ethic of the Buccaneers' Gruden make him tops in his sport. What Belichick did against the St. Louis Rams two championships ago is one of the most impressive coaching jobs in Super Bowl history. The performance and passion of all of these players and coaches make the NFL unique.

This book is in the same mold as that of several excellent baseball treatises by *Washington Post* columnist and author Thomas Boswell. However, instead of relying solely on past articles, a small number of which appear in this book, as well as portions of some of my previous stories and past interviews, I did extensive research to create a cache of new material and interviewed some 200 players, coaches, and union, team, and league personnel over a three-year period, as well as fans, agents, and even several dozen players' wives. Part of the reporting process involved following several people closely through all or portions of the 2002 season to get the kind of look at the NFL I had rarely seen before.

The Hall of Fame linebacker Lawrence Taylor once said that people outside of professional football have no idea how ugly the underbelly of the sport can be, which Taylor compared to the cold and gloomy dark side of the moon. But football also provides many breathtaking and warm moments, times when it captures the country, and the world. This volume attempts to shine light on both sides of the NFL and its bloody Sundays.

1

THE COACH

Jon Gruden

COACH CHUCKY

3:11 A.M.

When the alarm clock sounds, Cindy Gruden usually gives her husband, Jon, the turbulent and talented Tampa Bay Buccaneers head coach, a shove out of bed, which serves as a sort of kick start to his 20-hour day. "Go win me some football games," she tells him.

Jon Gruden is the best coach in football, and to be him is to be part brain, part unrepentant workaholic, and part sleep-deprived maniac. Indeed, such a delicious description of Gruden might apply to all NFL head coaches. "You have to be certifiable to do what we do," New York Giants coach Jim Fassel once said. If that's so, then Gruden should have been committed a long time ago. To be him is to stumble into the office at 4:00 in the morning, or 4:30 on the days he sleeps in, which means Gruden has become so familiar with seeing a sunrise that he could paint one blindfolded. He has also become best friends with winning. Because, when it comes to Gruden, that is what you get. You get the best and the brightest. You get a blue-collar guy with the work ethic of a coal miner and Marine fighting grunt all wrapped up in one. You get a man who off the field possesses a strong sense of right and wrong, but also one who will cut your heart out to get a win once the games begin. And don't ask

Gruden about war in Iraq. Don't ask him about the stock market. You'll be greeted by a stare and glance at his watch. Gotta go. Got players to coach. Don't care much about the outside world, man. He's got to go win some football games. Gruden thinks Eminem is a piece of candy. "Jon is dedicated, single-minded," Cindy says.

There is no coach in professional sports like the NFL coach. They are an obsessive lot, consumed by the job, and Gruden embodies the NFL leader—relentless, hyper-analytical, and media-savvy, able to leap the press in a single bound. Media smarts is a skill becoming increasingly vital in modern football. Since head coaches are like CEOs, they must be able to grapple with the power of television and the saturated media coverage teams now receive. Handsome, distinguished mugs like those of Jets coach Herman Edwards or Jon Gruden are something owners are looking for almost as much as coaching ability. "If a guy's good-looking, that's a plus," says one owner. "The head coach's face is going to be on television or on the cover of newspapers almost every day."

The pressure to look good, to look young, to look fit, is palpable. It is the burden New England offensive coordinator Charlie Weis felt last year when he decided to have gastric bypass surgery in June to, in his words, lose significant weight because he did not think owners and general managers would hire a fat man—at the time Weis weighed about 330 pounds. The surgery went so terribly wrong that Weis suffered from massive internal bleeding and almost lost his life. At one point his wife, Maura, had a priest read him his last rites. Weis recovered but now suffers nerve damage in his legs, and ironically, by having the operation, Weis admitted to the rest of the league that he had a weakness—in his case, food—and admitting flaws in the macho football world can ruin a coaching career. He told *Sports Illustrated:* "I think I'm ready to be a head coach. If what's happened to me is a deterrent to that, well, that'll be a shame. Owners should want to hire the best coaches, and whether you're fat, thin, black, or white shouldn't matter." But all of those things *do* matter to some.

The primary job of an NFL coach is to lead, and like many good generals, an NFL coach keeps a roster of often short-tempered and moody players with the attention spans of pimpled teens focused and inspired, pushing them through dreadful pain and frightening collisions, by using a variety of tactics, from gentle ego stroking to taking a player's soul and slicing it apart like a tomato. Coaches scream, cajole, trick, caress, and lie to get a player to function at his best. Some coaches do this while not only managing a frenetic, brutal game for three hours at least once a week but also while co-running the draft, making key free agent signings, and keeping the one eye that hasn't dozed off on the salary cap or a defensive lineman's girth. The responsibilities of a head coach in other sports pale in comparison to those of an NFL coach, especially beginning last decade, when football became a year-round sport. Ask an NFL coach what his job is, and to the man, he will give a good chuckle, like he was just told a great punch line. "No coach in this league has just one job," says Edwards. It's more like three. First, in this age of rabid football free agency, head coaches must transform teams that have seasonal, dramatic turnover into cohesive units. Second, a coach must devise winning schemes, while also countering the tactics of the coach on the opposite sideline, something Gruden excels at, as does New England's Belichick, Mike Shanahan of Denver, and Mike Martz of St. Louis, whose Rams playbook includes a mind-numbing 120 different offensive formations. Third, head coaches have to motivate players who have heard it all before and are playing in an age when one contract could set them up for life and thus lessen their motivation to heed the coach's words or play the game with the required ruthlessness.

Coaches are challenged by their ever-expanding job descriptions and hours, and there is a belief among some in the NFL coaching community that their terribly single-minded, overstressed careers—many coaches have memorized the phone numbers of both the local pizza delivery place and a heart specialist—may actually be shortening their lives. Still, make no mistake: they are handsomely rewarded for their blood and sweat. It was a true indication of a head coach's value when the Buccaneers traded valuable picks, two first-round and two second-round selections, to the Oakland Raiders, as well as $8 million in cash, to sign Gruden, without even first meeting him face to face, to a contract that pays him $17.5 million over five years. While some coaches like Minnesota's Mike Tice earn the NFL coaching version of minimum wage at about $600,000 a season, most head coaches are immensely well compensated. Washington's Steve Spurrier left the comfort of the University of Florida for the pressure cooker of the NFL, but he has a plump bank account to fall back on should his professional career turn into a miserable failure. Owner Danny Snyder, the little man with the big pockets, handed Spurrier a five-year, $25 million deal, the richest NFL coaching contract ever. Spurrier is not the only coach making big money. The average NFL coach earns over $1 million a season, double from just ten years ago.

There is, of course, a large dose of responsibility that comes with earning all of those zeroes, as well as a price to pay. Some coaches joke that with each game their cholesterol count increases by a factor of ten. Gruden has set the standard for work ethic among coaches and in the process generated admiration, disbelief, and jealousy all wrapped up into one spiked emotion. There are coaches who even privately claim that Gruden lies about what time he arises in the morning—which is 3:11 A.M. each day, six minutes earlier than he did as coach of the Raiders. Gruden's nickname among some of the players is "311"—a way of respectfully giving Gruden his props for climbing out of the sack so early. Gruden says he does so because he isn't as smart as other coaches and must work harder. "I'm not the smartest tack in the box," Gruden says. "I definitely believe in overkill. I'd rather be overprepared and have my players overprepared." Gruden's claim that he lacks an intellectual bent is not false modesty. He truly believes it. But you discover that this alleged dumb streak is sham upon meeting him. Gruden is single-minded. He is selfishly obsessed with winning. But he is not dumb. Not by a long shot.

Baltimore coach Brian Billick, only half-kidding, once said when asked what time he gets up in the morning: "About a half-hour before whatever time Gruden lies about coming in." But Gruden's schedule is not fabricated, and players and coaches on both the Raiders and Buccaneers attest that he is indeed familiar with the three o'clock hour.

Gruden's intensity is notorious. "Go, go, go—all the time," is how Tampa Bay wide receiver Keyshawn Johnson describes him. At 40 years old, he is young enough to maintain a schedule that would burn out three presidents without thoroughly wrecking his body—at least so far. "I worry about his health every day," says Cindy. "But I think he's built for the NFL coaching lifestyle." Gruden rarely napped as a kid and for most of his life has been an early riser. Players call Gruden a genetic freak, and one refers to Gruden not by his name but as "the coach who never sleeps." Gruden revels in his reputation as an uncompromising winner, but there are moments when he is quick to point out that his lifestyle is shared by many others in the sport and he does not sit atop Burnout Hill alone. I think there is a small part of Gruden's personality—a teensy, tiny part—that wonders if the way he lives his life is indeed the right way, though you would have an easier time cracking the genetic code than getting him to ever admit this possibility. He tells a story, with an almost defensive tone, of how he arrived at the Buccaneers' sleek facility at One Buccaneer Place in Tampa, around 4:00 A.M. one morning during the 2002 season, and defensive coordinator Monte Kiffin was crashed on a cot, sound asleep—he had spent the night at the team's complex after an evening of studying tapes. "I guess I'm not the sole crazy guy in this sport," Gruden laughs.

No, he's not, but he might be *the* craziest.

Gruden and some other NFL coaches, like New York's Edwards or Tennessee's Jeff Fisher, remind me of a different era, before stock scandals and finger-waving presidents, when it was simply about whoever worked the hardest and had the most talent grabbing the rewards. That is what makes NFL coaching so interesting to follow. An unrelenting coach with talent leading a team of average players will usually beat a great team with an average head coach who sleeps in and makes all of his daughter's softball games. That is the cruel reality of football. In baseball it's all about the players; managers do little, no matter the claims of the sport's romantics. The same goes for hockey and especially basketball. Football is a high-tech, modern sport, which makes it the perfect partner for television, but the game's coaches, the men who bring order to on-field chaos, are retro-1950s.

There is only one question. What does such a lucrative yet exceedingly demanding lifestyle do to the insides of a man who chooses this profession? Or better yet, what does it do to his family? To be a successful NFL coach, you must work at least twelve-hour days, eleven months a year, and be willing to spend most of your waking minutes away from friends, family, and lazy Sundays. The lifestyle, according to an NFL executive who has studied the profession, has led to a divorce rate in the past two decades of about 70 percent. Larry Kennan, head of the NFL Coaches Association, disputes that number but acknowledges he is scared for some coaches mainly because "so many seem to be facing dramatic health problems. It is something coaches don't like to speak about, but it is a plague on our profession."

Cindy Gruden is deep and astute. She is also no weeping willow. She has strong opinions about her husband's profession and is willing to share them. She expresses appreciation for the comfortable standard of living that coaching provides her and their three young children, Jon II, Michael, and Jayson. Yet she admits that part of being married to Jon Gruden, part of being a coach's wife in general, is losing a piece of yourself to the coaching lifestyle. Marriage is always about compromise, but being a coach's wife is more than that—it is about spending a great part of your married life, well, almost husbandless.

"We just don't see each other a lot, but you sort of get used to it," says Cindy. "I knew that going into the whole thing. Since we moved to Tampa, I've done a lot of wallpapering and painting." Then she chuckles: "I'm not real needy. That's what it takes to be married to Jon. So I think he married me because I bothered him the least. I've met a lot of coaching wives, and they are the same way. They are extremely independent. You have to be, because you spend a lot of time without your husband. One of the players' wives told me once, 'I don't make many friends, because I don't know when we're going to move.' I guess the same could be said for the wife of an NFL head coach."

"Jon has never changed," she says. "I admire that about him. I fell in love with that. We met when we were 24. I was trying to figure out what I was going to do with my life. But he always knew what he was going to do with his."

||

Larry Kennan, head of the Coaches Association, is normally a serial optimist, but when the subject of the health of coaches arises, his voice takes a right turn at solemn. He starts the conversation by reeling off a series of names, longtime coaching friends he used to laugh with, win with, and break bread with. Then Kennan quietly adds that they are gone now. They have all passed on. It is a roll call of the departed.

"There was Elijah Pitts, the Buffalo running backs coach. He was one of those guys that always worked. A real hard worker. He died of cancer in 1998. Bob McKittrick in San Francisco was one of the toughest coaches out there. Another guy who worked long hours. He gave everything to the game. He died of liver cancer a few years back. He was 64. Fritz Shurmur, too, yeah, he died of liver cancer as well. Fritz was a great guy. A football lifer. He was a big reason Green Bay got to the Super Bowl a short time back. I think he died in 1999. Dick Rehbein died of a heart attack in 2001. Right before the season. He wasn't even 50 yet I don't think. That was terrible. He had two daughters. There was Chip Myers in Minnesota who also died of a heart attack. That was 1999. He was just 53. Young guy. Ed Hughes was a lifer too. He was the offensive coordinator on the Bears' Super Bowl team. He died two years ago. I'm pretty sure he was in his early seventies. I'm forgetting somebody. Who am I forgetting? It's the coaching life, you know. It takes that kind of toll on the body."

Kennan is not an alarmist. He is measured and responsible and not prone to making grandiose statements. He is a good man who fights for the rights of coaches, mainly the lower-paid assistants, who spend a lifetime in the game but often walk away with nothing more than good memories, some nice NFL gear, and high blood pressure. But he is worried. Just since 1998, a handful of coaches, at least five, have died while on the job, and the majority of those men were in their fifties or younger. There has never been a study on the impact of the stress of coaching on the human body, so there is no proof that the increased demands on coaches, as Kennan is reluctantly beginning to believe, might be shortening their lives. Maybe the recent spate of deaths is unusual. Or maybe it's that coaches live longer than most people and what is happening is an anomaly, a glitch, one of those unfortunate galactic hiccups. At this moment there is no way to know for certain. Kennan, of course, understands that coaches have *always* worked hard, but something now is different, and his instincts are flaring, telling him the coaching profession is headed in the wrong direction. The coaching profession, he believes, might be killing its members.

"Coaches are going to be mad at me for saying this," says Kennan. "But I feel like I have to, because I want the coaches to understand how if they are not careful, if they keep working these crazy hours, it can drastically affect their health. I've been in the coaching business a long time, decades, and I have never seen the amount of coaching deaths I am seeing now. I can't remember so many coaches dying while they're on the job. It's frightening, and it's one of my biggest concerns as leader of the coaching union."

"We know that NFL coaches work three times more in one year than the average American worker," Kennan says. "I guess the question is, where do we draw the line? The philosophy now is, some is good, more is better, and too much is just right. I like Jon Gruden. He's a great coach. But if Gruden is in the office at 4:00 A.M., another head coach is going to say, 'I'm coming in at 3:45.' It's a competitive thing. That's part of the macho deal of this sport. We all need to be concerned about when enough is enough. The players have legislated that they want less hours, but coaches don't do that. There are more and more mini-camps and scouting, and there are just more things for coaches to do. It's getting worse and worse each year."

There is no evidence that a lack of sleep combined with high stress is leading, as some coaches believe, to the ruining of their health and bodies. But scientists do know that forced sleep deprivation exacerbates any chronic condition, particularly heart disease. Jed Black, director of Stanford University's Sleep Disorders Clinic, says that sleeplessness puts an increased stress on the cardiovascular system. "I don't think, based on my studies, it is outrageous to speculate that missing sleep puts an extra strain on the heart," he says, "and it's not just the heart. If you have diabetes, it gets worse. If you have some sort of ailment like cancer, it gets worse. That we know." So coaches, who are notorious for not taking care of their health, may be worsening conditions they are not even aware of by cutting out their rest. Black said another by-product of losing sleep that should concern NFL coaches has to do with decision making. Sleep deprivation can lead to making poor choices, and since NFL coaches make a number of decisions on a daily basis, their habit of skipping rest can be self-defeating. A small number of coaches—emphasis on *small*—are beginning to realize this. The Tennessee Titans coaching staff tries not to make crucial decisions at night, instead waiting until morning when they are more rested, relatively speaking.

The stress of the job has led to some spectacular coaching melt-downs within the past ten years alone. From Jim Mora to Mike Ditka, watching a man publicly disintegrate under pressure, the coaching equivalent of the China Syndrome, is both disturbing and fascinating. In actuality, these types of implosions are much more common than is generally known, but unlike some of Mora's outbursts, many others happen behind closed doors. That's what happened in the cases of former Detroit coach Bobby Ross and Cincinnati coach Bruce Coslet, each of whom took over one of the worst franchises in football. Late in Ross's tenure, which lasted from 1997 to 2000, players and officials in the Lions organization say the pressure of losing turned the normally affable Ross into an ogre. During a team meeting with a group of veteran Detroit Lions players in the fall of 2000, Ross threatened wholesale dismissals if the team did not begin playing to his standards. This kind of threat happens in football, but players who recall that meeting said Ross's words were vitriolic and out of character and it was clear to them that the stress of the job was tearing Ross apart.

" 'I don't care how many Pro Bowls you've gone to,' " a Lions player remembers Ross screaming as the team watched in stunned silence. " 'I don't care if you're going into the Hall of Fame. I don't care what would happen to our salary cap. I can still get rid of you.' " Several players who witnessed the outburst described it as one of the most emotional in Ross's time with the franchise. The scene occurred shortly before Ross shocked the Lions by resigning in November of that year.

Ross's coaching peers speak of him with great admiration. They say he was one of the most dedicated men in the league. When Ross coached the San Diego Chargers, going 50–36 and earning one Super Bowl appearance, Pro Bowl linebacker Junior Seau practically worshiped him. But in Detroit, as the losses mounted, Ross's relationship with his players quickly deteriorated. He had become increasingly frustrated by what he felt was a me-first attitude from some of his veterans. They, in turn, described Ross as paranoid, his outbursts increasing in frequency and intensity. Ross had never clicked with several of his key players and barely spoke to some of them, including then–star receiver Herman

Moore. The defeats began to wear on him physically and mentally. His temper shortened, and at practices he often looked exhausted, former defensive back Ron Rice said at the time. Players who only a few years earlier felt comfortable walking into his office to chitchat say they began avoiding Ross, never knowing when his temper would flare. "I think he felt that he really just burned himself out, physically and mentally," says the Lions' chairman and owner, William Clay Ford. "He really didn't have any more to give. The gas tank was empty."

Ross resigned following a tough loss to Miami on November 5, abruptly leaving a 5–4 team in the thick of a playoff hunt; he was the second NFL head coach to step down during that season. Coslet had resigned in September after his team opened the season with three straight losses. "I just don't have the energy level that you've got to have for the job, however you want to put it," Ross told ESPN soon after quitting. "You need it for the good of your team. It's not my nature to do something like this. But I'm tired. I thought this was the best time to do it, rather than to keep struggling." Coslet also cited stress as one of the primary reasons he resigned, saying he was barely sleeping, his health had deteriorated, and he was treating people in the organization poorly. It was the first time since Bill Johnson left the Bengals and Tommy Prothro walked away from the San Diego Chargers in 1978 that two coaches had resigned during a season.

Interviews with more than two dozen NFL head coaches and assistant coaches indicate that burnout is a constant danger in the profession. One assistant coach says that his fifteen-hour workdays ruined his marriage. Another says that several years ago, when his team was on a losing streak, he could not sleep for two days. One team stocks a storage room with blow-up mattresses so that coaches can sleep in the office overnight. Several assistant coaches say that alcohol abuse is a problem among a small number of their peers who drink to dull the pain of losing. Kennan says that some of the coaches he has heard from over the past few years have been told by their doctors that they have one form of cancer or another, and that the stress of the job contributed to the development of the illness. Heart disease has plagued a number of celebrated coaches over the years, including Bill Parcells, Dan Reeves, and Ditka.

Reeves missed the Atlanta Falcons' final three games of the 1998 Super Bowl season because of open-heart surgery.

That same season, with the Giants struggling with a 3–7 record, head coach Fassel noticed that he was losing substantial amounts of weight, at one point dropping 20 pounds in a few months, despite eating cinnamon rolls, cookies, and ice cream to bulk up. "My initial thought was that a player had been messing with the scale so they could make weight," says Fassel. "I got really nervous. I knew something was wrong, because I had been eating a lot. It was the stress. Coaching stress is the greatest diet in the world."

Dick Vermeil became a symbol for burnout when he stepped down as coach of the Philadelphia Eagles in 1983 after seven years of eighteen- to twenty-hour days. He would return to football, but only after many years and therapy sessions. Joe Gibbs led the Washington Redskins to four Super Bowls in twelve seasons, winning three. He was so obsessed with work—extremely Gruden-like in his hours—that he ordered the clocks removed from the room where game plans were formulated. The only way some assistants knew the time was by tracking the landing of the Concorde at nearby Dulles Airport. When it landed, they knew it was close to 6:00 A.M. The difference between coaching then and in the 21st century is that there is even more work to do now than when Gibbs was sleeping in the office almost daily.

"There's no part-time way to do this job," Fassel says. "You give everything up: spending time with your family, your social life, everything. Everything is geared toward Sunday, and if you lose you think, 'I put all that work in it and I didn't win?' That's when coaches start losing it."

Former San Francisco coach Steve Mariucci says that his wife, Gayle, like Gruden's spouse, worries about the effects of coaching on his body and mind. "My wife doesn't want me to stay in coaching very long," Mariucci explains.

When asked about his health, Mariucci says it is fine, other than "the weight gain I sometimes experience because I'm a nervous eater." Then he offers this comment: "I got checked out in the off-season [following the 2001 season] because of some concerns, but everything was fine." Mariucci would not elaborate about what those health questions were.

"It's a killer business, and there is not any doubt about that," Parcells says. "I was looking at the first coaches' photo I was involved in. There was only one guy still left in the first one I was in. That's Dan Reeves. I can recall the first picture that I was in, in 1983. Bud Grant was in the picture, and he was standing right behind me. He said, 'This is like taking pictures with bomber pilots. When you come back next year, there will be a few missing.' "

These men hate coaching and they love it, they pine for it and they despise it, but most of all, they stay in it, and some, like Parcells and Jimmy Johnson, retire to cushy, high-six-figure jobs as television analysts, enjoying free lunches and foot massages, but then go crawling back to the profession, the way a crack cocaine addict stumbles back to his favorite back alley to get a fix. But why? Jimmy Raye was a star college player at Michigan State, played defensive back in the pros, coached in college, and then in 1977 began an NFL career that has thus far spanned 25 years and 9 teams. Raye says it is easy to figure out why coaches, especially the assistants, stay in the game despite the at-times destructive effects it has on their lives.

"There is just an irresistible competitive urge a lot of us have," he says. "The feelings you get when you see your game plan and effort come to fruition on Sunday is incredible. The downside is, when things go wrong, players don't usually get fired, the coaches do. Assistants, many of us, are the low men on the totem pole, so we can get sacrificed first. And for a black assistant coach it can be even tougher, because nine times out of ten the black assistant coach is at the bottom of the rung. So when things go bad, we're the first to go."

Raye adds, "We're conditioned to be scared. Assistants are. We're afraid of being replaced, because in the back of our minds—and the owners know this—the NFL is the biggest show in town. So you don't want to lose your spot, because once you're out of it you don't get back in. So you keep driving and driving and working hard, and when you're in your twenties or thirties it doesn't seem so bad. When you're twenty, the age of fifty seems old. Then one day you're suddenly fifty, and you look around and see the guys you came into the league with, guys like

Elijah Pitts and Bob McKittrick and others, are all gone, and you start to wonder. You start thinking, 'Am I going to be the next one who just coaches until he dies on the job?' "

Raye is like many other assistants I interviewed in that he appreciates his situation and loves to coach. He doesn't want to sound like a complainer, and that is not his personality. But his words and those of others reflect the reality of their situation.

There is no question that countless people in many different professions have demanding work situations that cause extreme anxiety and lead to serious health issues. They, too, die on the job, and coaches acknowledge this. Then there are coaches who make life more difficult for other coaches, like Parcells, who retires and from the television studio lobbies for the jobs of other employed coaches. A short time ago, before Gruden, Parcells negotiated with the Buccaneers to become that franchise's head coach while Tony Dungy still held the position. It was a nasty, cutthroat maneuver, and Parcells repeated it just a year later when he met for five hours in late December 2002 with Dallas owner Jerry Jones about the possibility of taking over that head coaching position, which at the time was held by Dave Campo. My belief is that Parcells, who has always wanted to get back to the Giants, with whom he won two Super Bowls, saw how the Giants were struggling late in 2002. Expecting them to lose their final two games to Indianapolis and Philadelphia, Parcells met with Jones initially to let Giants ownership know that if they didn't fire Fassel and hire him, he would go to division competitor Dallas. When the Giants did not bite, Parcells made his move to the Cowboys. Parcells is that manipulative and sneaky. Before the Giants played Indianapolis, a game New York would win, Colts coach Dungy, who had been submarined by Parcells in Tampa Bay, read in the New York papers one columnist's musings that the team should fire Fassel and hire Parcells. Dungy approached Fassel during the pregame warm-ups and said, "I see Parcells is doing to you and Campo what he did to me." Parcells, whose primary rule has always been, help thyself first, and who has earned the nickname Stealth Assassin among some in the coaching community, demonstrates that sometimes coaches hurt their own cause.

Few occupations in the public eye are like coaching, which is so hyper-analyzed. It is only a game, but professional football is often treated like life or death. That is why there is so much pressure on the backs of coaches.

The NFL has benefited tremendously from a massive media following. Every game is available on satellite television. ESPN has two-hour pregame shows with more analysis of football than CNN's coverage of Operation Iraqi Freedom. Billions of bytes on the Internet are dedicated to nothing but football. The downside of this saturation coverage is that every move a coach makes is seen, analyzed, and commented on, and then again, and then yet again. When a coach makes a mistake, it is not only Groundhog Day (without Bill Murray) as ESPN replays the mistake repeatedly on highlight shows, but the mistake is also discussed on various websites and in chat rooms. A coach can be ridiculed and called a moron from sea to shining sea.

"People are very quick to criticize, and I think people gravitate to that," says Fassel. "I think we are so heavily scrutinized with so many things, in terms of talk shows, media, and pregame shows. That really magnifies it, but more than that, the people who are paid to do those shows, they aren't paid to be in the middle of the road. They are paid to be controversial, get on the guys, and stir the fans up. That is what they are paid for, and that is what they are doing. After a while, it's pretty hard to survive it, because everyone is going to go through some tough times. That is the way it is. I'm not feeling sorry for myself. That is just the way it is."

In late November 2002, Detroit coach Marty Mornhinweg discovered this firsthand when he made one of the worst coaching decisions of the last several decades and subsequently stumbled into football legend. The Lions won an overtime coin toss against Chicago, and instead of electing to take the football, he decided to kick off, thinking the 17-mph wind was a factor. He should have taken the ball, and that would have given him a chance to win the game on the Lions' first possession in OT—just like Detroit did a month earlier against Chicago. This time the Bears took Mornhinweg's gift and won the contest on a Paul Edinger 40-yard field goal. When asked if he regretted the coin toss decision, Mornhinweg admitted, "Knowing the outcome of this game, I wouldn't do it again." The next day Mornhinweg's decision was ridiculed on talk shows and ripped by sports broadcasters across the nation. One headline in the *Detroit Free Press* blared: "Blown Chance Shows Coach Is an Airhead." Mornhinweg was fired in January 2003.

Parity puts additional pressure on coaches. The final NFL week of 2002 saw 19 of 32 teams in the NFL either already in the postseason or playing for a spot, the biggest playoff logjam since the league went to a 16-game schedule in 1978. Twelve of 16 games that weekend had playoff implications. More than half of the games from that year were decided by eight points or less, and records were set for everything from overtimes, touchdowns, and points scored to television ratings. All of these things are good for fans and the health of the NFL, but they put remarkable pressure on coaches. A good coach can make a difference in a league where all of the talent and teams are closely aligned; a bad one can lose a season.

You want to know what really pushes coaches over the edge? Ridiculous expectations. The fans and news media members who do not understand what it takes to do the job. At the end of the 2002 season, as San Francisco wrapped up a playoff spot, the fourth in six years for Mariucci, a reporter asked him immediately following their game at Arizona about rumors regarding his job security. It was a fair question, since at the time there was some concern about Mariucci not having signed a contract extension. But did the query have to come at that moment? Couldn't Mariucci have been given a moment or two to digest the victory? "Do you think any other coach who's just clinched a division title has to answer questions about that?" asked Mariucci. Later that week the *San Francisco Chronicle* published a letter from one fan that partly read: "I have been a 49er fanatic since the late 1950s—they have been the love of my life.... [But] this is a boring football team, and I don't care much about them any longer. If Mariucci continues beyond this season, I will never again waste my money to see this football team."

This kind of criticism of a successful coach is dumbfounding, especially since any team that has the flamboyant wide receiver Terrell Owens on it could never be called boring. Mariucci's situation in particular has been puzzling. He has always struck me as a highly talented coach, beginning when he won 11 games his first year, despite losing quarterback Steve Young on the fifth play of the season to a severe concussion, and Jerry Rice on the 27th play to a blown-out knee. San Francisco legend Bill Walsh, the team consultant who hovers over the organization like an overbearing father, averaged 9.2 wins per regular season in ten years, playing with Hall of Famers Joe Montana and a healthy Young; Mariucci averaged 9.5, playing with a beat-up Young, who was at the end of his career when Mariucci took over, and Jeff Garcia. Mariucci presided over the rebuilding of a once-legendary franchise that is now back on solid turf but during his tenure the team endured different ownership, multiple personnel directors, and three general managers. Moreover, because of horrid salary cap situations, up until the beginning of the 2002 season the team has averaged a loss of 30 players a year to free agency, among the highest such number in football. (Mariucci used to keep photos in a small folder with lines crossing out the players who were missing each year.) The financial problems were horrific, so bad that following Mariucci's 12–4 season in 1998, the franchise was a stunning $28 million over the cap. Still Mariucci won thirteen, twelve, four, six, twelve, and ten games in his six seasons, and over the last two years only Philadelphia and Green Bay have won more games than the 49ers. That's a pretty darn good record. Still there were complaints. When Mariucci's 49ers overcame a 24-point deficit in the opening round of the playoffs against the Giants, the second-biggest comeback in postseason history, Walsh remarked after the game: "He needed to break out and win one game against a top-flight team." Such comments are nonsense. Mariucci more than proved himself with an impressive track record during the most difficult times in the team's history.

Mariucci says the occasional, puzzling lack of fan appreciation, and even the lack of respect in the past from Walsh, can be explained in something Young once told him. "In San Francisco," the quarterback remarked, "anything other than a Super Bowl is a train wreck."

"I think some of the problems some people had with me is simply that I didn't have a Lombardi Trophy," Mariucci explains. "That's where it all begins. The standards, the expectations, are higher than many other organizations. Some teams have never won a Super Bowl. We have five Super Bowl trophies in our trophy case."

He adds, "We do have a sophisticated fan base. We're here in Silicon Valley. They're smart, prideful, and successful. They understand the salary cap, the transitional period we have experienced, but that doesn't mean they're going to be patient." The 49ers in January 2003, following the team's postseason loss to the Buccaneers, fired Mariucci.

Over the past few years the NFL has recognized the real danger that coaching burnout poses and taken steps—some coaches say not nearly enough—to ease the stress. The league pushed back by two weeks the start of free agency, so coaches have more of a breather when the long season ends. Kennan has been relentless in his pursuit of a better lifestyle for coaches, particularly assistants, with his main goal being the reduction of the official retirement age from 65 because, in his words, "there are very few old coaches. Many either don't work or don't live to see those benefits." With fewer than 7 percent of the league's over 400 coaches 60 or older, many coaches believe there is rampant age discrimination, something the NFL denies.

Kennan was an assistant coach for 15 years, rising to offensive coordinator for the Patriots, and understands the harsh lifestyle, which is why the coaching establishment trusts and respects him. Kennan also has a stern but noncombative personality, an asset that allows him to negotiate calmly and effectively with owners, who automatically become confrontational when demands are set. Before Kennan, NFL assistants were ready to engage the owners in a bitter, protracted fight for improved retirement packages using a variety of more aggressive tactics. Most of these struggles went unnoticed by the public and news media. In 1997 a number of assistant coaches were so fed up by what they felt was an arrogant and unresponsive ownership that they met with Jeffrey Kessler, perhaps the most renowned sports antitrust lawyer in the country, in a hotel ballroom in Indianapolis. The topic of conversation? The NFL assistant coaches were considering suing the league for antitrust violations. One of the assistants' biggest complaints has been that since the NFL office keeps track of the salaries of almost every coach, and individual teams can find out approximately what those salaries are, there is almost a built-in salary ceiling. Some coaches wanted to sue to remove those restraints. The NFL says it in no way violates antitrust laws. Eventually the idea fizzled because the assistants were worried that a lawsuit would destroy their careers (which it would have).

Coaches found other ways to express their displeasure. In May 1998, approximately 50 assistant coaches walked into a league-sponsored coaching symposium 15 minutes late as a protest, an act commissioner Tagliabue called "silly." Then the coaches' association later that year joined forces with the NFL Players Association, which one owner labeled a hostile act. There were plans by assistants, later abandoned, to wear black armbands at a game to show solidarity, or to turn in game plans one day late across the league, or to have a one-day strike at a training camp.

Assistant coaches don't ask for sympathy. They realize police officers and firefighters and soldiers lose their lives while serving their country, and do so for far less money than assistants earn. In 1988, according to the league, there were 291 assistant coaches making between $86,000 and $175,000, while just ten years later there were 405 assistants making between $148,381 and $475,000. Now the average salary for a top position coach is about $225,000 a year. The average coordinator earns between $375,000 and $400,000, with a half-dozen in the $600,000–$850,000 range, including former head coaches such as Norv Turner in Miami and Wade Phillips in Atlanta. Money may not buy health or happiness but it's a hell of a down payment. Four decades ago head coaches earned $17,000 a year.

The money is good but the turnover is high. The association says that assistants are fired, on average, every one to three years. At the beginning of the 2002 season there were eight new head coaches (including the expansion Houston Texans). One season before there had been seven new head coaches. That means that in just two years the NFL experienced a 45 percent turnover (not including the Texans) of its head coaches, and possibly hundreds of its assistants. There are few professions where people become unemployed with that kind of regularity—unless you count the job of circus knife catcher.

Kennan eventually got his wish of a lower retirement age for the membership. Coaches wanted to use a formula that would allow them to receive retirement benefits once a combination of age and years in service reached 75. In other words, if an assistant was 50 years old and had coached in the league for 25 years, he would be eligible to retire and receive benefits. In May 2000 owners approved that new retirement formula by a vote of 30–1. It was a huge victory for Kennan, though assistants were not completely happy with the agreement, fearing it was still somewhat limited. There were other concessions by the owners. The NFL standardized the health and dental insurance plans for the coaches. In the past, different teams had different plans. One team's package might be considered excellent, while other plans were severely lacking. Now there was a single policy for all assistants. Second, the life insurance policy of each assistant was doubled, to $500,000 from $250,000. The deaths and long-term illnesses of some assistants played a factor in this agreement, Kennan says.

"What we basically did was get better protection for the older assistant coaches," says Kennan. And that is the subplot, the elephant in the room. Coaches in the NFL are becoming younger, and there is fear that the old guys are being squeezed out and the next head coach will soon be wearing diapers. Because Gruden is so good, and so dedicated, and so young, because his handsome mug is flashed so much on television and he was once named one of *People* magazine's 50 Most Beautiful People, he is a constant topic of conversation among coaches in football, whether they want to admit it or not. Once you get beyond some of the petty sniping—"I hate when you fuckers in the media anoint the next great head coach," said one coach, "Gruden's nothing special"—there is grand admiration and respect for Gruden's work ethic, his skill, and his ability to motivate players. They relish competing against him because some believe he is the hottest thing in football since the zone blitz, and beating the best always leads to a rare good night's sleep. They love Gruden—and they hate him. If Gruden and more like him come into the league and win like he has, then owners will believe only whippersnappers in their thirties can do the job.

Yes, they like Gruden, but they murmur, with an almost smarmy assuredness, that Gruden's lifestyle, in all of its sleepless glory, will catch up to him, somehow, some way, and snag him from behind like the Ghost of Burnout Past. Just wait, they say. Just wait.

II

"Har-vey fuck-ing Will-iams," Gruden says, his words purposely stammered for effect. I ask Gruden how he got his nickname, which is

"Chucky," after the doll from the movie *Child's Play* who dices and slices his way through the horror flick. Gruden responds to the question by naming the former Raiders running back who tagged him with the moniker. The star of the movie has a crazed look on his face, and the star of the Buccaneers has several bizarre facial contortions himself. Gruden's trademark sideline smirks are captured weekly by television cameras; sometimes Gruden contorts and coils his mug so much, twisting his eyebrows, sporting that sinister grin, he looks like a man suffering from food poisoning. For a guy who sports such a youthful *GQ* look, his face becomes butt ugly when the offense temporarily freezes or a pass route is run errantly. In 1998, Har-vey fuck-ing Will-iams was receiving an earful from Gruden after running the wrong way on an audible call. As Gruden was letting him have it, Williams thought he looked like the Chucky doll's twin, and a nickname was born. Gruden has never been overly fond of it. Years later, during Gruden's first team meeting with players from the Tampa Bay Buccaneers, he would tell them: "You can call me Coach. You can call me Jon. But don't call me Chucky."

After Gruden quickly disposes of that explanation, he approaches the subject of his coaching days in Oakland, and he does so cautiously, the way an explosives expert slowly advances upon a suspicious package. "I really don't want to go there, talking about Oakland. I don't want to get all emotional and shit like that." But there is a rise in Gruden's voice, and the blood is clearly flowing a little faster. The Raiders are a touchy topic, and not just with Gruden. Some players and officials on the Raiders dance around the matter of their former coach like skilled ballroom performers, while others have no fear in taking a bite out of their former coach's hide. Gruden approaches talk of his old team by first cautiously dipping a toe in it; then, pretty soon, he wades up to his knees in silver and black, and after a few minutes that passion in his voice, a sort of nuclear growl, heats up.

"I haven't spoken to many of the Raiders players," he says. "It's too sensitive. I'm told they feel I abandoned them or left them and that some of them are upset I have not contacted them. My leaving was emotional for all of us. I thought it was important to let them move on and for me to move on. I've got to worry about the Buccaneers."

"The guys in Oakland know how I felt about them," says Gruden.

"I loved a lot of those guys. They know that. But it doesn't help if I come out in the newspapers every day and say that because it would just make things worse. If they feel like I have betrayed them or whatever, they're wrong, and one day I hope to sit down and have a cup of coffee with some of them and give them my side of things." Gruden did stay in touch with Raiders quarterback Rich Gannon, since a bond had been forged between the two men that neither distance nor the NFL's tampering rules could break.

To understand the true power of Gruden's personality—he reminds me of a young Gibbs or a tad less obnoxious Parcells—one need only examine what he did in Oakland and then later in Tampa Bay. In Oakland, Gruden performed one of the best coaching jobs of the past ten years. He not only transformed the product on the field but changed the entire atmosphere of the Raiders organization. While it was always unfair to whisper, as many in football did, that owner Al Davis had become nothing but a meddling old goat who had lost touch with modern football, it was true that something had happened to the Raiders. The franchise had grown stale, like month-old chips, and Davis's head coaching choices were questionable. In two seasons coach Mike White went an unimpressive 15–17 from 1995 to 1996. After White came Joe Bugel, and he lasted just one error-plagued 4–12 season. It was not uncommon for players during the Bugel regime to show up repeatedly late for team meetings or to mouth off to the coaching staff. Once wide receiver Tim Brown, frustrated by the lack of progress on offense, threatened to call his own plays from the huddle.

Davis hired Gruden on January 22, 1998, after Gruden had spent seven seasons as an NFL assistant. Gruden's baby face and age, just 34 years old, caused the rest of the league to pause and take note of what had just happened. No one was used to seeing someone so young take the helm of such an important franchise. The word was that Davis had bungled another hire. The players themselves were at first cautious. "When he got to Oakland," says former Raiders wide receiver Terry Mickens, "there were veterans on the team who were actually older than he was. Guys were initially saying, '*He* has to prove himself to *me*.'" Gruden did—quickly—and the veteran-heavy roster noticed right away that Gruden would be different from his two immediate predecessors. Some who showed up early to the team complex to work out or go over game film would see Gruden already there, stashed away in a dark room watching film like a mad scientist with his test tubes. Word of his early rising habits spread through the Raiders like wildfire. The players and others were impressed. *He was always in the office.* Soon he began having meetings with the quarterbacks at 7:00 A.M.—early even by NFL standards—and that was before the regular offensive meetings. Gruden also started demanding more professionalism from the players, and he let them know that tardiness was unacceptable. One player remembers his first encounter with Gruden. The player says he was about three minutes late for a team meeting during training camp, and afterwards Gruden pulled him aside.

"Do you want to win?" Gruden asked.

Gruden's face was flushed and his lips tight. The player says at first he thought Gruden was engaged in a poor acting job, but after a few seconds he realized Gruden was serious.

"Yes, Coach."

"No, no. Don't give me that 'yeah Coach' shit," Gruden replied. "Do you want to fucking win?"

"Hell, yeah!"

"That's what I'm talking about!" Gruden responded. "Don't be fucking late again. That's losing shit. That's what losers do." The player said he was never tardy for another meeting while Gruden was coach.

After about only a month on the job, Gruden possessed a firm grip on the strengths and weaknesses of each player on the roster, especially the ones on offense. Knowing his players so well (and not leaving it up to his assistants to debrief him)—players like the cerebral wide receiver Brown and later the all-universe Jerry Rice, who, like Gannon, was brought in by Gruden—allowed Gruden to insert massive amounts of plays every week in the game plan—100 to 120 and over 50 running plays. Gruden's favorite player, Gannon, a career journeyman who joined the team as a free agent from Kansas City in 1999, was perfectly suited to digest the volume, since Gannon always preferred more to less. Gannon was an accurate thrower, and Gruden's passing offense functioned mainly between the hashes—few deep balls—and that worked to Gannon's advantage, cutting down on his potential to be intercepted. Even after Gruden packed his bags for the sun of Tampa Bay, Gannon would prosper, and the Raiders' offense, the best in the league in 2002, would continue to run what in effect were Gruden's schemes.

Gruden tried to prepare his players for every contingency, which is where the lack of sleep would come in, since he spent hours breaking down game film and opponent habits, far more than most head coaches. Gruden had a pickup for every blitz and an audible for every pass play. Though two-hour practices are the norm, most Raider practices under Gruden were easily three hours in length because Gruden inserted so much. In the classroom Gruden sometimes walked into player meetings and began firing questions, usually at Gannon and the quarterbacks. "Bam! Rich! You get cover 3. Who is your primary? Let's go!" Gruden had his offense so primed that it was rarely surprised by anything once game time rolled around.

Gruden's blistering intensity shook the Raiders down to their cleats. At first they didn't know what to make of the way Gruden would get excited over game planning, sweating profusely as he drew formations on the blackboard. He would spice up practices, which can be remarkably mundane, by scampering between drills like a wild man, barking orders at the players, challenging his offense. As players went through their routines, they could hear Gruden in the background, his raspy voice screaming, the words sounding like machine gun bullets: "I need to feel you! I need to feel you! Let me take you up to the gas station and fill you up with high octane! If you don't feel it, at least fake the enthusiasm!" Gruden would get orgasmic over the day's scripted calls—the list of practice plays. At one practice in 1999 he approached running back Tyrone Wheatley and screamed, "Hey, Wheat! I got a script for your ass! You're going to love it!" A week later: "Hey, Wheat! I'm going to bust your ass with these scripts. I'm going to bust your ass, big boy!" *Juice* is a word Gruden uses often, as in, either you have it or you don't, as in, if you do he will try to squeeze every bit of it from your body.

"This guy loves his job like no coach I have ever seen," says Wheatley. "The thing with him was that he was always right. I mean it. He rarely got things wrong because he studied so much. You couldn't argue with him because he could go tit-for-tat with you. He would come right back at you if you argued with him, and his point would usually be right. Some cats would complain about him. 'It's either his way or the highway.' But they didn't get it. He just wanted guys to work as hard as he did."

By the end of his first two seasons Gruden's program had taken complete shape, and his maniacal methods were paying dividends. An off-season workout program was in place for the first time, or at least a program that brought what the Raiders did up to par with some of the better franchises. He instituted a more modern system of play calling, film review techniques, and team meetings. Overall, he changed the institutional mind-set of the organization, which was stuck a decade in the past. The success of the reborn Raiders only served to reinforce Gruden's feelings that he needed to push himself, and those around him, at warp speed to stay ahead. His work schedule grew more intense as he stayed at the office later and awoke earlier.

One day in the winter of 1999, he received a phone call from San Francisco offensive line coach Bob McKittrick, whom Gruden considered the best coach he had ever seen. As an assistant in San Francisco, Gruden had watched the way McKittrick worked—the passion, the long hours, the smarts. McKittrick was who Gruden wanted to be when he grew up. Gruden expected advice or congratulatory words from McKittrick, but instead he heard something else—a warning. McKittrick informed Gruden he was dying of cancer and had a short time to live. The statement shocked Gruden, but before he could respond McKittrick told him that life should not be solely about football and that he needed to spend as much time with his family as possible. "Don't be like me," McKittrick said. But Gruden was *exactly* like him. Instead of offering some phony promise to change—because he knew he never would, never could—Gruden simply listened. Soon, McKittrick's words would fade, becoming a distant fog, and by the time the Raiders won their first division title with Gruden at the helm, in 2000, he was working even harder.

||

Gruden is able to do something, quite naturally, that some other NFL coaches fail miserably at: he can motivate players, getting inside their heads. Ideally players should be able to inspire themselves—they are paid handsomely to play football, so the responsibility to go hard every game should lie squarely on their own broad frames. Yet that is just not human nature. Even world-class athletes need a kick in the tights on occasion. Only a handful of coaches in history have been skilled at stirring their players. One of the more celebrated moments goes back to 1928 and Knute Rockne's famous "Win One for the Gipper" oration for Notre Dame players. Former Buffalo coach Marv Levy, a Harvard graduate, addressed the Bills one day following their painful 20–19 Super Bowl loss to the Giants in 1991. Levy read them a version of "The Ballad of Sir Andrew Barton."

> *Fight on my men, Sir Andrew said*
> *A little I'm hurt, but not yet slain*
> *I'll just lie down and bleed a while*
> *And then I'll rise and fight again*

Following that reading, a dozen players asked Levy for a copy of the poem, and the Bills went on to make three more championship appearances.

No one in the history of the modern NFL excels at mind games like Parcells, who one day will be inducted into the Hall of Fame. Parcells can be funny, nasty, and cruel—all requirements to be a distinguished head coach in the NFL. His tactics, both gentle and abrasive, are infamous. When Parcells was coaching the Jets, the team had won a particularly physically brutal game against New England in October 1997. It was a great win, but the celebration was tempered because linebacker Pepper Johnson had ruptured a tendon in his leg and was going to miss the remainder of the season. Johnson had been with Parcells for six years, on the Giants and now the Jets, and their relationship was almost like that of a father and son. With the injured Johnson sitting on a table in the training room, Parcells crowded the team around the linebacker and proceeded to say how important Johnson was to him, not just as a player but also as a person. Those present say Parcells had tears in his eyes as he spoke, and the moment proved to be a truly unifying one for the team, a sort of rallying point. A short time before that, when Parcells was coaching the Patriots, one of his players, Bob Kratch, spent nine days in the hospital with pneumonia and a staph infection. The 290-pound player lost 25 pounds, was being fed intravenously at one point, and missed eight weeks of the season. Though Kratch eventually made it back to the field, his early practices were understandably rusty, but that didn't matter to Parcells. When Kratch made a mistake during one of those first practices back, Parcells, in front of the entire team, barked, "Kratch! Stop worrying about your lungs!"

The former Washington coach Joe Gibbs says that before many of the Giants' big games against the Redskins in the 1980s Parcells would tell Lawrence Taylor that the Redskins thought he couldn't play anymore. It would always fire Taylor up. It didn't matter that the Redskins never said that or that Parcells used the tactic over and over again—what counted was that it worked. Another time, during a Giants practice in training camp, Parcells made Kratch run laps in the heat because he had failed to chase down a defensive player who made an interception. Kratch felt humiliated as he trotted around the field, teammates and fans laughing at him. But after that Kratch always hustled in similar situations, the punishment laps fresh in his head.

There was also a telling incident in Parcells's first season with the Patriots in 1993. During a team practice Parcells called receiver Greg McMurtry a coward in front of the entire team because he had failed to execute a block to Parcells's liking. McMurtry says Parcells asked him to do an illegal maneuver, something Parcells has denied. Whatever the case, Parcells's outburst demonstrated to the other Patriots players that a new sheriff was in town. Two years later, during the 1995 season, the Patriots had lost two straight games, and Kratch, a favorite Parcells whipping boy who nevertheless followed Parcells from New York to New England, was being moved from right to left guard. Before practice one day Parcells, with the other players present, told Kratch: "If you don't play better, you're going on the street. I'm cutting you." Kratch thought for sure he was gone. But he wasn't, and in the next game, he acknowledges, he did play better.

During the Jets' loss to Buffalo on November 30, 1997, the then-rookie Dedric Ward, who had been benched earlier in the season, made at least one bad play on special teams. The following week in practice

Parcells exploded at Ward in front of the entire team, cursing him out and questioning his intelligence. But that week, with Parcells's explosion as motivation, Ward practiced hard. Then there was the disastrous game against last-place Indianapolis about a month later that year. As the Jets, riddled with injuries on the offensive line, fell further and further behind in a game that was essential to their playoff chances, Parcells became increasingly irate. One of the targets of his anger was offensive lineman Lonnie Palelei, who was more of a natural guard than a tackle but had been forced to replace the injured Jumbo Elliott at left tackle. The fact that Palelei was playing out of position didn't matter to Parcells. After Palelei let his man beat him for a sack of quarterback Neil O'Donnell, Parcells was caught by television cameras chewing out Palelei. According to Jets players, one of the things Parcells told Palelei was, "You will never play for me again." In fact, Palelei was subsequently benched for a practice-squad player. Palelei explains that Parcells never told him he was through with the Jets. "All I'll say is, he told me I was playing horrible," he says. Every Monday after a game Parcells usually addressed the team. The Monday after that loss to the Colts he didn't. Players said at the time it was the first time during the regular season he had failed to do so, and it clearly seemed to be Parcells's way of showing how dissatisfied he was with the way the Jets had played. But the yelling, brooding, and benchings all worked because the Jets crushed the Buccaneers in the next game to put new life into their playoff hopes. In those seven days they had gone from bad to terrific as Parcells again found a way to get to his players.

For Parcells, like Gruden, when it comes to motivating his players, no tactic is too outrageous. When Parcells took over the Jets, they were the league's laughingstock, and he was determined to change that, at all costs. During a preseason game against his former team, the established and legendary Giants, Parcells was speaking with a Giants staff member about the pregame procedure of introducing the starting lineups to the fans at Giants Stadium. Parcells put his arm around the staff member, asked how he was doing, and at that moment acted as if they were best friends. Later Parcells was five minutes late in bringing the Jets out of the locker room. The Giants were forced to wait for the Jets since the visiting team—the Jets—was supposed to go onto the field first. Eventu-

ally Parcells emerged and began walking toward the field, his Jets players in tow. The same Giants official approached Parcells to make sure
everything was all right. Parcells got within two inches of the official's
face and began screaming obscenities at him, basically telling the man
he knew the rules. "Needless to say," the official says, "I was shocked."

So were a number of the Jets players. But a few of them privately
admitted they felt a sense of pride watching Parcells hollering at a
member of the Giants. After two years of public pummeling under former coach Rich Kotite, someone was finally sticking up for them. Later,
on the field, when he made eye contact with the same official, Parcells
winked at him. The incident was typical Parcells. By bringing out the
team late, he was making a statement—the game waits for my team and
me. As for the sudden change in personality when speaking with the
Giants staff member—going from friendly to nasty in a blink of the
eye—well, Parcells was in front of his Jets team the second time around
and basically sacrificed the Giants official to make an impression with
his players. It's us against them. That was the not-so-subtle message.
Few coaches have the gall—and credentials—to pull off such a stunt.
Many of the men who have played for Parcells loved him, and about an
equal number despised him, but almost all of them, to the player, say his
techniques made them play harder, made them play better. Some have
felt an intense loyalty to Parcells that borders on fervor. When Curtis
Martin won the team MVP award in the 1999 season with the Jets, he
gave it to Parcells, along with a note that said without Parcells he would
have never achieved so much in his career. Parcells wept upon reading
Martin's tribute to him, and to this day that trophy is among Parcells's
most prized possessions.

Parcells is up to his motivational tricks again as head coach of the
Cowboys. He lowered the temperature in the team's training room to
make it uncomfortable for players to hang out there and to force players
to think all football, all the time. To let the Dallas players know who is
boss, he banned games of dominoes and loud music in the locker room
and no longer allows players to use the Internet or telephone in the
equipment room. He posted signs throughout the complex. One read:
"Dumb players do dumb things. Smart players very seldom do dumb
things." Another sign stated: "Losers assemble in little groups and bitch

about the coaches and the system and other players and other little groups. Winners assemble as a team."

The ability to stir players emotionally and quickly bring a team together has become more vital than ever. Free agent movement has increased, and the window to make a championship run has become not five or six years, but two to three. Every team that starts training camp in August is significantly different from the one that ended the season the previous December or January. So coaches are now utilizing every possible ploy to build a cohesive, focused group.

Baltimore's Billick has shown movies to his players like *Saving Private Ryan* and *Wise Guys*. In 2000 the Giants' Jim Fassel, his team stuck in an ugly two-game losing streak, publicly guaranteed his team would make the playoffs, and they did. The Giants won their next seven games, making the Super Bowl against the Ravens. Though New England's Bill Belichick does not have the typical coaching background, he has proven to be a gifted motivator, almost as good as Gruden. He attended the liberal Wesleyan University in Middletown, Connecticut, where he played lacrosse, squash, and football while studying economics. Belichick has emerged from 29 NFL coaching seasons, including head coaching stints in Cleveland and now the Patriots, as well as four trips to the Super Bowl, as the best defensive coach in the history of football, finishing, in my opinion, ahead of Buddy Ryan and Bud Carson. Once known as Dr. Doom for his dour moods and lack of communication skills, Belichick adapted his style with the players and began to look for more inventive ways to reach them (though Belichick retains his sometimes paranoid and overly secretive ways when it comes to his dealings with the news media), especially during the Patriots' Super Bowl XXXVI run, which might be the best championship coaching job ever.

Some of Belichick's approaches have been devilishly clever. To break the monotony of training camp he once showed a film about the life of Sir Ernest Shackleton, who, with his 28 men, survived in the Antarctic from 1914 to 1916 following the destruction of their ship. The message: a group of men, if they work together, can survive anything. During Super Bowl week Belichick responded to players' complaints that their hotel rooms were too small by taking turns giving his own suite away to them. The following season, during training camp, he

invited Hall of Famer Bill Russell to speak to the team about the keys to
repeating.

Throughout the entire 2002 season Belichick never mentioned the
franchise's impressive Super Bowl victory to the players—until 24 hours
before their December 29 contest against Miami, both teams' final
regular-season game. A playoff spot was on the line for both, and Belichick
decided some extra motivational strategy was needed. Belichick lugged
the Lombardi Trophy to a team meeting the night before the game, and
the eyes of everyone in the room lit up like scoreboards. "There's a reason why this is here," Belichick told a quiet room. "Because we're still
the champions." New England won in overtime, 27–24, but the win
came too late—the Patriots missed the playoffs, as did their Super Bowl
opponent, St. Louis, showing just how difficult it is to navigate an NFL
season.

Gruden is approaching the level of a Parcells or Belichick when it
comes to drilling inside a player's head, always finding that little something to fire up his team, using information to get under players' skin,
the way a thorn irritates a lion's paw. Sometimes he relays a story or
prank to calm and focus them. When Tyrone Wheatley in 1999 was
preparing to go against his old coach, Dan Reeves, Gruden decided to
make sure his running back was at ease. Reeves and Wheatley had a
tense relationship when the two were with the Giants, with Wheatley
eventually leaving New York and rejuvenating his career in Oakland.
Wheatley going against Reeves for the first time was a major topic that
week around the Raiders.

One day after practice Wheatley arrived home to find a large bou-
quet of flowers sitting atop a desk. Wheatley's wife stared at him cross-
eyed, also curious about who had sent Wheatley the nice flora. Wheatley
opened the card, which read: "I can't wait to see you. You've always been
my favorite player. Love, your boy, Dan Reeves." It took several days for
one of Gruden's assistants to admit that Gruden was indeed the flower
bandit. The move allowed Wheatley to have a laugh during what might
have been an anxious week for him and illustrated that Gruden is always
thinking of his players.

One Raiders player remembers another example of Gruden rallying around his troops, though this example is a bit grittier—some would

say nastier. The week Oakland was scheduled to play Miami in 1999, cornerback Sam Madison, a strong man-to-man defender who hides the power of a bear under a slight frame, was a hot topic in Raidersville. Gruden and some of the Raiders players thought Madison was too big a talker, and that Oakland's corners were better anyway, chiefly Charles Woodson, the number-one pick from the University of Michigan. Gruden caught wind of the chatter among his players and decided it was time to teach the mouthy Madison a lesson. When Gruden was speaking to a group of offensive players, he told his receivers he wanted Madison punished.

"I want his ass knocked out of the game," a Raiders player recalls Gruden saying.

"But what about the fine?" one wideout asked. Such a move would surely draw the ire of the NFL and lead to a hefty financial penalty that would come straight out of the offender's pocket.

"Shit, I'll pay the fine," Gruden replied.

Gruden's request backfired. When the Miami contest arrived on October 31, none of the Raiders were able to get a clean shot on Madison, though several tried. When Raiders wide receiver Terry Mickens made contact with Madison, it wasn't the knockout blow Gruden was allegedly looking for, but it wasn't a kiss on the cheek either. Still, the hit failed to either put the corner out of the game or shut his mouth, and Mickens was called for pass interference on Madison. The penalty nullified a 48-yard reception from Gannon to Brown, which would have given Oakland the ball at the Miami 12-yard line. Instead, the Raiders faced a third-and-17, and Gannon was sacked to end the drive.

"Jon walked up to me during one practice and said, 'If you get a chance, knock him out, knock his block off,'" Mickens recalls in an interview. "I don't remember him saying, 'Take him out.' He didn't use those exact words. But you read between the lines. You just understood that Jon wanted him out of the game. So I tried to do it. It happened on a crossing route, and I had a chance to get at him, so I tried to smash him. That's what the coach asked me to do. He could get players to do almost anything."

Such a scene is disturbing for several reasons, and one of them is that players cannot complain about the long-term toll the violence of

the sport takes on their bodies and then become almost on-field hit men,
trying to take out a fellow competitor on a coach's whim.

The request was one of the few missteps Gruden has made
throughout what has been an almost flawless start to his NFL head-
coaching career. Gruden's star rose quickly inside the Raiders organization and around the league, especially after the team started to ignite.
There were two pivotal moments in Gruden's Raiders coaching tenure.
Oakland's recent history was more black and blue than silver and black,
as few NFL franchises were mocked for ineptitude like the Raiders, but
Gruden, with a refined Gannon (thanks to Gruden's offensive system), a
star in Brown, and a solid running game rejuvenated in part by Wheatley, stormed to the American Football Conference title game on January
14, 2001—the first time the Raiders had traveled that far in the postseason in a decade. But Gruden's Raiders were outclassed by one of the top
three defenses of all time, one that featured the all-world linebacker
Ray Lewis. Oakland fell behind 10–0, and once Gannon was knocked
out of the game early with a shoulder injury, the Raiders never had a
chance, losing 16–3.

The following year Gruden again brought the Raiders to the playoffs. In the divisional game against New England on January 19, 2002, at
a snowy Foxboro Stadium, the Raiders had a 13–10 lead with 7:53 left.
After the two teams exchanged punts, the Raiders faced a third-and-1 at
their own 44-yard line with just over two minutes left. If they had converted, the game would likely have been over, and the Raiders would
have traveled to Pittsburgh for the AFC title contest—and probably
would have won. But on that third-down play, Zack Crockett was
stopped for zero yardage. Later, with 1:50 remaining and New England
possessing the football at Oakland's 42, Woodson blitzed and hit quarterback Tom Brady, who clearly fumbled, but a replay review overturned
the fumble call and ruled that Brady's dropped ball was an incomplete
pass. The Patriots would go on to make the tying field goal, and Brady, in
overtime, completed all eight of his pass attempts, including one on
fourth down, to set up the game-winning kick. Thus, the "tuck rule"
was thrust into football lore, and the Raiders, who have battled the
league for years, cried conspiracy—everyone except Gruden.

To him the devil was in the details, not in the tuck, and when asked about that snowy, frustrating day, Gruden responded only as Gruden could, telling a newspaper columnist: "We had the ball third-and-1 at midfield with two minutes left. We ran 14 Blast. We were 15-for-16 on third down with 14 Blast. Steve Wisniewski, guard, on a thread pull, Zack Crockett the ball carrier, with Jon Ritchie leading on Bryan Cox— basic front we've worked on since Day 1. We're 15-for-16! But their linebacker starts quivering. Our right guard—I'm not being critical here—makes a hard call. You don't make a hard call. No one blocks the three technique. We get hit in the backfield for no gain. Punt the ball, hit a squib, Troy Brown runs it back to the 40, they go down, and [Adam] Vinatieri hits an amazing kick in a freakin' blizzard, 47 yards in a foot of snow to send it to overtime. We got what we deserved. We lost that game on 14 Blast. It wasn't a conspiracy. It wasn't the tuck. It wasn't the kicks. It was 14 Blast."

In football a successful tactic or coaching technique is often copied. When a handful of teams started to perfect the zone blitz in the early 1990s, that defense became one of the more utilized in the NFL. Then there are those franchises that don't bother with copying; they would rather simply steal the brains that dreamed up the strategies in the first place. That is what happened with Gruden. His winning style, his aggression, his football-is-life mentality, his expert play calling—the best in football—attracted suitors, and late in Gruden's tenure with Oakland the rumors started flying. He was being linked to almost every high-profile job opening there was, including the University of Notre Dame and Ohio State, two top-ten college offers he turned down. Several times, before team meetings, Gruden assured the players he wasn't going anywhere. "I'm going to win a Super Bowl with the Raiders," he stated flatly in one team session. Wheatley remembers that "a lot of guys predicated their futures on the fact that Jon said he was staying. Some guys had opportunities to go elsewhere, better opportunities, with more money, better deals, you know, but they stayed for Jon, and Jon told us he was going to win a championship with us. Most of the guys loved Jon and believed him." At the end of the 2002 season players packed their lockers and headed for home, thinking that next year Gruden would be back, and the team was primed for a championship jaunt.

What many of the players did not know was that Gruden was outgrowing the Raiders. He wanted more say—a lot more—in personnel matters, which is a no-no with Al Davis running the show. Coaches in this situation are not necessarily being greedy or power-hungry; a head coach simply wants to control his own destiny. Some figure that if they are going to be the ones scrutinized and criticized, sliced and diced by fans and the news media, fired, and then fired again, they should be able to pick the players they are going to coach. Parcells's famous quote prior to abandoning New England for the New York Jets following the 1996 season embodies these feelings perfectly: "If they want you to cook the meal, then you've got to be able to buy the groceries." By 2002 some 13 head coaches had final say on personnel matters. Gruden did not need *all* of the power, but he wanted more. He was ready for a bigger challenge, and he was ready to get away from Davis.

Thousands of miles away, Gruden's destiny was being played out on the Florida coast, where Tony Dungy, the soft-spoken defensive strategist, had led the Buccaneers to the playoffs in four of his six seasons, including 1999, when Tampa Bay made it to the conference title game. It was a solid record but not good enough in today's football, which says a lot about how high expectations have become for coaches. Dungy was fired, and the debacle that followed was comical. After making runs at San Francisco's Mariucci, then considering Marvin Lewis—a choice by general manager Rich McKay that was later overruled by ownership— the team next settled on luring Parcells out of retirement. Owner Malcolm Glazer and the Glazer family had consistently denied to the public that they had even conversed with Parcells, despite massive evidence to the contrary, including Parcells's attempts to hire a staff. The Glazer family protestations were, of course, some of the more scurrilous lies ever told in the long history of professional football. Not only was the team speaking to Parcells while Dungy was still the coach, but the Glazers had actually signed him to a four-year contract. The Buccaneers were stunned, however, when Parcells took his signed deal and backed out on the team at the last minute. Tampa Bay, highly embarrassed, frustrated, and desperate—morale was so low within the organization that McKay, while scouting players in Alabama at the Senior Bowl, felt the need to give a pep talk to his scouts, right there, on the practice sideline— decided to throw everything into the pot and go after Gruden. The bounty the team offered Davis to get the star coach was rich—two first-round selections, two second-round selections, and $8 million in cash. Tampa Bay ownership should have tossed in a free meal at Shula's Steak House while they were at it. While I feel that even at that steep price a talent like Gruden is worth the expenditure, the Buccaneers could have gotten Gruden much cheaper but were desperate after the Mariucci, Lewis, and Parcells flops to retain the franchise's dignity.

Gruden didn't tell some of his closest friends on the Raiders he was leaving until the last minute, which to this day still disappoints, and angers, some on the Oakland coaching staff. Bill Callahan, who would replace Gruden as Raiders head coach, has been a close friend of Gruden's for over a decade. They met while Gruden was with the Green Bay Packers and Callahan was at the University of Wisconsin. When Gruden became coach of the Raiders, he signed Callahan to the staff, and Callahan would remain a Gruden assistant for Gruden's four-year tenure, serving as a tight ends coach, offensive line coach, and offensive coordinator and calling the running plays every year. Still, as friendly as they were, Callahan wasn't sure exactly what was going on until Gruden was practically out the door. One Monday morning in mid-February, Callahan strolled into Gruden's office and asked if he wanted to walk together to the meeting room, where the staff was gathering. "Why don't you go run the meetings today," Gruden replied. "I'll catch up with you later."

That would be among the last moments Callahan would see his friend Gruden for months. Gruden bolted the Raiders with the abruptness of a cat burglar who had just tripped an alarm and knew the cops were on the way. "When Jon first left," Callahan explains, "we were all taken aback." Gruden became the seventh head coach in Tampa Bay history when he signed a five-year deal on February 18, 2002. Signing with Tampa Bay gave Gruden even more standing in the NFL and branded him as the hottest coach in the sport. Gruden had become Raiders coach at just 34, the youngest in the league, and four years later he was coach of the Buccaneers, with a résumé that included 40 victories before his 40th birthday, something few men have accomplished in modern NFL history.

Back in Oakland, Davis, who loathes the news media, called a press

conference, which is about as common an occurrence as a Bigfoot sight-
ing. Davis wanted to gloat, and he had a right to, since he had taken
some masterful beatings at the hands of other NFL owners as well as the
press in the pre-Gruden era. Now it was time for Davis to chirp: he had
pulled off a heist not seen since Butch and Sundance. In a masterful
stroke that was typical Davis, he signed all of the Raiders assistants to
contract extensions before letting Gruden go, so Gruden could not take
his coaches with him to Tampa Bay.

Some of the Raiders players were talking as much as Davis but saying different things. There was an initial sense among some of the
Raiders that Gruden had abandoned them and that he should have met
with the team to say good-bye. Jerry Porter said that the day before Gruden departed he was at the team facility rehabilitating his shoulder.
Gruden walked in and asked trainer Mark Mayer if Porter would be
ready to play in the coming season. Mayer said yes. Porter explained that
Gruden looked right at him, smiled, and said, "I love you, bro'. I'm
counting on you." Gruden then suggested that the two men see Michael
Jordan play with the Washington Wizards when they came to Oakland.
"That was the last thing he said to me," Porter says. "I turned on ESPN
the next day: Jon Gruden, Tampa Bay Buccaneers."

"I'm not going to lie to you, I felt betrayed at first," says Wheatley.
"But after some time had passed I understood. First, that's just the way
football is. Everyone pretty much looks out for his own self-interest. As
players, we try to get the best contract we can and the best situations we
can. Jon was doing the same thing everyone else in the NFL does. This is
a game where people move on." Callahan also expressed understanding
about Gruden's departure. "I learned a great deal from Jon Gruden,"
Callahan explains. "I couldn't even begin to start with the vastness of
what I've acquired from him. He's an outstanding coach in every respect
and every facet. There's nobody I've ever been associated with that has
as much passion and energy for the game of football as Jon Gruden." At
the time other Raiders, like Brown, said that Gruden's in-your-mug style
had worn thin. Offensive lineman Lincoln Kennedy said that Gruden
"was like a little man who wanted to be a big man and wanted to rule
the world. He had kind of a Napoleonic complex." (Gruden would later
joke, when asked to comment on Kennedy's remarks, "He's exactly right

about that.") Guard Frank Middleton also sounded off on Gruden: "It was kind of hard to concentrate on football last year. Every week somebody had a different story about Gruden: 'He's going here. He's going there.' He was trying to downplay it a little bit, but it kind of made it hard. This year we've had no distractions. We have a coach that's going to be here and wants to be here." In actuality most of the Raiders liked Gruden, because he won, and were upset that he had departed, especially Gannon. Hurt—that is the word one player used. *Hurt.*

"I understand their bitterness," Gruden says. "I did not leave communicating very much. I left very quietly. I believe that's the only way to do it. I don't want to say anything negative, I don't want to say too much, and I don't want anything I say to be repeated. I expect some of those guys to have bitterness. Some guys you'll never please. That's one thing I have discovered. Hopefully down the road we'll be able to play a round of golf and all will be forgotten, man."

‖

An eerie sense of calm initially settled, at least on the surface, on the now-Gruden-led Buccaneers training camp in July 2002. As players prepared to move into their summer digs, a scene that most players were unaware of took place during a meeting between town officials from Celebration, Florida—host city of the team's camp—and Buccaneers representatives. It was the first time in almost three decades that the franchise held its camp in a place other than its home facility in Tampa. Buccaneers management picked Celebration because of its plush surroundings, but town officials were a bit concerned about football players moving into their pristine neighborhood (guess who's coming to dinner). A Buccaneers official recalls something that was said by a Celebration representative in what was supposed to be a welcome-to-our-city speech: "Basically we're a wealthy town that has a certain type of person. The residents don't want to hear loud music or see guys that look like thugs. You guys can train here, but we expect you to watch your players." The Tampa Bay representative says: "Basically what the guy was saying was, 'You can come here, but keep your niggers in check.'" Ironic, especially since Celebration, conceived by the Disney behemoth and located near one of Disney's massive theme parks, was supposed to be a socially engineered community of racially and economically diverse people. It never panned out. The scene is a reminder that no matter how much a black professional football player accomplishes, no matter how glamorous his job looks to many segments of our society, no matter how decent he is, to some people he is just a thug, a criminal.

None of this had anything to do with Gruden. He was unaware of the ugly scene, and once he firmly took control of the team, the initial serenity surrounding the opening of camp, which only lasted about a millisecond anyway, was shattered by his ferocious intensity. The Buccaneers were immediately Gruden-fied, or as one player put it, Gruden-fried, because anyone who came across the coach was roasted by that trademark fervor. The Gulf Coast would never be the same.

There is a saying: the toe you stepped on yesterday may be attached to the ass you have to kiss today. Gruden has never cared about making a lot of friends in football, or enemies for that matter. He is about doing the job, and only about that. In dealing with other people, he thinks only about who is good enough to come along for the ride, and who is not. If feelings get stepped on, well, too bad. This is football, Gruden reasons, and if you do not like it, there is a bowling alley up the street. There is no better evidence of this thought process than Gruden's initial months with the Buccaneers. He stomped through the organization with the same kind of ruthlessness he displays on the field as a play caller. It was a shock to the team's system. For years Buccaneers officials and players had been used to the gracious Dungy, one of football's gentlemen. Gruden can at times turn into a jackass, a description that matches the drill sergeant demeanor that other head coaches try on now and then. There are exceptions, but most of the time nice men do not win big in the NFL. In football the sensitive coach doesn't just finish last—he doesn't finish. Oh, Gruden did display a note of kindness here and there. He made sure to be respectful of Dungy's legacy since so many players were intensely fond of him. Gruden invited a group of former Buccaneers to dinner and gave quarterback Doug Williams, a football legend among many black fans in Tampa and around the country, a jersey with his name on it. "I can't believe it took 20 years until someone invited me back," Williams says. A sweet moment indeed, but other moments like it were few and far between. Many initial meetings between Gruden and team officials did not go smoothly, as Gruden was often gruff and blunt. When one team official tried to coax Gruden out of his office for a league event, Gruden replied, "I can't go anywhere. I've got to figure out how I'm going to win with all these turds on offense." McKay has publicly recounted that when he first went over the team roster with Gruden, that famous Gruden sneer emerged in full effect. "Jon gets going with, 'This guy stinks, this guy can't play, this guy has to go,'" McKay remembers. "I say, 'Jon, calm down, hold on, we've done okay here the past few years.'"

Gruden was not one to tiptoe around anything. Depending on whom you speak to, Gruden acted like a tyrant who would stop at nothing to win, or he was simply doing what the Buccaneers had long needed, which was get rid of the deadwood and laid-back attitude. One thing everyone agrees on: Gruden was not shy in those early days. He asked for anything and everything and often got it. At one point in the summer the Buccaneers were $70,000 under budget. Gruden told one team official: "I need more money to get the coaches I need. Let's get it done." Boom. It was. Such a request is one Dungy would have never made, and if he had, it probably would have been rejected.

Two days after Gruden took the job he called defensive lineman Warren Sapp, one of the team's leaders, into the office and started the meeting by making one of those classic, twisting Gruden faces, before proceeding to rail about how he needed the defense to improve its already hard-hitting reputation. Sapp wasn't intimidated by the Gruden stare, but Gruden still got his attention. *He's so different from Dungy,* Sapp thought. *He screams. He yells. He's in your face.* No question— Coach Chucky was in town.

Gruden's exclamations and high-velocity coaching style are indeed the norm for him—he is incapable of toning it down, the same way a cheetah in the African wild is incapable of becoming a vegetarian. But there was something else going on inside Gruden. He felt an immediate and steady pressure to justify the picks and cash the Buccaneers had surrendered to snag him. So his already fanatical work ethic went into overdrive. The Buccaneers saw Extreme Gruden. Players' descriptions of their initial encounters with him, from the various minicamps up until

training camp, almost sound like religious experiences. The Buccaneers'
practices were more energized as Gruden began demanding that players
run from drill to drill instead of walking. Safety John Lynch and Gruden had a conversation that started with Gruden saying how much he
liked Lynch as a player. Then Gruden suddenly blurted: "Enough with
the bullshit. I'm watching film on how to isolate number 47 in this first
minicamp, and let me tell you, the first time you bring that weakside
free safety blitz, I'm going to buzz a slant right by your fucking head.
You won't know what hit you." Lynch is the consummate pro, and he
was stunned when, later in the year, during a team meeting, Gruden
called him out, saying he needed even more production from him.
Lynch wasn't angry—quite the opposite. He was pumped. Lynch went
home and excitedly told his wife the story.

On the practice field Gruden energized what had been a one-
dimensional, poorly schemed offensive attack by inserting his more
aggressive, multifaceted system. In minicamp the Buccaneers ran more
than 1,000 plays, and by the time training camp arrived Gruden was trying to jump-start the offensive tempo by cramming dozens of plays into
eight to ten minutes.

Gruden was always in the faces of his players, especially the ones on
offense, and mainly the quarterbacks, particularly starter Brad Johnson,
the laid-back thrower who grew up on a dirt road in Black Mountain,
North Carolina, and whose personality was the polar opposite of Gruden's. The new Buccaneers coach was not at first sold on Johnson, which
is why the team brought in Rob Johnson, a free agent from Buffalo. Gruden was also never shy about expressing his affection for backup Shaun
King. Brad Johnson's casual personality and weird quirks—Johnson is a
neat freak who keeps several clean jerseys, pairs of socks, and elbow pads
in a metal case available for quick-changing if he gets a little too dirty
for his liking—sometimes frustrated Gruden. And the way Gruden spoke
so harshly initially got under Johnson's skin. "At first their relationship
was a little shaky," says Buccaneers running back Michael Pittman.

During a practice Gruden pulled Johnson aside when he thought
the quarterback failed to shout a series of fake audible calls at the line of
scrimmage with enough exuberance. "On the dummy audibles," Gruden told Johnson, "don't be a dumbass yourself." Johnson always kept an

open mind about the coach, despite the early moments of discomfort, because he had heard nothing but good things about him. When Gruden was hired, Johnson phoned Gannon, a former teammate in Minnesota, and the two chatted up the topic of Gruden, with Gannon on his cell phone, chomping on a hot dog while watching a hockey game. Gannon raved. "You're going to love playing for this guy," he explained. "You will never be more prepared for a game than you will be with Gruden as your coach."

Eventually Johnson and Gruden would use Stan Parrish, the quarterbacks coach, as a sort of buffer during games, when Gruden was the most fired up. As the season progressed, and the Bucs began winning, their tolerance level for each other increased and they began spending four, five, and even six hours a day together without too many feelings getting bent out of shape. "He knows how to challenge us, and he jabs us with different strokes," says Johnson of Gruden. And no player is exempt from Gruden's pokes. Keyshawn Johnson says that some of Gruden's swipes were so personal and vitriolic that he would force himself to walk away from Gruden after one of these pointed comments, because if he didn't, the two men would get into a heated argument. "By walking away," Keyshawn Johnson says, "I kept the peace."

One afternoon in training camp Gruden exploded after watching what he thought was a lackluster effort from the offense. So he did something I would think was impossible. As a prop for his latest mind trick, he used the team's pirate ship mini-replica, a sort of mascot located in the team's stadium end zone that comes equipped with a crew that fires mock cannons after a Buccaneers touchdown. After a dropped pass, Gruden called the offense into a huddle, himself in the middle, and not happy. "Look up there, damn it! See that fucking pirate ship? See those guys up there?" The ship was not in sight, since the Buccaneers weren't at the stadium, but instead at a training camp practice field. He was asking the players to use their imaginations. They got the point. "If we don't get in the end zone, they can't do their fucking jobs! So let's put these guys to work and get in the fucking end zone, all right?"

Once the season began, Gruden continued to push and probe the players, catching their attention, earning their respect, and occasionally angering a small number of them, all at the same time. Gruden's goal was to get his team always thinking. His weekly Saturday speeches were invigorating, and he alternated between Thoughtful Gruden and Psycho Gruden. During one practice session before playing underachieving Minnesota midway through the season, Gruden went ballistic, threatening wholesale player firings and benchings. Another time Gruden used old game film of Lawrence Taylor to inspire his defense. In November 2002, after a 23–10 victory over Carolina that gave Tampa Bay an 8–2 record—the best 10-game start in franchise history—Gruden did the same thing the Wednesday following the game, as the team prepared for Green Bay, that he had done each Wednesday since the season began.

"Who's the best team on our schedule?" Gruden said to the players.

"Green Bay," the players responded in unison.

"And why is that, men?" Gruden asked.

"Because they're next," the players said.

After that Wednesday gathering players arrived at the complex for Thursday practice, and on a table in the middle of the locker room was a gargantuan slab of granite, weighing several hundred pounds. Gruden's message, which was embraced by the players: Be that blue-collar player who is pounding the rock every day. Keep chipping away at it. To Gruden the rock represented the season: getting to a Super Bowl would take constant, persistent effort by every player on the roster to wear down that piece of stone.

Some of Gruden's motivational ploys failed to reach everyone. There were players who thought they were childish and unnecessary. In Oakland, wide receiver Porter had been a favorite target of Gruden's. Feeling that Porter was failing to get the most out of his ability, Gruden constantly berated him. Raiders players describe the tactics Gruden used on Porter as thoroughly humiliating. They claim that during one practice, before members of the team, Gruden called Porter a "dumbass motherfucker." In another practice, players claim, Gruden said to Porter: "You'll never make it big in this league because you're too fucking stupid." Porter says that when Gruden left Oakland, "at the time, I had a sigh of relief. I felt I didn't have to fight with my coach anymore. I felt I didn't have to worry about having confrontation after confrontation with him and getting pissed off all the time just because of the way he was talking to me."

Porter barely played under Gruden but exploded into a receiving force once Gruden departed the Raiders. While Porter hated Gruden at the time, he is quick to point out that Gruden did make him a better player. In the Raiders' 2002 Super Bowl season Porter had one touchdown every 5.7 catches, tying him for first in the NFL.

In Tampa Bay, wide receiver Keyshawn Johnson, a tough, smart, and opinionated player, likes Gruden, but the two have never completely clicked. By December 2002, they were still attempting to decipher one another. They engaged in a sideline shouting match during one contest, and Johnson said in several interviews late in the regular season that he was frustrated by his lack of involvement in the offense. "He's still trying to figure me out," Johnson told me. "He has to know that I will jump over the wall. I don't need a coach to tell me how to jump over the wall. Just point the way." One Buccaneers player says: "Sometimes I hate coach Gruden. He's the biggest son-of-a-bitch I've ever played for, but he's also the best coach I've ever played for. He gets everything out of you, even if he goes overboard sometimes."

This reaction is something that happens to all successful coaches. The good ones are indeed hated, sometimes despised, but they manage to push their players hard, dragging the team into the postseason screaming, kicking, cursing—and when the winning starts, the moaning is quieted.

In Oakland, Gruden's spirit single-handedly revived a lifeless franchise. In Tampa Bay, the situation was not nearly as dire, since the Buccaneers had visited the postseason for three consecutive years before Gruden arrived, and under Dungy they had once almost reached the Super Bowl. Still, Tampa Bay, on the offensive side of the ball, lacked confidence. When the Buccaneers clinched a playoff spot by beating Detroit 23–20 on December 15, 2002—with that win Gruden joined Mike Holmgren as one of only two coaches in league history to take two different teams to the postseason in consecutive years, another impressive achievement on Gruden's résumé—Buccaneers players were privately saying that the road to the Super Bowl would go through Tampa Bay. That turned out not to be the case, but Gruden had the players so confident that they believed the Super Bowl was theirs to take, and they believed Gruden would lead them there.

"What we were definitely missing was a screamer and yeller," Keyshawn Johnson says. "Coach Dungy was a wonderful coach, but he didn't get the best out of everybody. Gruden is able to do that."

What cannot be understated is Gruden's skill as a tactical offensive coach. It is true that Gruden, like almost every offensive coaching mind in history, has stolen bits and pieces of strategy from other systems—a little Walsh "West Coast" offense, a little Shanahan, and a piece of Holmgren have all made it into Gruden's playbook. But Gruden is best when it comes to two things: calling the right play for the right situation and disguising from the defense where the play is going and whom the ball will reach. Because of the shifting and motion Gruden creates before the ball is snapped, as well as his use of numerous formations— he occasionally uses as many as 15 different formations in the first 15 plays, and then watches how a defense reacts—Gruden's offense presents the illusion that the play unfolding is a complicated one when it really is not. Against Carolina, a Gruden play call sent one Buccaneers wide receiver deep and another on a crossing route. The Panthers players clearly thought the two trotting wideouts were the principal targets and reacted by focusing on them. Wrong choice. Keenan McCardell, the third wide receiver, was the main objective of Johnson all along, and the confusion due to the shifting and route running left McCardell isolated on a linebacker—no contest. He made the catch.

Gruden creates many mismatches in the most dangerous part of the field for a defense, the middle, behind the linebackers and in front of the safeties. A missed tackle here in the Bermuda Triangle leads to an offensive player scampering for a touchdown or big gain. No matter how much some of the best defensive coordinators try to stop it, Gruden succeeds at creating what Giants linebacker Mike Barrow has nicknamed "jerk routes"—the mismatches that happen, for instance, when a fast wide receiver is covered by a slow, burly linebacker, who ends up looking like a jerk. Against Atlanta on December 8, in one of the biggest matchups of the 2002 regular season, the Buccaneers' defense stifled the explosive Michael Vick, but Gruden's offense, which thoroughly outsmarted the Falcons' defense, was a vital story line. On one play offensive tackle Lomas Brown lined up at tight end, encouraging a pre-snap read that a run play was to follow. But out of that run formation came a pass, and it completely hoodwinked the Falcons, who left tight end Rickey Dudley open down the middle for the catch.

As special as Gruden's offense is, it took some time for the players to grapple with its nuances and fully embrace it. Through the first eight weeks of the season the Buccaneers averaged just 15.1 points a contest. Then suddenly the tortoise pace at which the players were digesting Gruden's schemes quickened to the level of their head coach's pulse. During a five-game stretch that spanned from mid-November into December, the scoring average jumped 11 points, to 26.8 points a game, and Brad Johnson during that time tossed 15 touchdown passes and one interception, completing 65.5 percent of his throws. Johnson had 22 touchdown passes at this point, owning the franchise's single-season record with three games to go. The concepts Gruden had been preaching to Johnson, the blitz pickups, the hot reads, the plays themselves, all of which once seemed like nuclear physics to Johnson, were starting to make sense. Johnson remarked to teammates that he felt it would take two additional years to grasp Gruden's offense completely, but he seemed to be doing just fine now.

Johnson was always a solid quarterback, playing in Minnesota and Washington and for the London Monarchs of the NFL Europe, but he was never as hot as he was in Tampa Bay, where he finished the 2002 season as the conference's top-rated passer and in seven home games tossed 16 touchdown passes and one interception. Many coaches believe Johnson benefited from Gruden's system. "Jon and his system have taught Brad to be very efficient and an excellent decisionmaker," Mariucci says. "Brad has had some good years, but I think that was his best year." Gruden's system had thoroughly turned around Rich Gannon's career as well. Before arriving in Oakland, Gannon was seen as a career backup; in 1994, after coming off of shoulder surgery, there was such a lack of interest in the then-free agent that he telephoned well over a dozen franchises to see if any wanted him on their roster. Few did.

Gruden's relentless hard work in Tampa Bay, all those mornings and nights of breaking down film, the constant give-and-take with Brad and Keyshawn Johnson, and the offense, the mind games, the lack of sleep, had paid off already. The offense now embodied Gruden: it was smart, cocky, and aggressive.

Gruden's offenses, however, are not perfect—far from it. Sometimes he is too aggressive. Against Pittsburgh on December 23, 2002, Brad Johnson was sidelined because of a painful lower back injury, which gave quarterback King, whom Gruden liked, his first start since the 2000 season. There was little doubt that King would have cobwebs in his cranium after sitting on the bench for 31 games, but instead of protecting King by running the ball more, Gruden called for passes on eight of the Buccaneers' first 11 offensive plays. One of them was intercepted and returned 30 yards by Steelers cornerback Chad Scott for a touchdown. There were two lost fumbles, six sacks allowed, and three dropped passes in that contest overall—as well as the charge by Pittsburgh defender Lee Flowers that the Buccaneers were nothing but "paper champions." Gruden believes that if Johnson had started, the outcome might have been different; nevertheless, the loss was a setback for Gruden and King, as the quarterback was no mental match for Pittsburgh's complicated blitzing schemes, despite the fact that in practice all week Gruden had gone over blitz protection repeatedly.

The label of "top coach" is a highly subjective one. It's a label that Bill Parcells should have automatically, but his union with Dallas owner Jerry Jones will probably last as long as a Hollywood marriage—imagine what has to happen eventually with two sumo wrestlers, circling each other. Parcells might hit the eject button the moment Jones drops a hint about what play Parcells should call. Consequently, Parcells's candidacy for top coach must be temporarily suspended until he demonstrates that he can last in Dallas longer than the time it takes to cook Texas barbeque.

My top ten coaches in today's NFL go this way. After Gruden comes Bill Belichick of New England, the cleverest coach I have ever met, who won the Super Bowl over St. Louis with intellect and a dash of guile. Philadelphia's Andy Reid is flourishing in the toughest place to coach and has won 11, 11, and 12 games over the past three years through the 2002 season (though he is 0–2 in NFC championship games). Tennessee's Jeff Fisher just continues to win, even with a banged-up quarterback in Steve McNair and a runner, in Eddie George, who is wearing down. Brian Billick of Baltimore sometimes comes off as a little smug, but he is a solid leader. Mike Shanahan, like Belichick, wins through intellect. With John Elway's retirement four regular seasons ago, however, Shanahan is now 33–30 entering the 2003 season, so he drops on the list when normally he would be an automatic top-three coach. Bill Cowher has the Steelers in the Super Bowl mix every season. Mike Sherman of Green Bay is 33–14 in his three years as Packers head man and has the best regular-season winning percentage of any active coach—but he gets handicapped for having Brett Favre, one of the top NFL stars ever. Jim Fassel's Giants had the second-worst meltdown in playoff history with their loss to the 49ers in the 2002 postseason, but Fassel is 19–5 in December, and the team plays hard for him. Number ten is a tie between Steve Mariucci, who will turn around the Detroit Lions, and a coach who will quickly move up the charts in the years to come—Herman Edwards of the Jets, who mixes a quick mind and an ability to rally his players. On October 30, 2002, his team stuck at 2–5 and going nowhere, Edwards gave what is now an infamous speech to reporters when he responded to a question on whether his players might be quitting on the season. "This is what the greatest thing about sports is: you play to win the game. *Hello,* you play to win the game. You don't play to just play it. That's the great thing about sports: *you play to win.* I don't care if you don't have any wins, you go play to win. When you start telling me it doesn't matter, then retire, get out, because it matters. . . . One thing I know, I don't quit. That will not happen. That will not happen."

Edwards was in front of the press at a news conference, but he was using the media to reach his players, and the message was that anyone who refused to fight was not wanted. Go elsewhere. The Jets went on to become the first AFC team ever to open 2–5 and then win the division. It was a superb coaching job.

San Diego's Marty Schottenheimer, Atlanta's Dan Reeves, Dick Vermeil in Kansas City, Tony Dungy of Indianapolis, and Cleveland's Butch Davis—who took the Browns to the playoffs in 2002 for the first time since 1994—are other solid leaders who with a few wins here and there could easily leapfrog into the top ten.

Many times the only difference between a great coach and a terrible one is the players at his disposal. A small fraternity of coaches can take any roster of players, no matter how mediocre, and transform them into winners. This is what Parcells does so well, and why so many teams trip over themselves trying to lasso him, despite knowing he has more baggage than Continental Airlines. Despite the occasional bumps on the turf, Gruden is now on that level as well, simply because if you stuck him anywhere, on any team, whether it was the hapless Cincinnati Bengals or a top franchise like Philadelphia, he would win. A Gruden team will own a swagger. They become Gruden-fried.

What gives Gruden an edge over many other coaches are two tactics: turning around multiple franchises and doing so quickly. Both are terribly difficult to accomplish, but Gruden has made it look simple.

More than 150 men have debuted as a head coach in the NFL in the Super Bowl era, which began in 1966, and only three won 40 or more games by their 40th birthday. Entering the game against Pittsburgh, Gruden had a career mark of 49–29, and he was 39 years old. Steelers Coach Bill Cowher, who turned 40 before the 1997 season, was 53–27 from 1992 to 1996. John Madden, another ex-Raiders coach, was 70–21–7 before he turned 40. Cowher and Madden both made Super Bowl appearances, so Gruden is in excellent company.

When the Buccaneers won the National Football Conference South, Gruden became the first coach in league history to win two division titles with two different teams in consecutive seasons.

The December 23 Steelers-Buccaneers game did illustrate that holes can be found in Gruden's offenses, that there is kryptonite for his cockiness. Still, the Buccaneers had an aggressive tone on offense for the first time in years. Sapp, the mouthy defensive tackle, says the Buccaneers used to be "a blue-collar team that played the field-position game. Now, there's no such thing as a field-position game. Gruden gets the ball, and he thinks he can score from anywhere. You can put him in Afghanistan, he thinks he can score a touchdown."

II

Some say Gruden is a son-of-a-bitch, but actually he's the son of a coach. Twenty years ago Gruden's father, Jim, was an assistant on the Buccaneers' staff when John McKay was head coach. Jim was eventually fired, but he and his wife, Kathy, stayed in the Tampa area. The family was immersed in sports, and Jon took a liking to football almost immediately. He and his younger brother, Jay, would imitate the deep-throated snap count of Doug Williams. Jon caught the virus early and was full-blown infected even before the Tampa Bay days, when Notre Dame hired his father in 1978. As a young athlete, Gruden was not blessed with great athletic skill, but he was always much smarter than he thought he was, not just a "ham and egger," which is the term he has used for some time to describe himself. Gruden had a competitive spirit when he participated in high school sports, but that spirit failed to overcome his height disadvantage. Despite a solid quarterback career at South Bend Clay High School in Indiana, there was not a large demand from the top football factories for a five-foot-nine-inch thrower with mediocre arm strength and the speed of chilled pancake syrup. He stayed one year at Muskingum College in Ohio before transferring to Dayton, where he spent most of his career as a backup.

While at Dayton, Gruden filled out a questionnaire about what he wanted to do with his future. He wrote that he wanted to be head coach of Michigan by the age of 39. He would obviously have to settle for a little more.

It was at this point in his life that Gruden discovered just how deep his sleep deficit issues were. Nothing could keep his eyes closed for more than three or four hours—not throwing practice spirals at 4:00 A.M., not reading magazines cover to cover, not writing a half-dozen letters. He took sleeping pills and visited doctors, who told him there was nothing to be overly concerned about. Gruden did not know it at the time, but his inability to capture significant rest, which has had no negative effects on his health thus far, would become a priceless advantage.

Gruden took a graduate assistant position in 1985 at the University of Tennessee following his departure from Dayton, and it was there he met Cindy Brooks, a Volunteers cheerleader. The future Cindy Gruden never went out with another man again. "I loved his confidence, his dedication," she says. "He was also a perfect gentleman."

Once at Tennessee, Gruden's career took off on the kind of accelerated curve rarely before seen in modern football, and two Gruden trademarks punctuated his steady climb: constant film study, hours upon hours almost every day, and the study of his bedroom ceiling, since his sleep-deprived nights were a constant fixture. When Walt Harris, Tennessee's offensive assistant, was named head coach of the University of the Pacific, he took Gruden with him as receivers coach. Harris loved Gruden's work habits but was concerned about his sleep habits. Gruden lived with a group of coaches in a small apartment and would awaken his roommates by doing push-ups at two in the morning. He so annoyed some of the coaches that they moved him to another part of the building where his bizarre sleep habits would not disturb anyone.

A year later, in 1990, Gruden was hired by San Francisco for $500 a month, as an aide to Holmgren, who was the offensive coordinator under head coach George Seifert. Gruden ingested the "West Coast" offense scheme the way a fat SUV gulps gas. He was a convert, and his constant studying and hyperactive work ethic enabled him to pick up details and nuances of the system that had gone undetected even by men like Holmgren and one of the "West Coast" architects, and another Gruden mentor, Paul Hackett.

The future Hall of Fame thrower Steve Young was frustrated by his status as backup to Joe Montana. Irritated by his dealings with Young, Holmgren turned over coaching of the quarterback to Gruden, who turned the entire exercise into a game. He quizzed Young on aspects of the game plan, handing him a point when he got things right—What does this audible mean? Who does the back block in this coverage?—and subtracting a point when he was incorrect. Gruden, his mind a steel trap, would blow Young away.

There was nothing Gruden was not asked to do. He was the get-back coach during games, meaning it was his duty to keep the players behind the white line so officials did not penalize the team. He passed out jerseys. If the offense was short a quarterback during practice drills, in would step Gruden, who could throw some darts.

When his eyes again popped open at night, sleep failing to snatch him, he would digest Walsh's old game plans, which, to a coach, especially a young one like Gruden wanting to become an offense specialist, was the equivalent of a historian poring over an original copy of the Bill of Rights. Gruden took notes, spending hours by himself absorbing old school West Coast, logging thousands of his thoughts into stacks of notepads.

Holmgren became coach of the Packers in 1992, and he packed Gruden, who was an assistant at the University of Pittsburgh, and his energy into a suitcase, and took him along, naming him a Packers assistant coach. Holmgren later promoted Gruden to wide receivers coach, and the aggressive way Holmgren broke down film seeped into Gruden's coaching style. Wide receiver Terry Mickens played under Gruden in Oakland and Green Bay and remembers the new Packers assistant as cocky, excitable, and possessed of so much vigor he was a walking solar flare. Mickens recalls that Gruden rarely eased the receivers into practice after warm-ups, refusing to allow time for their bodies to adjust to the freezing temperatures. "If you think he's intense now, he was worse in Green Bay when he was receivers coach," Mickens says. "Some practices once winter rolled around got pretty cold, as you might imagine. After just a few minutes on the field he had us running routes, full speed, and you just prayed you didn't pull a muscle."

Gruden's energy level stayed nuclear when he was hired by Eagles' head coach Ray Rhodes to become the NFL's youngest offensive coordinator at 31 years old in 1995. Gruden punctuated his Eagles tenure like he has everywhere else he has coached—by rising early and outworking everyone. He would drive in the dark over the Walt Whitman Bridge at three o'clock to begin his day while other coaches were still snoozing. Philadelphia's offense was ranked third in 1996 and first in 1997, under Gruden, who made an impression on the Eagles players by running pass routes with them to demonstrate exactly how he wanted the offense orchestrated, sporting his hat on backwards, his tiny clipboard with plays and notes on it tucked into his waistband.

If his intensity has subsided since then, even one degree, it is difficult to tell. Late in the Buccaneers' 2002 season, as the playoffs approached, Gruden was again probing and pushing his way into the heads of his players. Historically Tampa Bay has performed miserably in the postseason on the road. The Buccaneers had never won a playoff contest away from the comforts of their home stadium in the franchise's entire existence, and like the mad scientist he is, Gruden began early on planting the seeds of the idea that overcoming that embarrassing obstacle should no longer be so difficult, because he was there, and he would lead the way. Gruden said, with a swagger, "There is a perception around here that we are going to curl up in a fetal position and die if we have to play a road playoff game. I say hogwash. Hell, we're in the playoffs. I saw the Ravens, close range, do it [two] consecutive weeks [in 2000]. They did it to me [in Oakland] and rallied and won the Super Bowl. So we are going to take that challenge of the playoffs when we get there. But it's not do or die. It's not like, 'Get homefield or we're out.' " Soon after that Buccaneers players were parroting Gruden's words, and the phrase "fetal position" became a favorite around Bucs practices.

The Buccaneers followed a tough loss to Pittsburgh on *Monday Night Football* with a solid victory over Chicago the following Sunday evening. The win gave Tampa Bay a franchise-best 12–4 record, but more important, the team ended an embarrassing streak in which they were 0–21 in games when the kickoff temperature was below 40 degrees. Before the Bears game Gruden said of the statistic, "I think that's for mentally weak people, personally. I think that's an excuse. It's hogwash. If we even bend to those standards, we're going to be distracted and find a way to lose the game. We're going to go play this game and play hard regardless of the circumstances." (Among Gruden's favorite non-expletives are "hogwash" and "turds.") Gruden's players obviously bought into his message.

After a week off following the regular season, the Buccaneers entered the playoffs, and in their first game, on January 12, 2003, against San Francisco and Mariucci, Gruden's team exploded, scoring 28 first-half points, more than the franchise has ever scored in an *entire* postseason game in its *history*, and the four touchdowns were one short of what the team scored under Dungy in six total playoff games. It was Tampa Bay's first playoff win since January 15, 2000. "This team here has a bounce to it," Sapp said. "I knew it as soon as we left camp. I don't know what it is exactly, but it's there. It has to start with Jon, because he's all about the juice. He means the world to this whole ball club. He'll touch every guy in this room with a 30-second speech. There's something special about him, something special about the Little Guy."

‖

It was January 2003, and Gruden, following another intense Tampa Bay practice, walked off the field sporting his dark red visor, which partially hid his boyish face. His hands were tucked away in his pockets, and his blond hair was slightly disheveled. His look was casual, and when speaking to a group of reporters Gruden had the low-key enthusiasm of a surfer about to hit the waves, dude. But as with many things when it comes to Gruden, there was much more to him than met the eye.

The Buccaneers were preparing for their NFC title game at Philadelphia, which meant Gruden had another dragon to slay. He spent the week working his team, trying to change the franchise's mind-set. The Buccaneers did not have one road postseason victory in six attempts, a miserable record, and they were playing at Veterans Stadium against the heavily favored Eagles, in the cold. Most observers gave Tampa Bay no chance of winning. Gruden fed off this perception, not backing away from it or refusing to address such an ugly playoff history, as some coaches might have done. Instead, he told his team that the cold weather issues the Buccaneers faced were the problems of the old Buccaneers, not the new ones. "Worrying about cold weather is for pussies," Gruden told a group of his offensive players, according to one of them, "and I don't see any pussies on this team. This team is made of men." Gruden relayed tales from other sports and manipulated them for his purpose. He talked of golfer Tiger Woods overcoming racism and baseball's Randy Johnson pitching from the bullpen in the final contest of the 2001 World Series. Gruden's message was simply that great players and teams always prevail, no matter the circumstances—or weather. "You have greatness in you," Gruden told the Bucs.

Whether it was Gruden's demand for poise in the Philadelphia frigid elements—which was 26 degrees with a wind chill of 16 at kickoff—or some of his tactical skills, or Tampa Bay's ferocious defense, or all of the above, a focused Buccaneers team made an appearance in that January 20 game. For Gruden's part, he thoroughly outcoached Philadelphia defensive coordinator Jim Johnson when he used the no-huddle offense in key situations, which frustrated the Eagles' vaunted blitz packages by keeping the defense off balance. Gruden had quarterback Brad Johnson use three-step drops when passing instead of longer ones, which helped Johnson avoid the pressure. And again, as he had done all season, as he has done for years, Gruden was able to create numerous mismatches, aligning speedy wide receivers with slower linebackers. Facing what is called a bunch formation, in which three and four wide receivers are grouped closely together on the line of scrimmage, then dispersed in different directions, the Eagles defenders were often confused about which player should cover which Tampa Bay receiver. Trailing early 7–3, the Buccaneers faced a third-and-2 at their own 24-yard line when receiver Joe Jurevicius lined up on the right side of the field in the slot position, ran a crossing pattern, and drew single coverage from Philadelphia's Barry Gardner, a linebacker. The play was smartly innovative because in past games the Buccaneers had usually run that play deep in an opponent's territory, not deep in their own. Gruden knew that Philadelphia knew what Jurevicius had previously done (sounds like an Abbott and Costello routine) and decided to change Jurevicius's habits. Normally Jurevicius would have run a whip route on that play, going inside, toward the middle of the field, and then reversing course, breaking to the sideline. On that big gain, a play called Triple Right 83 Double Smash X Option, Jurevicius stopped, faked like he was going to run that whip pattern by stutter stepping, but continued on across the middle, in what is called a shake route. Gardner didn't have a chance.

There was another situation that showed how Gruden's schemes outwit a defense. On a second-down play, when the Buccaneers used their two tight end, two running back, and one wide receiver package—a formation that indicates heavily that a run is coming—the Eagles countered by inserting their own big bodies to answer the expected ground attack. Gruden's film study anticipated that the Eagles would do just that, and thus the chess game began. Gruden inserted his two backs, Mike Alstott and Mike Pittman, his two tight ends, Ken Dilger and Rickey Dudley, and Keyshawn Johnson at wide receiver. Philadelphia was forced to remove their quick but smallish pass rusher in defensive end Hugh Douglas and top cover linebacker, Shawn Barber, whose speed is a great asset to the Eagles, because they believed they needed bulk, not swiftness, to stop what they thought was going to be a run.

Once Gruden's formation dictated the removal of two of Philadelphia's best defenders, he fooled the Eagles. Through shifting, he changed the formation from a run set to a passing one, moving three players to the right in a passing trips formation, Johnson wide to the left by himself, and in the backfield Pittman, who was covered by poor Gardner, a backup with pedestrian speed. Pittman beat Gardner easily. The play illustrated how good Gruden is at exploiting even the smallest cracks in a defense.

To counter Philly's aggressive, blitzing defense, Gruden utilized a combination of quick throws, maximum protection of Johnson, and rapid adjustments along the offensive line, sometimes basing Tampa Bay's formations on the pre-snap look flashed by the Eagles. Gruden and the staff encouraged the offensive linemen to look for hints of a Philadelphia blitz by occasionally peeking into the Eagles' secondary and watching for pairs of feet creeping up toward the line of scrimmage.

There is another example of how hyper-detail-oriented Gruden is. Gruden suggested to Brad Johnson that he wear a thin sport glove on his throwing hand during cold weather games. Passes would fly off his mitt with ease, Gruden claimed. He didn't make this proposition, however, the week of the Philadelphia game. Gruden spoke to Johnson in the spring, during one of the team's first minicamps, so he was thinking about the cold weather when the Bucs were practicing in shorts and T-shirts, months before the chill was a focus. Against the Eagles, Johnson used the glove, the first time in his career he had done so, and he sliced Philadelphia's secondary. "I couldn't have thrown without it," said the quarterback.

Before that game against Philadelphia, the Buccaneers, in three games at Veterans Stadium, two of them in the playoffs, had not scored a single offensive touchdown. In the team's postseason road history, from 1981 to 2001, it had scored a measly 42 total points and three touchdowns. Against Philadelphia in the NFC title contest, the team had 27 points alone on drives of 96, 80, 43, and 37 yards.

The Buccaneers were in the Super Bowl, and Gruden—not single-handedly, but almost—had transformed the franchise from a onetime laughingstock into a winner, by getting the team to believe. Believe they could beat the cold. Believe they could beat the Eagles. Believe they could be the best. Believe in whatever he told them to. "It's kind of like that movie *The Wizard of Oz*," Gruden said after the game. " 'Ding, dong, the witch is dead.' "

The Buccaneers players celebrated for hours following their momentous victory, and Gruden did as well, but he, of course, had one eye on his old team, the Raiders, who were beating Tennessee for the right to make their own Super Bowl appearance. If there was any doubt about what the Super Bowl would become, Oakland's radio play-by-play man, Greg Papa, left little when he exclaimed, in the third quarter of Oakland's contest, "The Raiders lead 27–24, and they're 15 minutes away from A Date With Gruden!"

Welcome to Chucky Bowl I.

At the beginning of Super Bowl week, Gruden took the unusual step of skipping a meeting with the media so he could stay in Tampa and work on the game plan. At 4:30 A.M. on Tuesday he boarded a charter flight—the plane was loaned to the team by Dallas Mavericks owner Mark Cuban—and was soon in San Diego, wearing a red Buccaneers jacket over a white polo shirt and answering every conceivable question posed to him by hundreds of reporters. Gruden was extremely complimentary of the Raiders organization and its players, preferring not to stoke their fires, since Oakland players were already using Gruden as a rallying point. Oakland showed little such restraint, and it did not take long for several Super Bowl swipes at Gruden from the Raiders to work their way into reporters' notepads. "Gruden is not the coach of this football team," offensive linemen Lincoln Kennedy said. "He jumped ship and left us behind. Gruden might have built this team, but Callahan finished it."

Gruden ignored most of the constant Super Bowl chatter and focused on his team. The mind games he had employed all year did not cease once the Buccaneers were in the big game. Gruden rode Simeon Rice much of the week, knowing that Rice would go against left tackle Barry Sims, a graduate of NFL Europe—which is professional football's version of a semipro system—and considered the weak link on a powerful offensive line. Gruden pulled no punches. "You know what, Simeon?" Gruden told Rice, according to a teammate. "You're going against a guy that was playing for the fucking Scottish Claymores a few years ago. If you can't beat this turd, then you ain't shit." Gruden added: "I need two sacks from you, and not when the score is 20–0. You need to be big in this game. You need to take it over. This is your time."

Gruden's opponent and friend played his own head games with the Raiders. Callahan's pregame speech to the team was another example of NFL head coaches using any tactic, no matter how low-down and dirty it may be, to inspire their club. Callahan spent the entire Super Bowl week—indeed many months before that—stating publicly that he held no bitterness toward Gruden for leaving. Then Callahan completely contradicted himself the Saturday night before the game. In front of the entire team in their hotel, Callahan played on the feeling of betrayal some Raiders still harbored against Gruden by telling them that the true reason Gruden bolted Oakland was that he did not feel this group of Raiders could win a championship. This was not a particularly truthful statement, but it didn't matter. Callahan was convincing the Raiders it was so, and they applauded Callahan after he was done speaking in what Raiders players called the speech of Callahan's life. "Why does the score have to be close?" he told the players.

Callahan's tactic, once Super Bowl XXXVII started, quickly became a distant memory, and soon after the game began it was clear that this was the Buccaneers' night—and in many ways it was Gruden's night.

Everything Gruden did, from the first time he ventured into the Buccaneers' team facility, to his initial practice, to the biggest game of his life, all came together marvelously in a brilliant first half of football. It is nights like the one Tampa Bay had in the 2002 Super Bowl that coaches spend all of their lives chasing, and why they work so many ridiculously long hours. Gruden has tasted this wondrous moment very early in his career. Tampa Bay did not beat up on Oakland because of Gruden's offense—they smashed the Raiders, 48–21, because of the Buccaneers' defense, which was well entrenched before Gruden's arrival. Tampa Bay *did* win because of Gruden's overall skill, smarts, and fire. The Bucs rode his emotions all week and all game, just as they had all year. No, defense won this game, but Gruden had his hand on that side of the ball as well. Gruden had warned the defense not to fall for Gannon's delicious pump fakes, which can sucker even the most disciplined secondary. Once the game began, the Buccaneers defenders were amazed that the Raiders ran almost exactly the plays Gruden had said the Oakland offense would. Gruden had gone a step further than just telling the defense during practice that week. When the scout team had simulated the Oakland offense, Gruden lined up under center, playing Gannon, imitating Gannon's cadence and occasional sidearm throwing style, and predicting what the Raiders would do on offense. As Gruden ran around the field, that blond hair bouncing around, it was like he was back throwing passes at Dayton.

There is also the fact that Gannon and Gruden stayed in contact once Gruden departed Oakland, speaking often, as recently as one week before the Super Bowl, according to coaches and players on both teams. Tampa Bay defensive players believe Gruden used the friendship to his advantage while preparing for the championship, somehow drilling inside Gannon's head, as he once did when both were with the Raiders, and picking up small, inside details about the Raiders offense, doing so without Gannon ever being aware he was being mentally pickpocketed. Well, that's what the Bucs say anyway.

The challenge Gruden gave Simeon Rice was another Gruden tactic that worked splendidly. Rice sacked Gannon in the first, second, and third quarters, thoroughly dominating Sims. Smacking Gannon around when the Buccaneers truly needed it, not late when the game was out of hand, was just what Gruden had asked Rice to do.

Gruden's offense made its own contributions, of course. Gruden knew that to win he would need to establish the run early in the game, and again, his inside knowledge of Oakland's team proved productive. Gruden focused on attacking the outside edges of the Raiders defense, which are vulnerable to a power ground attack because of the team's smallish defensive ends. On the second Buccaneers drive, Gruden used Johnson, the wide receiver who weighs 212 pounds, to lay a tough block on defensive end Regan Upshaw, who weighs 260 pounds. The block, along with several others, sprung running back Pittman for 23 yards and set the tone for Tampa Bay's physical dominance that was to come.

Brad Johnson had been extremely nervous the night before the game, waking up at 4:00 A.M. and pacing his room, and then the hotel hallway. That nervous energy quickly dissipated as Johnson played one of the best games of his career. In the passing game Gruden attacked Oakland's safeties, particularly Anthony Dorsett, again using the appearance of complexity—shifting and motion—to hide a simple play. Oakland's secondary became so frustrated by Gruden's offense that they began freelancing. On one play cornerback Charles Woodson made the horrid decision to blitz on his own in a futile attempt to create something that would stop that blitzkrieg. The maneuver failed. Oakland was in a total state of chaos.

The game was stunning. Gruden so thoroughly outcoached Callahan that few NFL observers could believe what had unfolded. Gruden knew Callahan was stubborn, almost arrogant, and that Callahan would refuse to alter his game plan, sticking with a strictly pass-oriented attack and abandoning the running game. This one-dimensional Oakland offense played right into Gruden's hands. It was unusual to see Oakland, so dominant late in the year, look so sloppy and ill prepared.

One thing stayed eerily familiar during the frenetic Super Bowl period. Tampa Bay coaches said Gruden slept a total of ten to twelve hours the entire week.

After the Super Bowl, Gruden, for the first time publicly, with cameras clicking and flashbulbs popping, acknowledged, ever so slightly, the impact his lifestyle has on his family. As he stood on a tall podium, smiling, with his wife, Cindy, and the kids at his side, the lean and glistening Lombardi Trophy in his hands, the coach with little time for anything other than football took a brief moment to reflect on his life. "A lot of times I've gone to work in the middle of the night, and Cindy shakes her head," he said. "I've missed out on a lot with my family, but to win a Super Bowl, at least it gives me some sort of explanation."

||

It was obviously a brilliant inaugural year for Gruden in Tampa. Gary Shelton, the fine columnist for the *St. Petersburg Times,* wrote that Gruden "rebuilt the engine of a moving car. He changed horses in the middle of the river. He took over a good team and made it better." The general manager McKay explained: "Any time a coach comes in . . . and you're able to improve, someone's done a nice job. I guarantee you if you look at other situations [on other teams], that isn't always the case." I wonder just how good this team will be when Gruden gets the players he *wants* in his offensive system.

Gruden has not, however, impressed everyone. The coaching fraternity is a hard-boiled, fickle group, susceptible to jealousies and pettiness. One coach remarked to me in January 2003: "If Gruden is so damn good, why did the Raiders excel even after he was gone?" Good question, easy answer. When Gruden led the Raiders in his final year in Oakland, the offense finished fourth in the NFL in scoring. Gruden relied heavily on the ground game; Callahan decided he wanted more of a passing offense and made two significant adjustments. He utilized Porter, not a Gruden favorite, much more than Gruden ever did, and Porter consumed a large number of fullback Jon Ritchie's downs. Then Callahan cut back from the number of rushes per game, from the high to low 20s. Gannon, with his accuracy, took full advantage of the pass-oriented attack, and Porter, with his speed, did the same. Gannon finished with 4,689 passing yards, seventh-best of all time, and was named the league's most valuable player, beating out Favre by four votes. The Raiders had a marvelous season, reaching the Super Bowl. Thus, superficially it seems as if Callahan reinvented the wheel. In reality, he simply tweaked what was already a great system. That was Gruden's playbook the Raiders used for all of those wins. That was his system. That was his quarterback, Gannon, who was not great until he became a Raider under Gruden. It was Gruden's decision to ask Rice to pack his bags and head to Oakland, and Gruden's decision to sign Charlie Garner. Basically the Raiders were still Gruden's team. Basically, Gruden had two franchises in the Super Bowl.

||

Despite the intensity, despite the work hours that drag on and on, Gruden still finds time to be a husband and father, though that may seem impossible. "I could not ask for a more dedicated family man," says Cindy. Gruden usually arrives home anywhere from 8:00 to 9:30 P.M. after bolting in the morning before 4:00. On a Friday he might make it home by 3:30 in the afternoon (wow—only a 12-hour day), while on Saturday the family does not see him much and on Sundays they see him following the game. Gruden manages the massive balancing act because he basically has only three interests—football, family, and fishing. Each spare moment is spent with Cindy and the kids—though the family has yet to take a spin on the small boat anchored alongside a dock in a gorgeous lake behind the Gruden house. The moments are precious, like rare minerals, but they are there, sandwiched between meetings and practices and Cindy writing the checks for all the bills because Jon doesn't have the time. He puts his kids to bed many nights and then pops a game tape in the machine so he can sneak in a little extra study. He took the kids fishing one November Saturday . . . at 2:55 in the morning. Hey, they bite early.

It is difficult for anyone outside of the profession to understand the obsession these men have, especially someone like Gruden. I have spent years around coaches, and I still do not completely comprehend their makeup. I do understand this: part of their neurotic and prideful existence is powered by competition, while another part is powered by fear—fear of being embarrassed before the sports world and their peers, and most of all, fear of losing. Losing boils their blood one week and can drive them into a state of serious depression the next. Dave McGinnis, coach of the Arizona Cardinals, a perennially losing franchise, tells the story of how one night during the 2001 season, with the team stuck in a three-game skid, he was getting ready for bed around midnight after a particularly long day of racking his brain to figure a way out of the slump. As he climbed into the sack, wondering what else could go wrong, he felt a pop on the bottom of his foot. A scorpion had stung him. The leg went numb, and when his wife exclaimed that they had to get him medical attention, McGinnis replied, his sense of humor still intact, "We've lost three games. If the poison goes to my heart, let it."

Losing hurts NFL coaches more than it does their counterparts in other sports. In baseball there are hundreds of games, and in hockey and basketball there are dozens. In those sports there are many other days. In the NFL there are only sixteen regular-season contests. One NFL game is essentially the equivalent of ten in Major League Baseball. That is ten times the pressure. That is ten times the scrutiny. That is ten times the joy—or heartache. A scorpion bite is nothing compared to an NFL losing season. I've seen NFL coaches after tough defeats—in the regular season, for goodness' sake—stand there and mumble to themselves after meeting with the news media, replaying over and over in their heads what they could have done better, and most of the time the answer is, not much.

Gruden has yet to experience the pain of a dreadful year as a head coach—and those kinds of seasons happen to the best. But I am not so sure he will see too many bloody Sundays, too many losses. Gruden has that combination of skill and fire that refuses to let him lose and will make him a legend in the sport. Oh, there will be tough times for the Bucs and Gruden. He is a grinder. His gritty, gruff style wears on players and others around him, the way Jimmy Johnson's coaching style did, or Parcells's does. Gruden will bump heads with general manager McKay—already has, in fact—because Gruden wants to control the roster. I would not be surprised if at some point an ugly power struggle developed between the two men, and in such a scenario McKay would lose. The Bucs owners, not exactly known for their loyalty, would toss out McKay faster than Gruden erased the team's losing image. One member of the Buccaneers' personnel department says in an interview: "When I talk to scouts or other personnel guys about Jon and Rich's relationship, the conversation is always the same. 'Jon's trying to bump Rich out the building, isn't he?' On the personnel side, we love Jon the coach, but we are not crazy about Jon the person."

Ouch.

Gruden has brought that kind of animosity on himself. At the NFL owners' meetings in the spring of 2003, Gruden complained to front office men and coaches *on other teams*, as well as to members of the news media, about the slow pace of free agent signings by the Buccaneers. He went even further and took direct shots at McKay, stating that the general manager was spending too much time involved with his duties on the competition committee and not enough on getting the players Gruden wanted. McKay had been through Gruden's fits before, but according to a member of Tampa Bay's front office, when McKay heard about what Gruden was doing at the owners' meetings, he became furious and said to friends that whatever trust was left between the two men was now completely gone.

Yes, the Bucs will wear on Gruden, and Gruden will wear on the Bucs. You can count on it.

Gruden will also have to face the uncomfortable fact that he will be a bigger target than ever, if that is possible for the current most high-profile coach in the sport. There is a head coach who has beaten Gruden over the last few years. When I interviewed him recently, the coach told me: "When I beat that cocky motherfucker, it was better than the first time I had sex." He told me this *before* Gruden was a world champion.

Still, no matter his bluntness, no matter how perpetually miserable he can be, no matter how many toes he steps on without blinking, no matter how much jealousy he faces, Gruden will win. That is what he does. That is the bottom line in a bottom-line business. Under Gruden the Yuccaneers became the Buccaneers. He wins the way Gibbs and Parcells did—without apology, without ever looking back. He is the 21st-century version of those two men. He will probably coach his way to multiple Super Bowl appearances—both with the Bucs and, after he wears on everyone's last nerve there and departs, with another team—or flame out trying.

"I know there are some people, even coaches, who might think the way I do things is over-the-top," Gruden tells me, fully aware his comment is soaking in a pool of understatement. "I feel like I have to work harder to be the best. Part of it is I have a sickness. This coaching bug has bitten me. I love what I do. I always will, and I don't know if I'll ever be able to change."

2

OFFENSE

Emmitt Smith

LONE STAR

It was April 1990, and Dallas Coach Jimmy Johnson, a cunning talent evaluator, had just made his first-round selection, the 17th overall, picking an undersized and moderately slow running back from the University of Florida named Emmitt Smith. Johnson liked Smith, but in the weeks leading up to the draft something stuck in Johnson's gut. Was this really the right guy for us?

On draft day Johnson stared at a piece of paper scribbled with Smith's vital statistics, focusing on two numbers: 5 feet 10 inches and 209 pounds. The figures stared back at Johnson like yellow caution flags. Running backs as tiny as Smith rarely lasted long in professional football. Smith was an NFL midget.

Johnson then turned to owner Jerry Jones and others in the draft war room. "I think we got a hell of a back," Cowboys officials remember Johnson telling them that day, "but we'll have to get another in five years. This one's gonna burn out pretty quick."

Three years later, just two seasons away from his supposed expiration date, it looked as if Johnson's prediction might come to fruition. On a cold December day, in the second quarter of the regular-season finale against the New York Giants, a game that would determine not just the NFC East winner but the winner of homefield advantage throughout the postseason, Smith limped toward the Dallas sideline, his right arm dangling like a broken tree limb. Smith had separated his shoulder, and the searing pain was intense, watering Smith's eyes and causing teammates who heard him scream from the throbbing pain think Smith was not just done for the day but for the upcoming postseason as well.

Dallas had a 13–0 lead early in the game, but with Smith on the sideline, hurt, the Giants came back, furiously, and tied the score at thirteen in the fourth quarter. On the bench Smith was getting edgy, and the Cowboys medical staff hustled to see if they could get him back in the contest, at Smith's insistence. He took two painkilling injections, then had a kneepad cut to form and taped to his shoulder as a way to provide extra cushion. Trainers next slid a harness over the entire jerry-built production. When they finished, half of Smith's body looked mummified.

What happened next was the greatest moment in a career of great moments. On Dallas's final eleven plays of the game, nine of them went to Smith, as quarterback Troy Aikman altered the way he handed off the ball to Smith to accommodate his debilitation. Smith took hit after hit on that painful shoulder: The Giants were aware he was hurt and began targeting his injury, like anti-aircraft missiles seeking the heat of a burning jet engine. Behind Smith, Dallas worked its way into field goal range, then kicker Eddie Murray's game-winner propelled not only the Cowboys onto the road to the Super Bowl but Smith onto the path to football immortality and the Hall of Fame. Smith finished that game with 32 carries for 168 yards, and 10 catches for 61. For the entire game Smith touched the ball 42 of the Cowboys' 70 snaps. Some Cowboys players would later quietly claim that Smith had exaggerated the pain so he could be the savior late in the contest. Such doubt is unfounded, since Giants defenders remember Smith's blaring yelps each time one of them managed to get a clean shot on the tender shoulder.

An exhausted Smith spent that night in Dallas's Baylor Medical

Center, but he believes the afternoon of pain was worth it. With home-field advantage throughout the playoffs secured, the Cowboys beat Green Bay and San Francisco before capturing Super Bowl XXVII over Buffalo. Smith was that game's most valuable player, gaining 132 yards and two touchdowns.

But for Smith it all came back to that cold day in New Jersey at Giants Stadium. "I can't describe to you how much it hurt," Smith says of his shoulder injury. "My teammates kept asking me, 'Are you all right?' I would say, 'Yeah, I'm okay.' But I was lying. I felt awful. I was seeing stars. But when [the trainers] asked me if I wanted to stay out of the game, I said, 'I am not coming out of this game.'"

||

October 27, 2002. Expiration date plus seven years. Emmitt Smith is 33 years old. The back whom many thought was too slow or too small and would be crumpled like a scrap of paper by the league's hard-hitting linebackers is in his 13th season. Smith's first burst is not scary anymore. His gallop through the hole has more of a hitch. Players no longer fear being embarrassed by one of his spin moves. But none of these things diminish what Smith does on this day against the Seattle Seahawks: rush for 109 yards to set the all-time career rushing record with 16,743 yards, surpassing the great Walter Payton's mark of 16,726.

||

Smith was the second of six running backs taken in that 1990 draft. With the exception of the University of Georgia's Rodney Hampton, who had a solid career with the New York Giants from 1990 to 1997, the other backs picked in the first round—Blair Thomas, Darrell Thompson, Steve Broussard, and Dexter Carter—were mostly dreadful. Smith would actually go on to rush for over 1,700 yards more than the combined career total of these five other runners.

Smith wasn't even the first player Johnson and the Cowboys initially desired—it was defensive lineman Ray Agnew, who had been snapped up by the New England Patriots by the time the Cowboys' selection came around. Smith was a bizarre pick for Dallas because the franchise had a roster full of backs, and NFL scouts that year deemed Smith a risk because of his diminutive size and slow recorded times in the 40-yard dash. Johnson thought he would be criticized by the news media for picking Smith, so when he met with the press he insisted that Smith's biggest proponent in the organization, scout Walt Yowarsky, accompany him to explain to the media jackals why another runner was being added to the stable of horses.

Smith is not the greatest runner in history, despite owning the title of biggest yardage gainer. That honor goes, without question, to Jim Brown, who never missed a game during a nine-year career. After Brown comes Gayle Sayers, the best open field runner ever. O. J. Simpson combined Olympic speed with elusiveness (though Simpson's legacy has become tarnished following the criminal and civil trials for the murders of his ex-wife, Nicole Brown Simpson, and her friend Ronald Goldman). Eric Dickerson was so smooth he made his galloping runs look easy, but he was an intimidating back who frightened defenses. Barry Sanders had too many negative rushing yards for my taste, but he was elite because he was almost impossible to tackle one-on-one. He is also the most intriguing of all the great runners. In only ten seasons with the often-talentless Detroit Lions, Sanders rushed for 15,269 yards. With Payton's record just one, or at most two, seasons out of his grasp, Sanders suddenly retired in 1999, quietly walking away from the game, never giving a definitive explanation. If Sanders had continued to play, he could have crushed the record, something even Smith admits. "Barry had not only the best chance of getting the record, but blowing the record way out, setting it in the 20,000-mark area," Smith says. "I felt very confident he had the ability to do so, and I thought he was going to do it. But upon his retirement, I was very shocked, like everybody else. I knew Barry had a chance of getting it before I did, so I knew if he got there before me, I'd be chasing after not only Walter but him as well."

Marshall Faulk, the greatest receiving back, is sixth on my list of stellar backs, followed by Payton at seven, a workout freak, and then Smith at eight, then the powerful Earl Campbell, who burned out at the age of 29, and Tony Dorsett, whose style is actually similar to Smith's.

What hurts Smith when the chatter about the best backs of all time arises is that none of the other greats—with the possible exception of Dorsett, and Payton did have the advantage of working part of his career with those exceptional Buddy Ryan–coached defenses—were surrounded by the kind of talent Smith was. For much of his career he worked with quarterback Troy Aikman, a definite Hall of Famer, and wide receiver Michael Irvin, a possible one. He ran behind lines that featured five Pro Bowl offensive linemen (guard Larry Allen is another Dallas player who is Hall of Fame caliber), a Pro Bowl tight end in Jay Novacek, and a Pro Bowl fullback in Daryl Johnston. That is enough talent for three teams let alone one—and that is just the offense. The simple fact is that much of Smith's production was the result of a symbiotic, and symphonic, relationship between himself, Dallas's strong passing game, and a great offensive line.

I have heard only one knock on Smith, and while the piece of criticism is petty, it is worth noting. Smith was aware—some say too aware—that he had a legitimate shot, beginning some time ago, to break Payton's record. Sometimes, a former teammate says, if Smith didn't get enough carries in a game, he pouted afterwards. So Jimmy Johnson began leaving Smith in contests that were Cowboys blowouts and handing the ball off to him when it would have been safer to sit Smith and not risk an injury to the star runner in garbage time, because Smith wanted to rack up yardage. In Smith's defense, he is not the only back to aggressively go after 100-yard rushing days, or the only player to hunt a prestigious record.

Smith might not be the preeminent back ever, but he is the most enduring. Smith estimates he's been hit tens of thousands of times, poked in the eye a few dozen, kicked about one hundred, and punched the same, all while running the football for 4,000 carries. Those numbers are what the record is about and why Smith's accomplishment is so impressive—he has stayed in the game for such a lengthy period at such a violent position. A number of runners who followed Smith into the league, players initially considered more sturdy and talented, have since retired, most run out of the game by injuries. The past five years alone saw a roster retired: Sanders, Terrell Davis, Robert Smith, and Jamal

Anderson. All were skilled. All except Sanders walked away for health reasons.

Playing the position destroys the human body, slowly. "Sometimes I wonder how I'm able to get up and walk after a game," says New York Jets runner Curtis Martin. A union study illustrates, with cold, hard facts, just how brutal playing professional running back can be. The career of a runner lasts an average of only 2.57 years, the study states, which is shorter than any other position, and almost a full year shorter than the average of all other players. The lives of fireflies last longer. An NFL running back also has only a 6 percent chance of reaching his tenth season in the league, as compared to 24.1 percent for an offensive lineman and 50 percent for a kicker.

Over its long history professional football has left strong, powerful men physically broken, even dead. Examining only a few of those cases illustrates the potential bodily damage Smith has dodged, utilizing both luck and skill.

II

Howard Griffith, a former fullback with Denver, estimates that more than half of his approximately 40 collisions a game were helmet to helmet and at full speed. He was forced to retire after ten seasons in the NFL due to a condition called foraminal stenosis, which is an irritation of nerves in the spinal column. That is what happens when a player becomes a human battering ram.

They study rats, you know. Scientists do. When they give these rats a blow to the head and then sacrifice them, they see no loss of brain cells. When the rats are given a second blow to the head and then sacrificed two weeks later, these scientists see a significant loss of brain cells because the rats are more vulnerable to a second injury during the window of time when the brain is healing from the first. It is believed by some medical experts that the process is the same in the human brain. "Brain injury is the silent epidemic," says Dr. Robert Cantu, medical director of the National Center for Catastrophic Sports Injury Research in Chapel Hill, North Carolina, and chief of neurosurgery at Emerson

Hospital in Massachusetts. When boxers suffer a concussion, they are forbidden in most states from returning to the ring for a month. A football player gets "dinged" in the first quarter, or has his "bell rung"—that's code for a concussion—and often he is sent back in by the second. Sometimes it is at the player's insistence; sometimes it is the coach's. A study by the players' union stated that more than 61 percent of former NFL players had concussions during their playing days and most were not sidelined after their injuries. The report was based on interviews with almost 1,100 players ages 27 to 86, 30 percent of whom had three or more concussions and 15 percent of whom had five or more. Overall, some half of the players had been knocked out at least once.

Former Oakland center Jim Otto, who retired in 1974, had over 40 operations, 30 on his knees alone, including an astounding six in one week. Over a 12-year career retired offensive lineman Mark Schlereth played in 156 games and three Super Bowls and had 29 medical procedures, including 20 knee surgeries. It became a sort of joke eventually. *Hey, Mark? Can you slip in a surgery during the lunch hour? Have you back on the field by dinnertime. Promise.* Schlereth could have given his battle scars nicknames, he had so many. Artificial hips. Artificial knees. Some of these guys had more plastic stuffed into their body than a Barbie doll. And the beat goes on. Former Jacksonville offensive lineman Jeff Novak sued his team doctor and called into question, as other players have done for decades, the role of team physicians, who are in the impossible, some say unethical, position of working for both the franchise and the player. Novak's lawsuit created all kinds of headlines. But behind the hype was the simple, agonizing pain Novak endured when, after playing an exhibition game, he awoke the next day in his bed in a pool of blood that went from his hip to his ankle. Novak says he later had blood and fluid drained from his right knee in a nonsterile environment that he claims led to staph and *E. coli* infections. Teammates said Novak's leg smelled like rotting meat. His career was done. Although a jury initially awarded Novak $4.35 million and $1 million to Novak's wife for loss of his services, a judge later threw out the verdict, finding no evidence of negligence by the team's doctor.

There was a time, before 1987, when players could not even select the doctor for their surgery; they could not get second opinions, or even see a copy of their own medical records. That has changed. Still, the beat goes on.

The old-timers are the ones who wear the most NFL scars. Super Bowl rings or lifelong friendships are not the only trophies they sport from their playing days. A heavy limp or hip replacement follows them to the retirement party. Joe Namath has compression between his sixth and seventh vertebrae that feels like a knife stabbing him in the back. The great John Unitas had both knees replaced. His right hand was so badly damaged from a 1968 injury that he could not hold a fork, comb his hair, or brush his teeth without some assistance. Before his death, when Unitas played golf, he'd use his left hand to wrap his lifeless right hand to the club with Velcro. The Pro Bowl defensive end from the 1972 undefeated Miami Dolphins, Bill Stanfill, another old warrior with an artificial hip, used to stash his hip socket in a mayonnaise jar over his fireplace. Earl Campbell, who played from 1978 to 1985, took so many pounding hits that years later arthritis has left him unable to walk long distances. When Campbell made an appearance at the Heisman Trophy presentation at the Yale Club in New York City on December 14, 2002, he could barely make it up the two steps to join past winners of the prestigious award grouped on the stage. Tacklers once feared Campbell. Now, not even 50 years old yet, he moves at the creaky pace of a man in his eighties. Linebacker Harry Carson suffers from headaches and memory loss after a 12-year career with the Giants filled with multiple concussions. He traces his problems to a violent head-on collision with former Washington running back John Riggins. Joe Jacoby, the former Washington offensive lineman, suffered two herniated disks during his playing days in the 1980s and now can't bend over. These men always say the same thing to today's players: Love the game but guard your health, or you will end up just like us. Always remember that the beat goes on.

"When you see some of the older guys, you have a moment when you wonder, 'Is that going to be me down the road?'" said Oakland runner Tyrone Wheatley, a power back who takes a number of hard hits. "You have to block those thoughts out. You can't play in fear of the future."

Some players ingest large doses of medication to deal with the pain. Shoot up, swallow up, and go back on the field. Favre admitted an addiction to the painkiller Vicodin in the mid-1990s. Other players in the recent past have described digesting massive amounts of painkillers to subdue the discomfort and becoming addicted to them. Once the team stopped prescribing them, for fear of the player doing damage to his body, some would go outside the NFL to get their fix by trading game tickets to pharmaceutical representatives for the drugs.

There are other problems. Mike Webster was the rock-hard center who played for the Pittsburgh Steelers from 1974 to 1988 and endured numerous shots to the head, sustaining multiple concussions, but he rarely took a game off. When he died of a heart attack in the fall of 2002, he was just 50 years old. Webster's death focused attention on another threat to players. As NFL men, particularly offensive linemen, increase their weight to get an advantage on opponents and better protect their bodies from the violence of the game, hypertension is apparently a constant companion.

The national study commissioned by the players' union states that heart disease is a major threat to these super-sized human beings. "Clearly, the increased body size typical of these positions is contributing to this substantial risk," the study says. "Although obesity has been linked to heart disease in several research studies, the study found one of the strongest associations to date between body size and death from heart disease. Players in the largest body size category, 64 percent of all linemen, had a six times greater risk of heart disease than those of normal size."

Mackie Shilstone, a conditioning specialist based in New Orleans who has worked with hundreds of professional athletes, including NFL players, believes that "within three years, an offensive or defensive lineman will die on the field from a stroke, because they are so big. I've seen the blood pressure of some linemen that was so high, the numbers would make you quiver."

Dr. Kevin Guskiewicz, research director of the Center for the Study of Retired Athletes at the University of North Carolina, has examined a variety of social and medical issues involving retired NFL players. He says that the preliminary findings of his research indicate that there is a higher incidence of hypertension and cardiovascular disease in retired pro football players compared with the general population. Guskiewicz says this is particularly true of offensive linemen like Webster. "It is higher than in the general population and appears earlier, at younger ages," he says. Perhaps even more disturbing is that linemen have grown significantly since Webster's playing days ended in 1990. (He played his last two seasons with the Kansas City Chiefs.) Webster's weight, 255 pounds, was low by today's standards—offensive linemen now routinely weigh more than 300 pounds. Since 1990 the number of 300-pounders has increased from 50 to over 300. The NFL's approach to the linemen's growing stature and the attendant health risks has been ambivalent. Team doctors and trainers routinely inform heavier players about the risks they face and urge them to have regular checkups for heart disease. But players say that coaches often ask offensive and defensive linemen to add weight, even if they are already a sturdy 270 or 280 pounds, to get to that benchmark of 300.

Pierce Scranton, a former team doctor for the Seattle Seahawks, told the *Washington Times* that heart disease is just one problem facing these gargantuan men. "We are creating a generation of super football players who will be crippled for the remainder of their life with arthritis," he said. "Their joints are not built to withstand the extra strain. In that individual's 40's or early 50's, all of a sudden they have severe back problems, spinal problems, arthritic spurs, knees, ankles, elbows that are worn out."

Players' mental health is also at risk later on. Dr. Cantu says that, while he did not treat Webster, he knows that studies have shown that repeated head trauma can lead to depression later in life. "There is substantial evidence that repeated trauma does occur on the football field, and those who have sustained this kind of trauma have a higher incidence of depression than those who have not," Cantu says. "It is also not unexpected that someone who has emotional problems significant enough to make him homeless would die a premature death."

Some experts, however, question whether the hits to the head that are commonplace in the NFL lead to lifelong problems for players. "We have no evidence, none, that there are lingering, long-term problems from repeated concussions," says Dr. James Kelly, associate professor of clinical neurology at Northwestern Medical School. "This is not boxing. They are two different sports."

The NFL has improved helmet technology since Webster's days by increasing the protective padding in the equipment to better absorb shock, among other things. Nevertheless, what makes playing on the offensive line, especially at center, so difficult is that a player is hit from many different angles, often in the head, and sometimes the padding is not enough to protect the brain. New York Jets center Kevin Mawae remembers a game several years ago in Indianapolis when someone hit him with a knee hard in his head and he was temporarily knocked unconscious.

"When you come to, you're worried about it, you have to check all of your extremities," he says. "The nature of the game is, you come into the locker room and you joke about it the next day. It was third down, so I was fortunate. I came out, shook it off, but when I came back in the game, I wasn't thinking clearly, made some bad calls, stuff I don't remember doing."

Part of the problem is that players do not police themselves. The 2002 season saw an unprecedented number of fines for helmet-to-helmet hits. By November of that year the NFL had suspended two players for such collisions, Denver's Kenoy Kennedy and San Diego's Rodney Harrison. From 1993 until that point, only one player, Mark Carrier, had been suspended for those types of vicious hits.

The NFL believes, correctly, that some coaches are teaching players, particularly safeties, to fly around the field like human rocket boosters, trying to deliver knockout blows to increasingly faster and more powerful wide receivers. The idea is to scare and intimidate. This, of course, is not a new strategy in football. Intimidation has been going on in the sport for a century. One of the more infamous examples occurred when Jack Tatum, a defensive back for the Oakland Raiders, paralyzed Patriots wide receiver Darryl Stingley in a 1978 exhibition game, leveling him with a punishing hit that far exceeded the force required to break up a developing play. Tatum subsequently authored a book titled *They Call Me Assassin*, in which he boasted, "I like to believe my best hits border on felonious assaults."

Players now have forgotten that tragic moment, and today some believe, naively, that the improved helmet technology can protect them from injury, and so they are unafraid to use their helmets as weapons. There is also this: safeties are faster and more bulked up than at any period in football history. In the past a 170-pound safety simply could not do as much damage as some of these powerful defensive backs of today. Dallas's Darren Woodson was fined $75,000 for a hit on Seattle's Darrell Jackson in week eight of the 2002 season. It was a hit that knocked Jackson unconscious and later caused him to have a severe seizure in the locker room. "The simple thing of the matter is, Darrell almost died," says Seattle coach Mike Holmgren. Woodson is a muscular 6-foot-1 and 219 pounds and outweighs by 16 pounds the heaviest safety currently in the Hall of Fame, Ronnie Lott. Around the same time Philadelphia safety Brian Dawkins, a respected player and football ambassador, was fined $50,000 for a smackdown on the Giants' wide receiver Ike Hilliard, who was knocked out for the year with a shoulder injury.

An advanced degree in toughness has always been required to play in the NFL. Former Pittsburgh Steelers owner Art Rooney recounted that he once witnessed a Steelers lineman in the locker room after a game, bending over, barely able to stand or take off his uniform, because he had been kicked in the groin. As Rooney drove home, he said to his sons, a hint of awe in his voice, "Now *that* is a real football player."

Is a new generation of beaten-up players now being created? Will today's players hold their grandkids in one hand and a cane in the other like those who played decades ago? The union and the NFL maintain that medical care in the 21st century is far better than in years past, and that doctors and trainers take more care to protect players from the damaging effects of the sport. That is partially true, but there is still the pressure that players put on themselves, and that teams put on the players, to get back on the field, at all costs. Players want to do it because they love the game, and teams push the players because they want to win. When Tennessee linebacker Keith Bulluck, following a short pass completion on the final play of the third quarter, hit Pittsburgh quarterback Tommy Maddox, Maddox lay unmoving on the field. As he was taken off on a cart, Maddox had no feeling in his extremities, owing to a spinal cord contusion and a concussion. It was a frightening moment. But just a week or so later, following a battery of tests that showed he was no longer seriously hurt, Maddox was talking about wanting to get back on the field. The traumatic hit was a thing of the past. That is the psychology of players. They have an unrestrained, competitive spirit that is both admirable and, frankly, self-destructive.

The scare involving Maddox occurred on November 17, 2002— eleven years to the day after Mike Utley, a former guard for Detroit, lay on a football field, not feeling his limbs, his heart pounding, the horror of what might be flashing before his eyes. Maddox eventually walked back onto a field, just two weeks later, but Utley never walked again.

‖

In 1999, eight years after the day he lost the use of his legs while pass blocking against the then–Los Angeles Rams, Utley read a letter from a young fan, scribbled in crayon. "I wish I could switch my legs for yours," the fan wrote, "so you could play one more game." Several years later, in the winter of 2002, Utley remembers the letter, and how it touched him, and how by then there were no regrets. He is asked again, all these months later, with all the doctors and physical therapists now as much a part of his life as his wife and children—are there regrets now? Knowing what you now do, would you play football again, would you go back on that field, for that play, on the day everything changed? The contemplative Utley gives the same answer he gave a friend who asked for his thoughts on the eerie coincidence of the Maddox hit occurring on the same day, at almost the same hour, of Utley's collision eleven years earlier. Utley had seen the replays of the Maddox play on highlight shows.

"A friend asked me, 'Mike, when you saw what happened, what goes through your head?'" says Utley. "I told him, 'To be honest, it's scary to watch.' Then the next question was, 'Do you think he should play again?' That question is so tough to answer. At one point I would always tell people that, unequivocally, I would make the same decision to play football. I would do the same thing all over again. That's how much

I love the sport and still love the sport. That hasn't changed. But now I have a little more perspective on things. If I were 26 years old and single and no kids, I would do it all over again. But if I was married and with kids at the time I was hurt, and I had the same choice, I don't know. I'd have to do a lot more soul searching." Utley is always reminded of his situation each time a player suffers a spinal injury. It was this way in the summer of 1999 when Cincinnati safety Kelvin Moore broke a vertebra in his neck while making a tackle against Detroit in a meaningless preseason game. It was this way in 1996 when Cincinnati guard Scott Brumfield suffered a spinal cord concussion that put him in a wheelchair for two weeks, and it was this way when Detroit's Reggie Brown injured his neck in 1997 and was forced to retire.

Before his injury, which occurred on a pass play and led to the fracture of his sixth vertebrae, Utley was an adrenaline junkie, a motorcycle-cruisin', bleached-blond thrill seeker, and professional football, the ultimate danger sport, fit those needs perfectly. Utley excelled at the guard spot on the offensive line, about as grunt as you can get. He was the type of player some of the older coaches in the league refer to as "gung-ho." He retained that fighting spirit after he was paralyzed.

Utley is medically defined as a quadriplegic, but he has extensive use of his arms and can drive cars and pilot boats. He also scuba dives, kayaks, skydives, and once even skied—until he separated his shoulder. He works out four days a week, lifting weights with his upper body and doing exercises that keep his legs fit, utilizes biofeedback therapy, and works with a chiropractor. Utley is a sturdy 240 pounds with just 10 percent body fat. Gung-ho. "When I go to teams and visit with players, they've been great to me," Utley says. "But it's also strange, because on the one hand they see how strong I am and they're amazed. Then on the other hand, no player ever wants to see a crippled guy. I think I remind players that they are not indestructible. Most players think they are, and then something like this happens and it makes you pause as a player, and no player wants to be reminded how fragile their bodies really are. Players just want to put out of their mind that what happened to me can happen to them."

Utley spends much of his time raising money through his organization, the Mike Utley Foundation, which is devoted to finding a cure for spinal cord injuries. Utley remains the same gregarious, contemplative person he was as an NFL player. He still watches lots of football, and when he is asked about the resilience of Emmitt Smith, Utley says he is awestruck by how a player so small by football standards could stay in the game so long. "Emmitt and Jerry Rice are some of the best football players I have ever seen," says Utley. "Darrell Green in Washington played for 20 years in the NFL. They've had such great careers. They enjoy the game, and that's the key. You have to enjoy football as long as you can, because you never know what will happen to you on a football field. You never know when your career is going to end, or how it's going to end."

∎∎

This is the carnage Smith has run through and around, and these are the odds he has beaten, which makes his eclipse of Payton's mark the most impressive of all the football records and, I believe, of all sporting records. Breaking the record doesn't mean Smith is the fastest, or the biggest, or the best athlete, or, as some may now believe, the best running back (which is not the case), but it does mark him as the toughest, the most determined, the most lasting of athletes, in what is the most physically demanding position of any professional sport. He is an armored tank. There are few human beings who could survive his kind of masochism and still produce at such a high quality. Smith played in his 200th career game in 2002, an accomplishment only Marcus Allen and Earnest Byner have matched. Smith has also carried the ball at least 250 times in eight consecutive seasons; Thurman Thomas and Curtis Martin are the only other players to achieve such a feat. During Smith's tenure in the league, players like Utley have been paralyzed, had their knees torn to shreds, seen their Achilles' tendon disintegrate, suffered concussions, fractured bones that ended careers, and all the while Smith has kept running and running. "If you know the history of the game with running backs," Smith says, "I'm two and three times extinct."

Cal Ripken's consecutive game streak of 2,131 was highly impressive, but Ripken never had to worry about getting his brains beat in by a

300-pound defensive lineman each time he stepped to the plate. Brett Favre had played in a record 173 consecutive regular-season starts by the end of the 2002 season. That is also a stirring feat, but again, Favre was never physically punished like Smith, who was hit on almost every running play, yard after yard, game after game, season after season, for thousands of carries.

I witnessed a scene that will probably stay in my mind forever, and it exemplifies the punishment a running back's body takes. Rodney Hampton was one of the toughest backs of the last decade. (Smith outlasted him too, just as he has outlived many other backs who came into football when he did.) In September 1994, while playing at Arizona, a Cardinals defender lowered his helmet and using it as a battering ram, hit Hampton, at full speed, from behind, the helmet smashing Hampton in the left kidney. The hit sent Hampton buckling, and he fell to his knees. "I don't remember ever feeling that much pain," Hampton said at the time. Hampton later discovered blood in his urine and was taken to St. Joseph's Hospital and Medical Center in Phoenix, where he stayed for several days in a small room on the eighth floor of the building while the Giants flew back to New Jersey. Hampton had a bruised kidney and back, and when I visited him in his hospital room at 6:45 A.M. the day after the game, I could not believe what I was seeing. The powerful Hampton looked so small and weak. He was hooked up to an intravenous feeder and was wide awake, despite being unable to sleep through the night because of the intense pain. It took him a great effort to just sit up in bed. Until that moment I had not truly seen the aftereffects of football violence up close and personal. It gave me a whole new respect for the men who play the sport, especially the runners like Smith.

When asked his own opinion on what is the most difficult record to shatter in football, Smith says, "I think this record, the rushing record, may be the hardest But even harder than that might be what Jerry Rice is doing. I mean, Jerry Rice is setting records so far out there that it's going to be kind of amazing to watch players come behind him and do things that he's been able to get accomplished. He's still playing, so he's setting the bar really high.

"But as far as the game is concerned, the running game is one of the things that most defenses and opposing teams try to stop right off the bat. I think as far as rushing the ball and running the ball, it makes it that much more difficult for a running back to get to 15,000 or 16,000 yards, because you have to go through a number of years to do so, and you've got to go through a number of defenses that are gearing up to stop you."

II

Smith made his steady, deliberate crawl into the record books despite the equally steady decline of the Dallas franchise since Jimmy Johnson departed the Cowboys in 1994, and owner Jerry Jones, who is the antithesis of Johnson when it comes to picking top college players, took over the personnel duties. Smith at one point basked in championships and division titles, working with the best talent football had to offer. That changed in the last half of his career. At the beginning of the 2002 season, it had been six years since Dallas made a Super Bowl appearance, five since it had grabbed a playoff victory, and three since it finished above 8–8. The end of 2002 saw Dallas suffer its third consecutive double-digit losing season. The team spent some $25 million in 2001 on players who were no longer on their roster, an indicator of horrific salary cap management.

And this last number is the most damaging statistic of all: only two of 67 post-Johnson picks have made the Pro Bowl. That's proof of miserable drafting; under Johnson half a dozen Cowboys players made the trip to Hawaii.

The Cowboys and 49ers were among the dominant teams of the 1990s, and both went through a drought after the years of success. But San Francisco was able to rebound quicker because the team's recent drafts and free agent acquisitions were more intelligent than those of the Cowboys. After overhauling their personnel department, the 49ers found young stars like quarterback Jeff Garcia and wide receiver Terrell Owens to refresh their rosters. At the end of the 2001 season, 12 of the 49ers' 18 draft picks over the previous two years had either started or played significant roles, and the franchise was yet again making regular postseason playoff appearances. By the end of that same year the Cowboys were still awful, going 5–11, with no surefire replacements in the fold for Aikman, Irvin, and Smith, though Troy Hambrick, a swift power runner, has a chance to be a decent Smith surrogate. Jones tried to find new quarterback blood, but his selection of Quincy Carter was a disaster, and he spent $3 million in bonus money on free agent Chad Hutchinson, who has spent most of his life playing baseball. Those maneuvers prevented him from drafting Joey Harrington, who could have stepped into Aikman's cleats.

In effect, the franchise crumbled around Smith, and 2002 brought another awful year, with the Cowboys again finishing 5–11, the third straight year one of the most prestigious franchises in sports finished with only five victories. As Dallas's passing game crashed and burned— it was ranked dead last in the league in 2001—the pressure on Smith increased. Taking more hits, because there was no other threat on offense, he faced a steady, choking diet of seven- and eight-man fronts. The Cowboys went from a team packed with greats to one: Smith, a single, lone star.

||

One of the more pleasing aspects of football, and sports in general, is that it constantly reenergizes itself. Ideas evolve, change, and are reborn. The base of player talent does the same. When Smith retires one day soon, San Diego runner LaDainian Tomlinson, who idolized Smith while growing up in Waco, Texas, and possesses Smith-like ability and stamina, is the best candidate to replace him as one of the premier backs in football. Favre, who threw more touchdown passes in the 1990s than anyone else, will also leave the game soon, and there are already some solid candidates ready to try to fill his rather large shoes. Indianapolis wide receiver Marvin Harrison, who plays with an understated elegance, is the next Tim Brown, while Kansas City running back Priest Holmes and Miami runner Ricky Williams are part of a strong group of backs who may well play in the NFL for the next three to five years.

A short time ago there was an almost leaguewide panic that the talent at quarterback had thinned like the scalp of a middle-aged man. For a while that was true. Not anymore. The position has become thoroughly invigorated, and the league is crawling with young, able arms. Midway through the 2002 season there were 17 starters under age 28, the largest such number of pubescent throwers in two decades. The list is impressive. Tom Brady won a Super Bowl for New England. Drew Brees is a solid performer for the Chargers. David Carr is the toughest quarterback in football and flashed a spark of ability in his rookie season despite playing behind a subpar offensive line. Chad Pennington is a Rhodes scholar from Marshall University who is the Jets' signal caller of the future. The only positive outcome of Detroit's disastrous last few seasons is that Harrington, with fluid arm mechanics beyond his years, has proven an excellent leader despite the misery surrounding the franchise. The presence of all these good players bodes well for the NFL's quarterbacking future. None of them, however, can match Atlanta's Michael Vick.

There is no more frightening vision for a defensive football player than Vick running in the open field, since he is almost impossible to tackle one-on-one. When Vick emerged as the best player entering the 2001 draft, San Diego had the first pick, but the team was convinced they would have trouble signing him to a long-term deal, so they made a swap with Atlanta. The Chargers received a package of picks that brought them Tomlinson, wide receivers Reche Caldwell and Tim Dwight, and cornerback Tay Cody. San Diego used a second-round selection to pick Brees. The philosophy of the franchise was that as great as Vick might be, he was just one player, and San Diego could rebuild its team faster with multiple picks. It was sound reasoning—and it was also wrong. What makes this, from Atlanta's perspective, the best trade in modern NFL history is that Vick is a Michael Jordan or a Lawrence Taylor, and when you have the opportunity to get such a talent, you grab it. Vick is so dangerous because his arm is powerful and accurate, and he combines those qualities with the fastest feet this side of the king of pop. "There're not many quarterbacks in the league who can outrun an entire defense," says Carolina linebacker Will Witherspoon. "It's like playing against a cheetah."

"He is Frankenstein," says Bill Polian, Indianapolis Colts general manager. "He is a monster on offense that no one has figured out how to deal with yet. He is like a throwback to the single-wing days when you had talented tailbacks that could both run and throw. With this guy, the play is never over." When Vick began to embarrass players and defensive coordinators, a rallying cry emerged across the league: let's make sure this guy doesn't humiliate us. No one wanted to be Vick-timized.

One team has learned how to slow Vick, and that is Tampa Bay. Gruden's Buccaneers, who have the most speed on defense of any NFL team, held Vick to one yard rushing in the teams' first meeting of 2002, and 15 yards in the second. They bottled up Vick by matching him RPM for RPM and smacked the quarterback in the mouth each time he tried to break into the open field. Indeed, as good as Vick is—and he is great—sometimes there is a little too much panting when NFL players and team officials discuss him. I haven't heard this much hyperventilating since I went to dinner with a Jets offensive lineman and he groped the dessert menu. "Can we let him get one banner up in the gym before we put him in Canton, please?" Parcells pleaded on ESPN. And the idea that there has never been a Vick in the history of the league is slightly misleading and demonstrates the occasional short attention span that plagues sports history. Otto Graham was one of the best rushing quarterbacks ever, as was Steve Young. The difference, of course, is that Vick is faster. Much faster.

Vick is *not* speedier, however, than a generation of black college quarterbacks who, because of discrimination, were kept out of the NFL or switched to another position. The Braddock study, prepared in 1980 by sociology professor Jomills Braddock, then of Johns Hopkins University, examined NFL rosters from 1960 to 1979 and discovered there were two patterns of discrimination in the NFL. First, blacks were kept from the head coaching ranks, and second, the NFL segregated players by position. Blacks rarely played what Braddock called "central" spots— quarterback, center, guard, or linebacker, positions that require intelligence, leadership, and interaction with others. During that time period, 175 of 178 centers, 278 of 288 quarterbacks, 340 of 398 guards, and 588 of 688 linebackers were white, according to the study. Meanwhile, 199 of 489 running backs, 126 of 289 fullbacks, 199 of 565 wide receivers, and 333 of 835 defensive backs were black. Braddock reasoned that the stereotype of black men possessing more speed than whites encouraged a disproportionate number of them to play at the so-called speed positions, while the thinking positions, like quarterback, were kept almost exclusively off-limits. This type of racism continued beyond 1980. One news organization looked at each NFL team's media guide in 1986—not exactly an eternity ago—and discovered that 85 of 88 quarterbacks, 101 of 118 guards, and 66 of 77 centers were white. Conversely, 172 of 206 running backs, 154 of 191 wide receivers, 86 of 131 safeties, and 144 of 150 cornerbacks were black.

In the past many blacks coming out of college had almost no chance of playing quarterback in the NFL, and make no mistake, some of these players, maybe dozens of them, were just as fast and strong-armed as Vick. They never received the opportunity, however, to show their skills. Marlin Briscoe was a 14th-round draft pick of the Denver Broncos in 1968 and as a rookie became the first black starting quarter-back in league history. Playing like Vick decades before Vick was born, Briscoe tossed 14 touchdown passes, a Denver rookie record that still stands. Despite the excellent start to his career, he was traded to Buffalo the next year after refusing Denver's request to convert to wide receiver, a move that seemed to be racially motivated. Briscoe spent the rest of his career as a pass catcher.

University of Tampa quarterback Freddie Solomon played in the 1970s. NFL scouts at the time thought Solomon was one of the fastest players they had ever seen. He was a great scrambler, once rushing for 182 yards against the University of Miami, and in his last game as a col-legian he rushed for 211 yards against Florida A&M. The Miami Dol-phins drafted Solomon in the second round, but they did not list his position as quarterback.

It was listed as "Athlete."

Seriously.

Solomon was switched to wide receiver once he got into the pros, and he spent the next eleven years at that spot, most of them in San Francisco following a trade from Miami. Present-day football features large numbers of black quarterbacks in college and the NFL because there is now little or no discrimination by coaches and personnel men when it comes to men of color playing the position. But imagine if that had been the case in previous decades. Is it so difficult to believe there would have been more Vicks playing in the NFL? Was there a genera-

tion of players like Solomon who never received an honest opportunity
to play quarterback? To become Vick? To become Graham? To become
Young?

This is not to downgrade Vick—his abilities go beyond the physical.
At Virginia Tech he was always the first player in the film room. He
spent the 2001 off-season painstakingly working on his fundamental
throwing mechanics, which are now excellent, and mastering the long-
winded verbiage and complications inherent to a Dan Reeves offense.
Vick also went to Young for advice—two lefties, chatting it up—and
picked the brains of an Atlanta Braves coach to learn better sliding techniques and thus absorb fewer beatings at the end of his wild scrambles.
At a young age, Vick has combined the physical and mental to produce
electrifying results, and his popularity is beginning to transcend the
sport. One game that will help define his career occurred against Minnesota when Vick won the contest in overtime with a play called Weakside Run Pass Action, Mirrored Out Cut. The result was a twisting,
darting run that ended in a 46-yard touchdown, with defenders colliding
all over the field while pursuing him, tackling puffs of smoke. He finished that game with 173 yards rushing, an NFL single-game record for
quarterbacks, a 28-yard touchdown run, and a 39-yard touchdown pass.
Several weeks before that game, in a game against New Orleans, Vick
tossed a 74-yard touchdown pass and ran for two more scores. Against
Pittsburgh his precision passing converted a third-and-22, third-and-24,
and third-and-27. One defensive coordinator speculated that a future
defense against Vick, for teams that do not possess the fast defensive
linemen that the Buccaneers and Eagles do, will feature playing eleven
defensive backs to stop him.

I have never been a big fan of Reeves's offensive systems. No matter
where Reeves coached or who the quarterback was, from John Elway in
Denver to Dave Brown in New York, he was always stubbornly conservative in his approach to the game. If Reeves had opened his playbook a bit
more and dusted off those pages that had deep throws on them, he
would not have gone winless in four Super Bowl attempts. With Vick,
Reeves has taken a *slightly* different approach. The Falcons designed a
number of plays to take advantage of Vick's explosive start and stop abilities, including reverse pivots, built-in runs, quarterback sweeps, and

keepers. The only concern with Vick is that, with all of the scrambling, he must be careful and delicate in his decisionmaking, or he could be concussed out of football like Young. During the 2002 season, in which he rushed for 777 yards—third most in history for quarterbacks—he suffered two separated shoulders and an injured thumb.

The Falcons made the Super Bowl before Vick, but his arrival, which has been like that of a Greek god riding a lightning bolt down from the heavens, has made the franchise both good *and* popular. In 36 years of NFL football, the Falcons have an unimpressive seven winning seasons, leading to a sense of apathy in the city as thick as chicken-fried steak. Those days are gone. Each game is a sellout, and in 2002 television ratings were up by 30 percent. It's the Vick effect.

People are saying, chanting, that Michael Vick is the Real Trick. Yes, as a star like Emmitt Smith prepares to pack his bags, another one like Vick comes into the picture, easing the ache, just a bit, of losing the old champion.

||

Smith was not a studier. His fullback Daryl Johnston, who cracked open holes in the sea of bodies for Smith with the same reliability of a bell-man opening doors at a five-star hotel, often took copious notes during offensive film meetings in the darkened rooms. The film projector flashed images on the barely lit screen, and Johnston juggled different colored pens as he scratched down his thoughts. Smith was known to take a nap or two at these strategy sessions and occasionally instructed Johnston, "Tap me when the lights come on." Smith, however, rarely made mistakes on the field or coughed up the football, fumbling just once every 151 rushes. Smith always picked up the correct blitzing line-backer and hit the right hole. With his practically psychic synapses, he displayed a feel for the game that only a handful of backs in the long history of football possessed.

The salary cap hampers teams from holding on to longtime players, even ones as special as Smith, and Smith's backup, Troy Hambrick, chirped that Smith had enjoyed his career and now it was time for Ham-brick to start his. It had been clear for some time that Smith's days in

Dallas were numbered, and in March 2003, he signed a contract with the Arizona Cardinals, joining other legends who refused to believe their careers were over and subsequently signed with another franchise—like O.J. Simpson, who ended his career with the 49ers; Joe Namath, who finished with not the Jets but the Rams; Johnny Unitas, who landed in San Diego after a Hall-of-Fame career in Baltimore; Pittsburgh's Franco Harris, who ended his career in Seattle; and Jerry Rice, now sporting silver black. The departure of a superstar is never pretty. When Joe Montana was being pushed out of the San Francisco offense in favor of the more youthful Steve Young, Montana lashed out that Young was trying to steal his job. Then Montana said: "I don't want to be on the bench ever." Montana bolted the 49ers and signed with Kansas City.

Smith's legs are definitely slowing—the 2002 season saw Smith finish below the 1,000-yard threshold for the first time since his rookie year. But there is still some juice left in that mature tank. On Thanksgiving Day, against a solid Washington defense, Smith rushed for 144 yards on 23 carries in a 27–20 win. It was the 76th 100-yard game of his career, and for a moment it looked like Aikman and Irvin were back on the field and the Cowboys were rolling to the Super Bowl. When asked if he was stunned that he still had that kind of performance in his old legs, Smith replied, "Why should I be amazed? It's my job. It's what I do."

Perhaps the most vital and precious aspect of Smith's style and personality is that he gets it. When the runner made an appearance two days before Christmas of 2002 on *The Late Show with David Letterman*, dressed in a dark, smart, pin-striped suit, light blue shirt, and gray tie, he talked of his love for football, and for playing on the Cowboys, despite the recent losing seasons. "I'm living out a childhood dream," he told the talk show host. Smith's words were sincere, not drenched in phoniness. He respects the NFL's tradition, something some younger players, like Randy Moss, do not understand or care about. Smith embraced Payton's legacy easily, with respect and with tenderness—a word not often used in football, but it is apropos. The two men met in 1995 during an awards ceremony in Dallas and struck up a friendship almost immediately. "My first memory of Walter was probably being so excited when I first met him," Smith says. "I spent some time with him, talked to him about his workouts, and we shared a number of conversations in terms of the game of football and the opportunities that football presents. We discussed how to try to capitalize on those opportunities, as well as achieve something good and giving back to people."

Payton told Smith only he and Sanders had a chance to break his record. The two stayed in touch after that initial meeting, and when Payton later revealed to Smith he was suffering from liver disease, the two men became closer. In the last year of his life Payton asked Smith to keep close tabs on his son, Jarret, who at the time was about to start college at the University of Miami. When Smith broke the record at Texas Stadium, Payton's mother, Alyne, and brother, Eddie, were in the stands. They congratulated Smith, the tough runner, the Payton of the 1990s. Then Smith, who never let intense physical pain stop him, paused to thank the fans, and wept.

3

DEFENSE

Michael Strahan

INDEPENDENCE DAYS

Tiki Barber answered the telephone one warm day in March 2002 and as soon as he heard the voice on the line Barber, a running back for the New York Giants, knew the next several minutes were not going to be cheery. It was Michael Strahan, his teammate, and Strahan wasn't much for pleasantries. One day earlier Barber had launched into a public riff: Strahan was greedy and selfish for rejecting the team's most recent contract offer. Now Strahan was calling to discover just what exactly Barber had been smoking to suddenly betray not just his teammate and friend but one of football's most accepted codes: players do not publicly criticize each other's contract situations. No, Barber knew this was going to be about as much fun as having his hair set on fire, if he had had hair.

"This is Mike," Strahan said. Then before Barber could utter a syllable, Strahan blurted, "What were you thinking?"

"I guess I got a little bit out of control, huh?" Barber said, chuckling.

Barber making a joke of what were some incredibly ugly remarks infuriated the normally friendly and gregarious Strahan even more. "Tiki, you used my situation to make yourself look good," Strahan told the running back, his voice rising. "You don't know my situation unless you've spoken to me or my agent, and you haven't. And you know what? You're a hypocrite. You're a phony. You're just trying to use me and suck up to [owner] Wellington Mara and make yourself look good." Barber knew this had been coming, but the anger in Strahan's voice nevertheless caught him off guard.

He should not have been shocked. Barber had been a teammate of Strahan's for more than five years. They were friends, at least up until that moment, often eating dinner together. Barber was even an invited guest at Strahan's surprise 30th birthday party. Barber knew Strahan as an honest person, a good person, a professional person, but Barber also understood that if you cross Strahan, get ready to rumble.

Teammates appreciate Strahan's directness. He has always said exactly what is on his mind, a trait that is admirable in the mostly plastic world of professional sports. But this characteristic has landed him in trouble on more than one occasion and led to what he called an "on-again, off-again cold war" between himself and Giants management for several years. But Strahan is much more than the mouth that roars. He is the most intellectual, benevolent, and thoughtful player I have met in my 16 years of covering the National Football League. His ability to examine the larger picture has made Strahan, rather quietly, one of the leaders of a movement of many star players across the league who are taking more control of their careers, creating a level of independence never before seen in professional football. The evidence of this movement is everywhere. Players are routinely challenging the advice of team trainers and physicians who might be pushing them back to the field too quickly after an injury, and they have even set up a panel of independent doctors specifically for players who need second opinions. They are requesting better practice facilities and more grass playing fields, which are easier on the body. They are closely monitoring their agents and financial representatives after a series of scandals rocked the sport's world. Hiring private investigators to look into the backgrounds of potential spouses. Increasingly ignoring the so-called voluntary off-season minicamps that have been traditionally mandatory. Pushing for more protective headgear to cut down on the chances of concussion. Retiring in their prime, as running back Robert Smith did in February 2001 at the still-effective age of 28, instead of waiting until their bodies are bruised and broken before leaving the game. "It's better to walk away early than limp away late," Smith says.

Further proving their mettle as individuals, players stood in rebellion against their teams after the terrorist attacks of September 11, 2001. On September 12, the NFL was considering letting teams play the weekend schedule of games, despite the fact that the World Trade Center, the Pennsylvania crash site, and the Pentagon were still smoldering. A small group of vocal players from the New York teams—one of the leaders was Strahan—vehemently objected and threatened to mutiny, to refuse to step onto the fields, if the league went ahead with its plans. The NFL learned about the players' plans and postponed the contests.

This new level of self-determination is not without its problems. A handful of players misuse these new powers, like superheroes turned bad. During the 2001 season the relationship between Pro Bowl wide receiver Terren Owens and his head coach, San Francisco's Steve Mariucci, completely disintegrated. The tension began after Owens, twice during a game against Dallas that year, dashed from the end zone after scoring to the huge star at midfield of Texas Stadium and struck a pose like a rock star following a triumphant concert. Mariucci suspended Owens for one week and fined him a week's pay, or $24,294, for the hotdogging. Owens stopped speaking to his head coach soon after that and later complained openly about Mariucci's play calling when he felt the ball was not sailing his way as much as he thought it should.

There was a time not so long ago when Owens's actions would have been considered insubordination and would have led to his being cut or traded, despite his great abilities. In the past football coaches, believing that outspoken players poisoned the team, would plot to clean house, at all costs. (When Dan Reeves took over the Giants in 1993, he brought in a number of players from his former team, the Denver Broncos. Longtime Giants linebacker Pepper Johnson was dismayed and nicknamed the Giants "the New Jersey Broncos." Only a few days after Johnson lobbed that insult, Reeves cut the outspoken player.) Now the salary cap prevents such moves, so coaches must almost bargain with their players, play kiss-up, and stroke their egos, when previously a hammer would have been used to quell any rebellion.

To repair the relationship, Mariucci, following the season, took the

unprecedented step of boarding a plane and going to see Owens in the
player's Atlanta off-season home. (One 49ers official suggested that Mariucci was prodded to go by team management.) The two wiped the slate
clean, but I can't remember a head coach taking the step Mariucci did.
By his actions, Mariucci, a sensible and logical man, conceded a large
dose of power to Owens. In the end, his poor relationship with Owens
was one of the reasons the 49ers fired Mariucci.

It was also Owens who pulled a signature move when, after scoring
on a 37-yard touchdown pass, he yanked out a Sharpie, took the football
and autographed it, then handed it to his financial consultant in the
stands. Owens received a barrelfull from his coach for this obnoxious
form of celebration, though funny and original. This incident was yet
another bit of evidence that today's independent players are embarrassed by little and fear no criticism.

At times the arrogance of Minnesota wide receiver Randy Moss has
sucked the exuberance out of the Vikings organization. His declaration
during the 2001 season that he "plays when he wants to play"—in the
wake of allegations that he takes some plays off during games by not
blocking on running plays or on downs when the ball does not go to him,
allegations backed up by game film aired on ESPN's hard-core football
show *Edge NFL Matchup*—was an embarrassment to everyone in the
sport. (Soon after his statement, a joke started making its way around
the league. What's the difference between Randy Moss and a dollar bill?
You can get four quarters from a dollar bill.) In just six NFL seasons
Moss is already one of the best wide receivers in the history of football,
and he knows it. Moss feels the rules need not apply to him.

That explains why in 1999 the NFL fined him $10,000 for verbally
abusing an official. Later that year Moss was fined $25,000 for squirting
water at an official who made a call Moss did not like. In 2000 he was
fined $25,000 for making contact with an official. In 2001 he was docked
$30,000 over the course of the season for three taunting incidents and
one dress code violation. Also that year the Vikings fined Moss $15,000
for verbally abusing corporate sponsors on a team bus, and he was subsequently ordered by the team to take anger-management counseling.
Then came the capper when in September 2002 Moss was arrested and
charged with three misdemeanor violations for careless driving, failure

to obey a traffic officer, and possession of marijuana, since a small amount of dope was in his car. (Moss said it was not his—"not my shit" is what he told one teammate.) Police said Moss slowly pushed the officer, who was on foot at the time, down a Minneapolis street after she tried to prevent him from making an illegal turn. In December Moss resolved the reckless episode by pleading guilty to two misdemeanor driving charges: careless driving and obstruction of traffic. As a result, the judge ordered Moss to perform 40 hours of community service. The marijuana charge was dismissed.

Other than those tribulations, Moss has been a great citizen. He is an example of independence days run amok, a player who believes, correctly, that his talent will always insulate him from the crimes he commits as well as the issues that arise like sea monsters out of the murky waters because of his serious lack of maturity. Wrote *Sports Illustrated*'s Paul Zimmerman on Moss: "He's falling into the role of a classic coach-breaker. The only question I ask is why did God, in his infinite wisdom, choose a jerk like this on whom to bestow such remarkable physical prowess?"

Former NFL player Randy Cross, now an opinionated analyst for *CBS Sports,* had this rather blunt view: He thinks some players are not seeking independence so much as just being flat-out, self-centered egoists. "Lost amid all the opinions and excuses offered up . . . regarding the Randy Moss mess is a deeper theme that this case only highlighted. There seems to be a growing lack of respect for most authority figures, be they traffic control officers, local policemen, assistant coaches, and even head coaches. For a generation of athletes so obsessed by 'respect and not being dissed,' as a group they rarely hesitate to disrespect any authority figure that has the misfortune to cross them. Since when has it been okay to ignore, and push with your car, a traffic officer? Since when, in the case of Tampa Bay's Keyshawn Johnson and Bucs head coach Jon Gruden, did it become okay to get in your coach's face on the sideline and challenge him for a national TV audience to see? How about Terrell Owens of the 49ers ripping head coach Steve Marriucci for 'lacking a killer instinct' because he wouldn't pour it on the Redskins? The bottom line is the message that they send to those watching that are the most impressionable—kids. Get a grip!"

Unlike Moss, Strahan's contribution to the new independence movement in the NFL has not been negative. Strahan has battled to maintain his individuality, something that is much more difficult in the NFL than one would believe. Football demands that players not just wear uniforms, but become uniform. It often disdains players who think clearly and out of the box. Football wants drones.

Players are increasingly unwilling to play that role. Several years ago a small group of New York Jets veterans went to then–new head coach Al Groh, a remarkably dense human being, and complained that some of the practice regimens were too brutal; they asked him to ease up. Groh is old school, and the thought of players making that sort of demand simply did not compute. He ignored their requests. The players responded by tuning Groh out the rest of the year. Groh lasted that one season before quitting. He now coaches the University of Virginia Cavaliers, where college kids still sport that subservient mentality the professionals are attempting to abandon.

Standing up to authority, as many NFL players are learning, is not always PC. Strahan is a superstar who speaks his mind. Sometimes his words are so brutally honest they make your hair stand on end. But unlike Tiki Barber, Strahan does not politic, and that has always made him interesting to cover. He has challenged the Giants in many different ways, from what he should be paid after setting the controversial all-time season sack record at 22 during the 2001–2002 season, to how the team markets some of its stars. Kept out of public view, the latter issue has been one of the thornier issues raised by Strahan. Several of the more high-profile Giants players have long been irritated—even insulted—at what they feel is the lack of marketing attention paid by the organization to the highly productive players like Strahan and former Giants linebacker Jessie Armstead. Former cornerback Jason Sehorn, who had an injury-plagued Giants career, was promoted more by the team, according to Giants players, especially when it came to issues like jersey sales, than practically any other player. The team released Sehorn in March 2003 after his physical skills, which had deteriorated considerably, could no longer insulate him from the repercussions due to Sehorn's increasingly bad attitude. "That is a battle I fought for some time," Strahan acknowledges. The Giants have consistently and vehemently denied such accusations.

Fueling Strahan's rage at Barber was that his onetime friend was siding with management and doing so in the most public of ways. But it was more than that. Barber had gone through his own lengthy contract talks several years earlier, and he had repeatedly complained to Strahan privately about his disgust with how the Giants treated him during those negotiations. Strahan would simply listen and console him and never thought of going to the media to criticize Barber.

Barber's ripping of Strahan in the press was perhaps the completion of a metamorphosis by Barber, an intelligent, likable, and vital player who majored in commerce at the University of Virginia. There was no question Barber was bright, and a key member of the team, but recently, as he had become a bigger part of the Giants' offense and more of a New York celebrity, Barber had changed. He was seen by a number of team-mates as someone who cared more about being a media icon than a foot-ball player. Barber had significantly increased his workload for New York television and radio stations as an NFL analyst. He hosted a show on the YES television network, worked as a talking head on a local CBS affiliate, gave commentary on ESPN radio, even reviewed films for the Giants' website. Barber was on TV more than *Law and Order*. Indeed, he had earned the nickname "Movie Star" among some of the defensive players.

There is, of course, a fine line between seeking off-field financial opportunities to secure one's future, once the playing days end, and being a super-sized hot dog. It is a line that players have a difficult time verbally defining, but as Supreme Court Justice Potter Stewart said of pornography, they know it when it they see it. To some Giants players, Barber didn't just cross the line with his comments about Strahan—he flew over it in a Learjet.

"For him to shoot off his mouth, acting like he's Mr. New York, yes, I'm ticked off about that," Giants defensive lineman Keith Hamilton said of Barber to the *Newark Star-Ledger*. "Who is he to shoot off his mouth? He talks like he's acting in the best interests of the team. Well, tell him to give his $7 million bonus back, since he's feeling so charitable."

The entire mess began with Strahan's bitter contract dispute—and shortly before the defensive lineman's phone soiree with Barber—when Strahan had rejected a seven-year, $58 million deal from the team. (Strahan's four-year, $32 million deal was set to expire.) The core of the recent offer—a $17 million signing bonus—was split into two portions. Strahan would have earned $10 million in the 2002–2003 season and $7 million the following year.

Football salaries are often misleading. Unlike professional baseball and basketball earnings, the contract is not guaranteed in its entirety, only parts of it, usually the signing bonus. Since football is by far the most violent of all sports, that uncertainty leaves many players in the dust when commonplace season- or career-ending injuries occur. Strahan was 31 years old. He probably would never have worked to the end of the proposed contract, since most defensive ends, according to a union study, last just 3.31 years in the NFL.

This was Strahan's tenth season. He knew he was playing with house money.

So Strahan feared he could be seriously injured. Then, after one season, he might be cut by the Giants and would earn only the first portion of the signing bonus—an unlikely, but nevertheless plausible, scenario. The Giants had completed split-bonus deals with Sehorn and Barber in past seasons (both received their money), but Strahan had seen too many players released by the Giants unexpectedly to trust management. He watched quarterback Phil Simms get dumped; Hall of Fame linebacker Taylor was shown the door; and recently Armstead, probably the most popular player on the Giants team, had been sent packing. (Armstead says the first he learned he was being fired was not from the Giants organization but from various leaked media reports.) Across the league salary dumping is extremely in vogue with management, as numerous players are cut over salary cap issues.

The Giants are considered the classiest organization in football, but after his release and subsequent signing with the Washington Redskins, Armstead challenged this reputation by revealing that he played part of the 2001 season with a torn hamstring but was asked by the Giants during the year not to disclose this fact to the news media. When Armstead's contract situation arose, however, Armstead says the Giants public relations office began leaking to certain members of the news media that he had lost a step, and thus they were forced to release him. The Giants maintain they have always treated Armstead fairly and with respect.

It was another Armstead fiery quote, this one to Jay Glazer of *CBS Sportsline,* that gave at least a bit of credence to Strahan's worries that he could end up a salary cap casualty like Armstead. "The next time they preach to these young guys about the Giants family, I hope they don't buy into that family issue," Armstead said. "View how your leaders are treated. I was a leader. Use me as an example."

Adding to the oil-and-water mix of Strahan and the Giants was this ingredient: Strahan's agent, Tony Agnone, had a sour relationship with Ernie Accorsi, New York's skilled general manager, a result of several rounds of sour contract negotiations with the team. There was zero trust between the two men, though Accorsi has always been a huge fan of Strahan's.

All of those issues led to Strahan's decision to decline the Giants' offer, which he explained in detail to Glazer. Barber followed that interview with one with the *New York Post.* Barber's words were remarkably personal—I cannot remember one player blasting another over a contract the way Barber did Strahan. What was more unusual was that Barber did not first voice his grievances with Strahan before speaking to the reporter.

In one of his worst barbs, Barber said: "[Strahan] basically said he doesn't trust the organization. When they made the deal with me it wasn't an agreement between Ernie [Accorsi] and I that the money would come through. It was from the owner of the team. My agent warned me about it, but we had the promise of Mr. Mara, who typifies integrity in this league. I felt confident if there was someone I could trust, it was him. It makes me mad. If you can't trust the Giants, who can you trust?"

Barber was being about as genuine as a toupee. During his own contract negotiations Barber had insisted many times, according to Strahan and other teammates, that he indeed did not trust the Giants and was concerned about a split bonus. Barber must have forgotten to mention that fact to the writer. Barber's hypocrisy angered Strahan more than anything. Strahan felt that Barber was being deceitful in order to make Strahan look like a greedy athlete when Barber himself once had the exact same concerns Strahan did.

Armstead says Barber should not have "kissed ass to the organization by trying to talk about another player's contract. You don't do that. Just like a fireman's got a code, a policeman's got a code, there's an unwritten code: you don't speak on another player's contract. We know it's a cutthroat game. A guy's got to get what he can get. And you've got the biggest example right here," Armstead says, pointing to himself. "Get what you can get, because you still can go to five Pro Bowls straight and play nine years and they can let you go."

The angry thoughts flowed through Strahan's mind as he spoke to Barber. Barber's mealy-mouthed excuses infuriated him. It was only a matter of minutes before the phone conversation between the two men turned ugly, complete with yelling and cursing. "Let me tell you something, Tiki," Strahan said. "In public I'm not going to say anything bad about you. I don't want our team to look like we're divided. I'm going to take the high road in public. But if I ever see you alone in a private moment, I'm going to kick your ass. If we're practicing and you come running through the hole near me, I'm going to knock you out." Strahan then hung up the phone.

Strahan was never going to attack Barber, whom he outweighed by 75 pounds; his anger had simply momentarily displaced his better judgment. Barber would actually later apologize publicly to Strahan following a preseason game in late August 2002 during a sideline interview with Glazer, who would be working the contest for WCBS-TV. Strahan eventually decided to coexist with Barber for the good of the team, though he would never forget what Barber had done.

"Tiki is opportunistic," Strahan says. "He took my situation and took advantage of it. There is a lot of jealousy. You don't think players get jealous of other players? Everybody wants to be 'The Man.' The thing is, Tiki and I were good friends. That's what blew my mind. Hey, in this game, not everybody has the same value system. Tiki's biggest thing is, he plays football for stuff outside of football. He wants to be a television star, and he plays football for that. Then you have the guys who play to be the best. That's what I want to do."

The dispute showed that the price of player independence is not cheap. Thus, a tide might be turning. NFL teams have always preached that allegiance to football comes before family, friends, church, and community. Players are expected to sacrifice their health to excel, as the 2001 heatstroke-related death of Vikings' tackle Korey Stringer showed. Indeed, no sport asks players to put aside their personal safety like professional football does, and the sacrifice has resulted in a huge human price, the cost of consent. "You go all out, sometimes no matter the physical price, because you know the guy next to you will," said Green Bay's Favre.

Yet quietly that mind-set is changing. In a strange way, the salary cap may have limited players' paychecks, but it gave star players more staying power, since cutting a high-cost veteran, or losing one to injury, can wreck a team's cap situation. Players know that in many cases they are in control, not the head coach, as the Owens situation suggests. And they are often exercising that control in one word—by simply saying no.

This resistance movement has led to an escalating push and pull between player and coach, and as the Strahan and Barber feud showed, between player and player. The seesaw bounces back and forth between who has the power and who does not, between who will get a big piece of the pie and who will get crumbs. Barber's preemptive strike slamming Strahan was a clumsy attempt to use Strahan's delicate situation to boost his own standing—after all, playing the greed card is about as easy as portraying Terrell Owens as a showboat—which could in turn lead to more endorsement or media opportunities.

Football stopped being simply a game long ago. It is as big a business as Microsoft or American Express, complete with all of the corporate trimmings: backstabbing, manipulation, and power plays. And despite wisely investing in revenue sharing and a salary cap, most football players are beginning to realize for the first time that the sports world is an entertainment medium in which everyone acts out of his own self-interest.

II

When Michael Strahan was nine years old, home for him was Mannheim, West Germany, where his dad, Gene, was a major in the U.S. Army. At that young age, like most boys, Strahan emulated his father. When Gene awoke at 5:30 every morning to work out, young Michael would scamper through the hills with his dad, jumping and running along the obstacle course used by the 82nd Airborne. When they finished the course, it was off to the weight room, or maybe the gym for a boxing lesson. Push-ups came later that night during commercials while watching television. Gene never forced his son or even asked him to come along on those runs. Michael just did it.

As Strahan grew older, the training regimen would turn him into a fitness machine. Ironically, he participated little in youth sports and did not play organized football until he was a strapping 16-year-old. Gene was aware that his son was on the verge of becoming a brilliant athlete, despite his limited exposure to sports. So Gene decided to play a hunch. He sent Strahan to live with his uncle in Texas. It paid off. Strahan played just one season of high school football and earned a scholarship to Texas Southern University in Houston.

But after his first semester of college Strahan was ready to go back to Germany for good, and he cleaned out his dorm room, taking every sheet, pillowcase, and eraser. He had not grown up in the United States and didn't understand or like the lifestyle. American football was a mystery to him. Other players knew how to move with more grace. They had football muscle and were mean and tough. Strahan was big but not as powerful as his teammates.

Strahan returned to live with his parents in Mannheim. Weeks went by. Then months. "Isn't it time for you to go back?" Gene asked. "What are you going to do?" Strahan told his father that he had hoped to never return to Texas and would stay with him. Then the army officer looked closer at his son and said: "No. What are *you* going to do?" It hit Strahan. His father had a plan, but he could not do it for his son. Strahan had to do it by himself.

Strahan intended to stick with one of the mottoes Gene and Louise

and the other six Strahan children had adopted: never start something
you cannot finish.

When Strahan decided to recommit to football and Texas Southern,
he went all out. No one worked harder. On Easter Sunday in 1990 and on
Thanksgiving Day in 1991 and 1992, Strahan did not fly back to Europe to
visit his parents. He stayed alone on the deserted campus for the holidays.
Strahan put the idle time to good use, strapping on his roommate's
weighted shoes and running the football stadium steps. Then came pounding the streets, followed by laps around the gym, and then more stadium
steps. When Strahan tired, his mind would flash back to the young kid running through the obstacle course with his father, and energy would again
flow through his muscles. After a workout Strahan would call Gene back in
Germany, who always said, "All of your hard work will pay off one day."

Gene knew what he was talking about. Besides being a standout soldier, Gene Strahan was an excellent boxer in the Armed Services tour-
naments, even going 1–1 against Ken Norton, a onetime top Marine
heavyweight who would go on to become world champion. One of
Gene's first jobs as a young adult was to chop and haul wood pulp, rising
out of bed at 2:00 A.M. for a five-hour ride to Louisiana. The job paid $35
a week. Louise earned money by sewing ROTC patches on uniforms.

Gene's toughness and unflappable work ethic were passed down to
Strahan as sure as his eye color was. Strahan still trains like the kid in
Mannheim, working harder during the season than almost any other
lineman in football, studying game film until his eyes can barely stay
open. And Gene's influence goes beyond the physical. His mental rigid-
ity and stubbornness, common among military men and women, have
become a part of his son as well. As Strahan would slowly develop from
a college kid intimidated by football into an NFL rookie, and then into
one of the top five defensive linemen of the past 20 years, his almost
unshakable belief in himself, to do the right thing, even if that thing
was unpopular or even incorrect, would constantly be tested. There
would be moments when Strahan crashed through the Giants organization like Godzilla in downtown Tokyo, taking on the team over issues
minor and grand, being alternately an invaluable asset to the franchise
and a major irritant.

11

The worst hit Strahan said he has taken in the NFL happened early in his career against the Washington Redskins. Strahan had pulled one of his distinguished speed moves, curving around the offensive tackle and locking his eyes on the target, which was running back Terry Allen. Strahan trailed Allen by about ten feet but closed fast. The more ground Strahan gained, the more he blocked out what was going on around him, which is why he failed to see wide receiver Michael Westbrook, running with a full head of steam, coming in the opposite direction.

When Strahan got within inches of Allen, a Washington offensive lineman was jammed backwards and tumbled in front of Strahan, causing him to leap unexpectedly. The jump was so sudden that Strahan's body was vulnerable, because he was using his hands to balance himself while he was airborne instead of to protect his body. Just as Strahan landed and put one toe on the ground, he was hit by Westbrook, who used his momentum and lower center of gravity, despite being outweighed by over 60 pounds, to bash Strahan thoroughly. In making contact, Westbrook applied the crown of his helmet to Strahan's jaw, and Strahan's head snapped back like a Pez dispenser. "He could have killed me," Strahan says. His words are not an overstatement.

The entire episode lasted just a few seconds and ended with Westbrook standing over Strahan and pointing at him, laughing. What made things worse for Strahan was that he was not wearing a mouthpiece, which can help absorb shock. (He now uses one every game.) For a few moments Strahan did not know who or where he was.

"I just sort of stumbled around. I knew I was done for the day. I was out of it," he says. "I didn't know where I was for a second or two. Then [Westbrook] started talking trash, and when I started to become more aware, I started to get pissed off. I was not going to leave the game with somebody making fun of me that way. I tried to talk shit back, but I don't know what the hell came out of my mouth.

"I had a concussion," Strahan says. "I was seeing stars. I was loopy. I was blinking my eyes to make the stars disappear. Then I started praying that the ball didn't come my way because if it did I was done. In the huddle a couple of guys asked me, 'Are you okay?' "

Strahan estimates that was his third concussion, and he has probably had several more. "These are things you simply cannot worry too much about when you are playing," he explains. "I've tried to take more control of things and maybe not go right back in the game immediately if I get my bell rung. But there's a fine line. You can't worry about injuries too much when you are playing because if you do, you'll be tentative. You won't be any good."

The hit by Westbrook jarred more than Strahan's skull. It led to a sort of personal awakening. Strahan would continue to be a fearless player, but he knew that in the end his career was remarkably fragile. So when various contract situations arose with the Giants, he was determined to get as much money—especially guaranteed money, a rarity in the sport—as he could. He was going to take more control of his life, on and off the field. The 1999–2000 season only reinforced his thinking. That off-season Strahan signed a $32 million contract extension but followed the signing of the deal with just five sacks. Frustrated during the year by his low sack numbers, Strahan became agitated around the locker room, combative, that gap-toothed smile gone from his face. Armstead, his friend, once chided him during a game to stop solely going for sacks and get back to being the all-around defensive player he was. Strahan's effectiveness returned after wrist and knee surgeries following that season.

This period was the beginning of Strahan's battles with some members of the New York news media, and these skirmishes began to reshape his thinking on how to deal with the press. "I caught a lot of heat that year I had five sacks," Strahan says. "Up until that point I had been nothing but nice and respectful to writers. So it became clear to me. No matter how nice I was to writers, if I struggled, I was just another dumb player to some of them. I realized a player has no real friends in the media. So I decided to control [whom] I talk to and when I talk. Time is the most important asset you have, more important than money or almost anything else, because you can't get time back."

"During a season everything is on a clock," he continues. "The few moments I'm not on the clock, I want to take control of those moments. It's the one thing a small number of players still don't get. They go through their careers like robots. They don't think they have control. We have a lot more control than some players understand."

"If I get 15 sacks one season, I'm a great guy," Strahan adds, clearly impassioned now. "If I get five sacks, I'm a bum. That's the way it goes. So I've learned to just speak my mind and be myself. I say what I say. I say what people are thinking. I don't live a lie the way some people do."

Strahan *can* be irritable. He *can* be hypersensitive. Glenn Parker, a former Giants offensive lineman who has always liked Strahan, once said of the defensive star: "I've met grapes with thicker skin than Mike." There have been times when I wrote things Strahan disliked and he didn't speak to me for weeks or sometimes months afterwards. It's never bothered me. Most writers are used to getting chewed out by players or given the cold shoulder following an unfavorable story. It is a part of the job. But when Strahan challenges or blows off certain Giants beat writers, it drives them bonkers. A handful of them have sought revenge, which is reminiscent of something Napoleon once said, that three hostile newspapers are more to be feared than a thousand bayonets. Strahan likes to be combative with some in the local media when a smile or a joke might ease the tension. Sometimes Strahan does not just give some members of the New York media ammunition, he locks and loads the weapon for them. In November 1999, while Jim Fassel was away attending his mother's funeral, Strahan told writers after one practice that the Giants' defense was carrying the load and they were tired of doing it. He didn't stop there. He went on to criticize the offensive players and Fassel's play calling. When Fassel returned, the offense and defense were in a full-blown civil war.

After the Giants' first home contest following the terrorist attacks of September 11, 2001, Strahan told a group of reporters about an emotional discussion he had had in the minutes before the game with a fan who lost her spouse in the collapse of the towers. (Since coming into the league, Strahan has been one of the more generous NFL players when it comes to charitable donations, of both money and time.) A *Newsday* reporter followed Strahan's vivid tale with a slow, fat curveball that Strahan should have knocked out of the park. "Earlier, Coach Fassel said he knew you were going to have a big game today," the writer asked. "How did he know?"

Strahan shot back, "Because you guys said I wouldn't." He continued: "Guy doesn't get a sack for one game, and people say he can't play anymore. You guys put me under the doo-doo pile. Stop doing that. I have feelings too." That kind of smart-mouthed response from Strahan just isn't necessary.

But some of the New York writers are at fault as well. One thing that always confused Strahan—and me as well—was why some writers picked his performance apart while Sehorn, who would sign his own lucrative contract extensions, often went unscathed by the wrath of these beat journalists, despite a rash of injuries that kept him off the field.

Several writers go out of their way to attack Strahan constantly, analyzing every syllable he utters and every tackle he makes, often with excessive and unnecessary venom. Other stars on the team rarely receive that kind of microscopic analysis. A veteran Strahan-hater once told a new Giants beat writer who had just been assigned to the job: "Don't trust anything Strahan tells you." A veteran beat writer told the *Village Voice* anonymously, and thus rather gutlessly, "No question [Strahan's] a very sensitive and moody guy. And it gets him into trouble."

One of the problems is that some of the Giants beat writers are uncomfortably close to members of the front office and public relations staff. Several of them who have been the most critical of Strahan over recent years have been regulars on a Giants-produced television show that analyzes Giants games. *The show is cohosted by the team's public relations director.* That's not just unnervingly intimate, that's inbreeding. The beat writers who are regularly paid $200 a week by the Giants to appear on the show are the same beat writers who are assigned to provide unbiased coverage of the Giants. This is a damaging conflict of interest; at best it presents, as the phrase goes in the journalism business, the *appearance* of compromised ethics.

How uncomfortably close are some of the beat writers with the team? When the reporter for the *New York Times* that covered the Giants departed the beat for a job at ESPN, the team's public relations director actually called the *Times* to recommend the beat writer from *Newsday* for the opening. That is just not supposed to happen. A reporter and a team are not supposed to become such close pals that the PR guy is acting as a job headhunter for the writer, because that level of friendship means the reporter is incapable of providing unbiased coverage. Needless to say, the reporter was not considered for the position.

HBO aired a smart documentary called *Journeys with George* about a former *NBC News* producer's travels with George W. Bush's 2000 campaign. The producer, Alexandra Pelosi, recalled that when Bush's handlers gave her not one but several cakes for her birthday while she was on the trail with Bush, she subsequently started to feel more fondness for the Bush campaign and the people who ran it. That made the journalist part of her soul somewhat uncomfortable, however, because she was supposed to be objective. Imagine, then, the impact of regular paychecks from the Giants organization on how these beat writers cover the franchise and how it deals with Strahan.

When Strahan has engaged in his tiffs with the team, this closeness between some members of the media and the Giants has sometimes manifested itself in attacks on Strahan on behalf of the team. A sort of mob mentality seems to develop regarding the star, something the military calls "incestuous amplification," which *Jane's Defense Weekly* calls "a condition . . . where one only listens to those who are already in lockstep agreement, reinforcing set beliefs and creating a situation ripe for miscalculation." This is not a unique phenomenon in NFL media-team relationships, but in all my years of covering a football beat I have never seen it to the degree it affects Strahan.

The strain between Strahan and some New York journalists has always struck me as bizarre considering that Strahan has a professional and comfortable relationship with most national media, as was evident, for instance, when *ABC Sports* selected him as one of two player-hosts for the network's pregame coverage of Super Bowl XXXVII. Good game or bad, Strahan is a stand-up athlete and will stay at his locker and answer questions when the norm in the NFL now is for players to hide from the media after a poor effort. He offers some of the more poignant opinions of anyone in football. In the media we often say we wish players were not so fake and could be more accessible. Then along comes a player like Strahan, who often returns phone calls and will meet for lunch and chat. He'll talk about who the best linemen are to go against, or discuss what the league needs to do to better protect its players from injuries, or what his thoughts are on the war against terror—in other words, any topic, any time. And sportswriters complain. When he spoke to the *New York Daily News* as part of the newspaper's periodic interview series called "Unplugged," he answered questions on everything from Senator Trent Lott's stroll down segregation lane to why he has never fixed that now-trademark gap between his two front teeth, to what he would do if he were commissioner for a day. Strahan doesn't do drugs. He doesn't get arrested. He has always been a good citizen off the field and a relentless worker on it.

I ask Strahan, why not try to get along better with some of the New York writers who dislike him? He answers quickly. "Because I'm not an Uncle Tom. I'm not going to suck up to anybody. I have to be me."

||

Strahan is driving on Route 3 in New Jersey one early fall day, away from Giants Stadium, away from another busy practice. His cell phone is crackling, and so is his sharp tongue. For a player who can at times be considered such a grouch by some, he has always possessed a notable sense of humor. A small number of NFL players find it difficult to leave the violence they experience on the football field there where it belongs, and it colors their lives, changing their personalities from cheery to nasty, especially after years of exposure to broken bones and torn limbs. Some players bring that violence into their personal lives, abusing domestic partners or brawling in bar fights. Strahan is not one of those men. He is immensely laid back away from the sport, especially with people he trusts, always chitchatting, always joking around.

It takes a lot to get him rattled, but should a player push the wrong buttons, the big softie is capable of wringing a neck or two.

During the Giants' training camp in 1994, defensive lineman Chris Maumalanga, a brute and former L.A. gang member, got into one of the worst fights I have ever seen, more fierce than any boxing match, when he beat up offensive lineman Scott Davis and, in the process, yanked off Davis's helmet and beat him over the head with it. The combustible Maumalanga had been in a number of altercations. In another incident in 1995 he and a small group of players were sitting around talking when the 6-foot-3-inch, 240-pound Mitch Davis joked that he wanted the 270-pound Maumalanga to go downstairs and get his keys. Maumalanga said no. Davis, half-joking, half-trying to embarrass Maumalanga in front of his friends, asked again. Maumalanga punched him in the face. One punch. Davis was knocked unconscious for several minutes. Maumalanga pounced on Davis as he lay sprawled on the floor. It took two players, the 242-pound Pete Shufelt and the 230-pound Armstead, both linebackers, to pull Maumalanga off Davis. A day later Davis's eye was still practically swollen shut. Maumalanga was feeling his oats and decided he would test himself against Strahan. Bad move. Several weeks after Maumalanga knocked out Davis, he started teasing Strahan over some silly stuff while the two were sitting around in the locker room, and since Strahan likes a good joke as much as anyone, he at first laughed along, which seemed to frustrate Maumalanga. So he then physically threatened Strahan, who told Maumalanga to calm down. Instead, Maumalanga took a swing at Strahan. He missed. The 270-pound Strahan, who has done some boxing, punched Maumalanga in the face several times, then threw him several feet before the fight was broken up. Maumalanga never bothered Strahan again.

Strahan's low-key nature was illustrated when he married his wife, Jean, on a riverboat that steamed down the Missouri River, with just 18 of the couple's friends and family attending. When he remembers that day, his voice is quiet, warm. As he drives on and the subject changes to sacks, his mood switches from introspective to humor-prone, and the jokes come rolling off Strahan's lips faster than a Michael Vick strike, each one punctuated by his contagious laugh—"heh-heh-heh." I tell him that when he broke Mark Gastineau's single-season sack record in the final game of the 2002 season and the former Jets player, who was at the contest, gave Strahan a kiss on the cheek to congratulate him, he was going to catch some heat from teammates. "Grown men are allowed to kiss," he says, "and we don't have to say anything more than that." Heh-heh-heh.

It is some months after he entered the record books following a controversial sack, and time has allowed Strahan to smile when discussing it. It wasn't always that way. Strahan broke the record because of a gift from Favre with less than three minutes remaining in the game, which took place at Giants Stadium on January 6, 2002. Green Bay Coach Mike Sherman, with his team comfortably ahead, called for a running play to Ahman Green. Favre changed it, without telling his offensive line, to a quarterback keep, meaning Favre was to fake a handoff and then run the opposite way—in this instance, toward Strahan's left defensive end spot. Since the linemen thought Favre was handing off, they did not pass protect and Strahan was free. He steamrolled right into Favre for a 7-yard sack.

Until that point Strahan had no sacks, three quarterback hurries, and two quarterback hits. He was not going to get the record. There is no question that Favre knew this, and that he changed the play so Strahan could snag the sack. "Strahan can get sacks on his own," Sherman said at the time, stressing that the original call was for a handoff. "We don't have to give it to him."

The news media went ballistic, implying, even stating outright, that Favre had tanked it for his friend Strahan. Bill Lyon of the *Philadelphia Inquirer* wrote: "Favre is a fierce, fiery competitor with an incredible tolerance for pain. His credentials are impeccable. But he has made it difficult not to believe that the record Strahan now holds is tainted. You don't like to think that Favre, even if it was a well-intended, well-meaning gesture, deliberately made sure that Strahan got the sack he needed for the record. That is an affront to the integrity of the game and is an insult to all the other pass-rushers who came close to 22."

The controversy overshadowed Strahan's remarkable year. Since 1982, when the NFL first began tracking sack statistics, only five players other than Strahan—Gastineau, Lawrence Taylor (20.5 in 1986), Reggie White (21 in 1987), Chris Doleman (21 in 1989), and Derrick Thomas (20 in 1990)—have had 20 or more sacks in a season. Of those players only three—Gastineau, White, and Doleman—were defensive linemen, which puts Strahan in some fairly rare company.

What has made Strahan such a formidable player, especially in the last five seasons, and the best defensive lineman in today's football, is that his game goes beyond the sacks. One of the few linemen who plays both the pass and run well, Strahan is immensely well rounded. He is usually among the top five in team tackles and has led in fumble recoveries—meaning he is always around the football. There are also few linemen who have displayed Strahan's kind of consistency, especially at such a violent position. Strahan had played in 112 straight regular-season games entering the 2003 season.

Instead of relying on brute strength—standing at 6 feet 5 inches and weighing a sturdy 275 pounds, he has plenty of that—Strahan studies the tendencies of his opponents, using extensive game film work, picking up tidbits that give away a weakness. To Strahan, the way a quarterback hitches his shoulder before a snap, or an offensive tackle twitches his right hand, are clues to whether the play is a run or pass. He is infamous for stealing a team's signals or guessing the correct snap count.

Strahan's feeling about the gift-wrapped sack have gone from defensive to indifferent. He starts to relay a story about it and is laughing before he tells it, showing that the sack criticism isn't so stinging anymore. Strahan attended Favre's charity golf tournament in Gulfport, Mississippi, the summer following The Sack. One morning he ran into Favre's mother, Bonita Favre, who promptly pulled him aside. *"Michael"*—Strahan is imitating her thick Mississippi drawl—*"are you getting as much shit over that sack stuff as my son is getting?"* Strahan says when he spoke to Favre he didn't ask the quarterback if he took a dive. Favre had denied to the media after the game that he intentionally allowed Strahan to sack him, and he told Strahan at the golf tournament, "All I did was tell those reporters the truth, but what I really wanted to say to them was, 'Fuck you, guys.'"

Strahan chuckles when recounting the story, but he becomes more serious when discussing some of his dealings with the Giants. Strahan claims that one of the things he has fought the team over for years is the issue of which players the team will choose to promote and market. Strahan says the Giants heavily promoted Sehorn but for years practically ignored him and Armstead, clearly the two biggest stars on the team when they both played together. "They would always pump Sehorn, so Jessie and I always had to go complain to the Giants," Strahan remarks.

The inequality manifested itself in several ways, Strahan says. The first has to do with player appearances. The Giants are like most NFL teams in that their players are often paid to attend events, like an autograph signing or the opening of an apparel store. Some of these appearances can pay tens of thousands of dollars. Strahan claims that the Giants handed most of the better, higher-paying, higher-profile appearance requests to Sehorn, while shunting the ones that paid little or nothing and were less high-profile to Strahan, Armstead, and others. The Giants have denied that they ever showed such favoritism.

The second issue is the way in which Giants jerseys are distributed in New York–area sporting goods stores. Though the issue surfaced years ago, it irritates Strahan to this day. He claims that the Giants manipulated how the jerseys were disseminated so that a larger number of stores had more jerseys emblazoned with Sehorn's name and number than with the names of other players on the team. Strahan says he protested repeatedly to Rusty Hawley, the Giants' vice president of marketing, about the lack of Strahan or Armstead jerseys in stores. Hawley, Strahan says, would always respond that the team did not promote Sehorn's jersey more than his or Armstead's. At one point Strahan's wife, Jean, as smart as her husband and equally feisty, got into the act by asking merchandise outlets how the process worked, claiming to have discovered information that she and Strahan thought confirmed Hawley had been misleading them when it came to the number of jerseys distributed.

What Strahan is saying is that the Giants stacked the deck in favor of Sehorn for a dual purpose—to get Sehorn more publicity and to limit Strahan's visibility as a way of punishing him for confronting the team over various issues. Again, the Giants maintain no such bias ever existed.

Does Strahan have a legitimate gripe? Or is he expressing paranoia on the level of Captain Queeg? There are two problems with Strahan's theory. First, there is no hard evidence of its veracity. Second, it seems that consumers determine jersey sales. If a fan wants a Giants jersey, he buys the one he wants, no matter how much the Giants may or may not promote a Sehorn jersey.

If Strahan is being paranoid, then Armstead must have inhaled a similar virus, because he believes the same thing Strahan does—and he believed it before he was released from the team, so it is not bitterness talking. Also, other Giants players who asked not to be identified, past and current, have expressed identical beliefs.

Perhaps the most important point is that Strahan believes this to be true enough to confront the Giants about it, which exemplifies how much the team's star player has at times distrusted the franchise.

What makes these matters even thornier is Sehorn himself. Players on the Giants and around the league have claimed that Sehorn received large amounts of media attention and favoritism from the organization because he is a white cornerback—a rarity in professional football. (Or as one writer put it, "the only one in captivity.") Tampa Bay defensive lineman Warren Sapp called Sehorn "extremely overrated. How does a guy who has never been to the Pro Bowl get so much attention?"

St. Louis coach Mike Martz has also bashed Sehorn. When Sehorn said after a narrow 15–14 victory over St. Louis during the 2000–2001 season that the Rams did not have a patient offense, which was true, Martz fired back. "Who cares? Do you think I need to worry about what Jason Sehorn thinks?" he said. "We just keep running by Jason, that's all I know." Later that year Martz added: "We threw the ball all over the lot against the Giants. I'd like to line up against Jason Sehorn every day of the week." Martz's comments, which he later apologized for, show just what kind of lightning rod Sehorn has become.

When Cris Carter played for the Minnesota Vikings, he went against Sehorn several times and once called him "the most overrated player in football." Now Carter, who is headed for the Hall of Fame, is an analyst for HBO's *Inside the NFL*. He puts the Sehorn phenomenon in perfect perspective. "A lot of African American players do not want to believe that a white cornerback can play well," says Carter, who competed against every top cornerback in the game. "It's wrong to think that, but it happens. It's the same way with [New York Jets wide receiver] Wayne Chrebet. I knew black players who said, 'He can't be any good as a wide receiver because he's white.' "

"But there was something else that happened that was just as wrong," Carter adds. "I think Jason was a good corner, but he never hit his prime because of all the injuries he suffered. But the media was putting him in the same class as a Deion Sanders or an Aeneas Williams. There are a lot of good corners in the league, and Jason was elevated above those good corners by the media. That shouldn't have been the case. The only reason that happened was because . . . I'm not going down that road, but you know what I'm talking about."

The road Carter will not traverse is race. But it is a road well traveled when it comes to Sehorn. As Sehorn's star grew, over the years, I interviewed dozens of league players for stories to be published in the *New York Times*. Invariably when I introduced myself and said I was from New York, a player, always a black player, usually at a skill position, would bitterly bring up the topic of Sehorn. The conversations, a number of them, were always the same: if Sehorn were black, he'd be viewed as just another cornerback by a mostly white football media.

Sehorn has displayed astounding, albeit short, bouts of athleticism during his career. Giants teammates nicknamed him "Species" because of his combination of size, speed, and athleticism, and former Dallas wide receiver Michael Irvin once called Sehorn "the awesome white boy." One of the best plays I have ever seen happened in the 2000 postseason when Sehorn dove after a Donovan McNabb pass, tipped it into the air, picked himself off the turf as the ball floated above him, then stretched upwards to catch the ball and returned it 32 yards for a touchdown.

What makes Sehorn thoroughly overrated is his lack of consistency. Part of being a great NFL player is staying on the field, but Sehorn has been unable to do that because of a series of injuries. He has had a torn anterior cruciate ligament, broken ribs, a broken leg, a busted ankle, and two knee surgeries, the second one repairing a microfracture in his right knee. Since becoming a starter in 1996, Sehorn has started in just 73 of a possible 101 games. Strahan hasn't missed a game since 1996, an incredible stretch for a defensive lineman. Armstead started 96 straight games at linebacker for the Giants before being released. But while members of the media bashed Strahan during his injury-plagued five-sack season after he signed a new contract, Sehorn received a $10 million signing bonus while being primarily a part-time player and was able to limp under the media radar like he was wearing a personal cloaking device.

What irritated Strahan and other Giants the most, and why there was such anger over the jersey issue, was their feeling that Sehorn was held to a different standard than other teammates. Indeed, at times in his Giants career no player thumbed his nose at the team's rules more than Sehorn. In the spring of 1999 he skipped the final week of a passing camp without informing the team, angering Fassel. At various points earlier in his career, during team meetings and practices, Sehorn openly disobeyed the instructions of coaches and spoke back to assistants in blatant acts of insubordination, usually without being punished. Fassel screamed at Sehorn one training camp in front of the team after

Sehorn mouthed off to him. Sehorn's nickname eventually changed from "Species" to "Rodman," after the mercurial former basketball star who constantly tested his coaches. (Interestingly, Sehorn has occasionally also treated some members of the local media terribly, but mysteriously, his actions are not held against him by some in the media the way Strahan's occasional anti-press stances are.) Meanwhile, Sehorn's endorsement opportunities quadrupled as his star rose, and the team began promoting Sehorn perhaps more than any other Giant.

Players often felt that Sehorn was never severely disciplined for his actions because management was infatuated with him. Wellington Mara, the best owner in the history of the sport, told the *New York Times* in the summer of 2002 that when Sehorn was in his prime, "he was as good as I ever saw playing his position. I used to watch him practice, so athletic and it came so easily to him, and yet he applied himself 100 percent. It was great to watch." Mara's knowledge of football is second to no one's. However, Mara's statement is a stretch of epic proportions. Sehorn simply did not present enough raw materials on the field to merit such a conclusion.

Fassel did try to reel Sehorn in several times, but recently Sehorn's own actions began to show publicly just how much of a malcontent he can be. His true colors showed in November 2002 when Sehorn, relegated to a reserve cornerback role because he'd been beaten out by younger and more talented players, was asked about defending against Minnesota wideout Randy Moss, whom the Giants were going to face. Sehorn replied: "It doesn't matter—I don't play anyway. Why are you talking to me? Talk to the two starters." Sehorn was as bitter as a ripe lemon. I can only imagine the roasting Strahan would have received had he made such a selfish remark.

There is no question that star players, or players simply perceived as stars, have always been treated differently than ordinary grunts. Former Dallas coach Jimmy Johnson has told the story of cutting one of his backup players who kept falling asleep in meetings. When asked what would happen if the star of the team, quarterback Aikman, had also repeatedly dozed off, Johnson replied, "I'd get him a pillow."

Sehorn's actions—skipping off-season workout programs, talking back to coaches, working out in California instead of the area—could be seen as smacking on a slice of his own independence pie. But there is a difference. Though Sehorn is slightly more grounded now, he has acted like an aloof prima donna in the past. Strahan is a legitimate star but has never held himself to a separate standard. He rarely misses a practice or is late for a meeting, and in his decade-long career with the Giants he has never departed in the off-season for an extended period of time, instead choosing to stay around the Giants' facility to work out there. And Strahan, unlike Sehorn, has not told coaches where they can shove their whistles. That may be one of the main reasons Sehorn was let go. He had agreed to a pay cut of more than $3 million requested by the Giants in the winter of 2003, but the team still released him. I believe the Giants simply tired of Sehorn's act, and Sehorn's skill was no longer good enough to protect him from his at-times crappy attitude.

At one point before Sehorn's release, when Armstead and Strahan began seeing, according to the two players, Sehorn, who had lived by a different set of rules for so long, promoted more than them, it of course struck a nerve with the two players. The situation remained freshly sensitive to them. What may be the most important aspect of this dispute is that Strahan *perceived* a slight from the Giants. That is how acrimonious the relationship has occasionally been. Strahan sometimes—sometimes—is so distrusting of his employer that he is unwilling to give the organization the benefit of the doubt, and some in the Giants organization were too arrogant—we don't need to explain ourselves to him, he's just a player—to fully explain to Strahan how the jersey distribution process worked.

Strahan was so furious that several years ago he began a sort of protest. The Giants, like most teams, ask players to sign replicas of their jerseys, which are then given away for various promotional purposes. Strahan had been cooperative for much of his Giants career, but for a brief period a short time ago he began refusing to autograph his jerseys. Members of the organization, including Hawley, would continue to ask, and Strahan would continue to firmly say no.

According to Strahan, Hawley once tried to pull a power play. During Strahan's signing boycott, Frank Mara, the son of Wellington and the team's director of promotion, asked Strahan to sign a jersey. Strahan says that when the younger Mara made the request, Hawley was in the background. "He stood there with his arms crossed," Strahan says of Hawley. "I guess he thought I wouldn't turn down the owner's son." But Strahan did.

Strahan says the team went so far as to request team psychologist Joel Goldberg to speak to him in an effort to smooth things over. After one particular practice, Strahan was told that Goldberg was looking for him. Strahan says he intercepted the therapist. "Doc, I'm not crazy," Strahan told Goldberg. "I may be angry, but I'm not crazy."

II

Why didn't he just sign the damn jerseys, I ask him? Why cause yourself a headache? Why not cooperate? Why not make it easy on yourself? And by the way, Michael, haven't the Giants treated you well by paying you more than $60 million in your career? There are a lot of people who would love to be disrespected in that way.

His responses make a great deal of sense.

To Strahan, his past disputes with the Giants were not just about simple slights. They were about the organization punishing him for being outspoken and independent. The Giants tuned him out when he brought up concerns off the gridiron. It was their way, Strahan reasons (and I believe correctly), of trying to regain control of him.

There are two separate issues. An organization pays a player millions for a contract because it needs that player to be successful. Players can be grateful, sure, but they have earned that money, especially players like Strahan. From the $17.6 billion television contract alone, each NFL team is funneled $77 million. That doesn't include the revenue generated from sweetheart stadium deals and other sources of football-related monies. Owners make money without apology, and so should athletes—above all, professional football players, many of whom will lose the ability in later life to walk without a limp or think straight after a series of brain-scrambling concussions.

What I always tell people who think athletes gripe too much is that some do. Sure. Still, use your imagination. You're in a good job. You're paid well. You work hard. You follow the rules. But the guy down the hall misses half of the week because he is sick. When he does come in, he tells his bosses to screw themselves. He spends more time doing things outside of the job than on the job. No matter. The company gives him raises. His picture is all over the place as Employee of the Month even though you know he blew off a mandatory meeting. Several meetings, in fact. But there you are. Constantly doing your job. You make a lot of money. But you were one of the big reasons why the company finished in the top two in productivity in the nation, so you more than earned your cash. But the other guy, the golden boy, gets the company's attention. None of this would irritate you? Of course it would.

This is not to say the Giants are the complete bad guys. Of all the organizations I have covered as a beat, the Giants are the most loyal to their coaches, front office employees, and fans—despite Armstead's feelings to the contrary. Mara is the classiest owner in the NFL because he has spent his life considering the interest of the league before his own, something the likes of Daniel Snyder and Jerry Jones do not. The team's other co-owner, Preston Robert Tisch, is respected by everyone in the sport. George Young, the former general manager, was the most generous executive I ever knew, and his replacement, Ernie Accorsi, is among the smartest. (His selection of tight end Jeremy Shockey in the 2002 draft was one of the better picks the Giants have made in years.) Fassel is a nice guy who wins, a rarity in football.

The Giants just get it right.

Strahan is one of the few exceptions to the rule, and it has to do with the Giants' irrational desire to control everything around them, every player, every member of the franchise, every reporter, every blade of grass. Some teams want to have power over some of these things, but few care or have the energy to exert control over all of them. The public relations department tends to reward players and writers who cooperate and follow the team's lead, and it nastily bad-mouths and retaliates against those people who refuse to do so. The way to deal with an independent, productive, and opinionated player like Strahan, who is also a responsible, mature player, is to let him be. Let him talk. Let him have his fits. Because in the end trying to put a stranglehold on Strahan is counterproductive; he will only fight back as hard as you fight him.

At one point the two sides began tuning each other out. When Strahan's $9,000 Rolex Daytona watch was stolen out of his locker following the Green Bay game (just one of several thefts of players' belongings that year), he says the Giants did not immediately help him find it or offer reimbursement. So Strahan pushed for the team's insurer to pick up the tab. When the company refused, he continued to fight the Giants on it. To Strahan, the struggle became less about the watch and more about providing a secure atmosphere for players and their possessions. Another battle, another front in the cold war. (The Giants should have handled the situation the way Jimmy Johnson did. Twenty-four hours before the Cowboys were to leave for one of the Super Bowls, the Super Bowl tickets of Chad Hennings, the team's defensive end, were stolen from his locker. If sold to scalpers, they could have brought tens of thousands of dollars. Upon hearing about the theft, Johnson told his team: "If the person who did this does not come forward with the tickets by breakfast tomorrow, I will find out who it is. I will cut your sorry ass. Then I will call every coach in the National Football League and tell each one of them to never, ever hire this sorry SOB because he is a no-good rotten turncoat who steals from his teammates." The tickets were turned in the next day at 6:30 in the morning.)

Some skirmishes Strahan has gotten mixed up in had nothing to do with his own team. As so often has happened, Strahan did not start the fight, but he also did not shy away once the adjectives started flying. When Sapp mocked the sack record by saying it deserved an asterisk, Strahan responded by calling Sapp "a jackass." Then Strahan sent word through Armstead—a friend of both men and, like Sapp, a University of Miami alum—that if Sapp wanted to keep lobbing grenades, Strahan was only getting started. Sapp, fearing a verbal sparring match he could not win, instantly shut up. Strahan simply does not back down—on anything.

II

The day after the terror attacks of September 11, 2001, a group of Giants players walked onto the practice field, located a mere ten miles from the devastation where the World Trade Center towers once stood. The smoke from the fall of the buildings still covered part of Manhattan, creating a thin, ugly layer of smog. The players could see it all. And it wasn't just that image that brought tears to some of their eyes. It was the knowledge that only a few feet away from their grass outdoor practice field, inside the indoor practice dome used when the weather was disagreeable, the bodies of some of the victims were spread across the floor. The facility was now a makeshift morgue. Rescue vehicles dashed in and out of the parking lot. The Giants were in no mood to play football.

The NFL, like the rest of the country, remained stunned following the suicide airplane crashes, but the league was still considering playing its slate of 15 games, despite safety issues and logistical concerns about hundreds of players flying around the country. Approximately half of the league's 32 owners wanted the games to go on, citing the importance of returning to normalcy. And that might have happened. Then something remarkable occurred.

On Wednesday night, one day after the towers fell, union leader Gene Upshaw, a former offensive lineman for the Oakland Raiders, a Hall-of-Famer, and as skilled a leader as there is in all of professional sports, held a conference call with the player representatives from each franchise. At first some of the reps were ambivalent about whether to play that weekend, while others agreed with ownership, that playing might help the country heal. Strahan grew impatient and, as he always does, spoke up forcefully and effectively.

"All of you need to understand something," Strahan said. "At our practice fields we can still see the smoke. They're taking bodies into our practice bubble. I don't know about any of you, but I'm not playing this weekend. I can't do it. And I know a lot of my teammates won't either. They're still digging bodies out of the rubble here. If we played, it would be disrespectful to the people who died. It's as simple as that." Strahan stressed that the horrors were not just pictures on a TV screen. Jets center Kevin Mawae echoed Strahan, his words equally as fervent. Clearly, if the NFL did decide to continue, players on the two New York franchises would not.

The majority of reps sat in stunned silence following the words from Strahan and Mawae. The players on the call voted 17–10 not to play, with one abstention. Upshaw spoke to Tagliabue and relayed what had happened. He made sure Tagliabue understood just how vehemently opposed to playing the games were the players in New York and even those in Washington, where the third jetliner had crashed into the Pentagon. Opposition isn't the correct word; the league would have had a mutiny on its hands.

Buffalo player representative Phil Hansen remembers the speeches by Strahan and Mawae and how they moved everyone. "Hairs stood up on the back of my neck after they spoke," Hansen says. "After they said their piece, it was hard to dispute. How are you going to play in the Meadowlands when you have people under the rubble right across the river?"

The postponement of the games was the first-ever for nonstrike reasons by the NFL, which had received widespread criticism for opting to play following the assassination of President John F. Kennedy in 1963. The league played through World War II, the San Francisco earthquake in 1989, and the Persian Gulf War—but this was just *different.* Following the NFL's decision, there was a postponement parade in the sports world. Five hours after football announced its plan, Major League Baseball postponed its weekend games. All Division I-A college football conferences, some of which earlier in the day had said they would play that weekend, called off their games once the NFL did. NASCAR called off a Winston Cup race in New Hampshire.

The potential boycott was simply one of many factors that led to Tagliabue's decision—the league imagined the frightening but realistic scenario of another hijacked plane crashing into a crowded stadium—but the voice of the players was paramount. Tagliabue consulted numerous league executives and many outside of the sport, including officials from the Bush administration and from the office of New York Governor George E. Pataki. But in the end it might have been the voices of two simple grunts, Strahan and Mawae, that had the greatest effect of all on the course Tagliabue took.

|||

In the off-season of 2002, Strahan, as he always does, attended most of the off-season workout program and voluntary minicamps. In actuality, "voluntary" is not the proper word. Minicamps are required. Giants coaches nicknamed these practices "VM" for "voluntary-mandatory."

More NFL players, especially veterans, are increasingly skipping these practices, in small but noticeable numbers. The union received numerous complaints from the membership about teams requiring players to show up almost daily in the off-season. Some veterans have taken measures into their own hands. When Giants defensive lineman Keith Hamilton skipped a "VM" day to take a little time to himself, he would monitor his caller ID system closely: if the Giants' office number popped up, he would allow the voice-mail to kick in.

Strahan was taking his own day off that summer when he got a phone call from Charles Way, the former Giants fullback who now headed the team's office for player programs. "Hey, Mike, it's Charles," he said. "Listen, Coach Fassel wants to talk to you." Fassel got on the line and simply wanted to know why Strahan wasn't there—it was unusual for him not to be—and by the time the two hung up Strahan had made it clear that practice was voluntary and there was something he had to take care of. The conversation was polite, and Strahan told Fassel he would make it the following day.

Strahan had watched earlier that month, in the middle of June, when 22-year-old Sean Guthrie, during one of the off-season practices, tore his right patellar tendon while participating in a pass-blocking drill. As he tried to circumvent tackle Jeff Hatch, Guthrie's knee buckled and he crashed to the ground, writhing in pain. He was gone. Done. Injured during a meaningless practice in the spring, he would be forced to miss the entire 2002–2003 season.

These are the internal battles NFL players constantly fight. Teams do not always look out for the health of the players. So now players are choosing which rules to follow and which ones to ignore in order to keep their bodies intact. Again, the line between selfishness and independence is razor-thin. Strahan skipping one or two days of a voluntary-mandatory, I would argue, is a good thing. The league has turned football into a 12-month affair, and players should be able to spend a short time away from the sport. What Sehorn has done in the past—in spending an entire off-season working out in California—is more of a selfish act; the vast majority of players spend their off-seasons working out around the team complex minus several days or so. So Sehorn should have done so as well.

In an article for *ESPN: The Magazine*, Pro Bowl running back Edgerrin James told his story of a game against Detroit on October 29, 2000. Then-coach Jim Mora, with the Colts ahead, told James to fall down and run out the clock. But as James wrote, he decided to disobey Mora. James stated in the story: "I've got too many incentive clauses in my contract for that. Every yard is money, man. So I started laughing in the huddle when I heard what coach wanted. And then I kept running past that first-down marker until I had my touchdown. And I heard a cash register ringing the whole damn way, too. Coach was mad as a mother, but how mad can your coach really be when you score a touchdown for him? I know the haters think that's selfish, and I understand that. But I've got a contract that forces me to be selfish. That's why I want to renegotiate. You want to change my attitude? Then change my contract. Because I lost $3.875 million in incentives last season when my knee exploded, and the haters weren't crying for me then."

Mora claims that James's version of what happened during that game is completely false. Yet James's vitriolic, possibly exaggerated, words illustrate how the specter of crippling injuries transforms the attitude of some players. They want to get as much money as they can, as quickly as they can, because an NFL player never knows when his situation will suddenly resemble that of Guthrie or James himself, who missed an entire season with a busted knee, or the players who have been permanently paralyzed. Or Stringer. James also wrote: "Let the haters get down there in goal-line situations and feel what I have to feel to make my money, and then we can talk about selfish. Look at my hands, man. I dislocate my fingers during a play, and I pop them back into place on the field—even though they are all messed up, like spaghetti—because I need to stay in the game every play. . . . Look at these players who can barely walk when they're done playing. That's gonna be me, so I've got to squeeze everything I can out of this now. We're not guaranteed the money in our contracts like basketball and baseball players are. I ain't hating on nobody in baseball, but I know I'm speaking for every NFL player when I say it ain't right the best baseball player [Alex Rodriguez] gets $252 million and our best player, Marshall Faulk, just signed for $200 million less than that. Ain't no crazy 300-pounders trying to break no baseball player's legs."

▌▌

In the early 1980s wide receiver Phil McConkey had a tryout with the Giants but was subsequently released. The Giants realized that letting McConkey go was a mistake and after one season brought him back. He would remain with the team from 1984 to 1988. McConkey had never wanted to leave in the first place, and when he returned to Giants Stadium, he went into the locker room, where there was a large chalkboard, and wrote in bold letters: "THE GRASS IS GREENER MY ASS."

Somehow, despite the turmoil, despite the dozens of contrasting egos and wildly divergent personalities, an NFL team stays together, bonded by the pursuit of winning, or the pain of losing, and most players, especially the brainy ones like Strahan, understand how fortunate they are to make massive amounts of money playing a sport they love, despite the physical dangers. Few people truly understand how deeply Strahan cares about the game or how hard he works. Part of that is Strahan's fault; part of it is also the media's fault. Too many times the media focus on some of the controversial things he says, or his moodiness, and not enough on what he does on the field. Strahan is one of perhaps a handful of star NFL players who go just about each down in practice, even serving on scout team drills. This is almost unheard-of. Most stars are allowed, even encouraged, to skip a series or two, so practice doesn't beat too much out of their frames. Strahan stays in because he feels that, as a leader, he must set the example for the rest of the team. He has done this bravely but also at a price: his wholehearted participation in practices has worn down his body faster than it would have otherwise, and for the first time last year Strahan began to feel, well, *tired*. He began to sense his mortality catching up to him.

Yet it did not show. Strahan in the 2002–2003 season failed to equal his sack record. He was double- or triple-teamed almost every passing down, yet he remained dominant, as dedicated as ever, occupying blockers so that other teammates could make plays, inspiring the team with his words, and ripping into teammates he felt did not take their jobs as seriously as he did. In week two, prior to the Giants' improbable upset of the Rams, he sat next to teammate Kenny Holmes on the plane ride to St. Louis. Holmes had been struggling since the

Giants signed him as a free agent the year before. Strahan told him about his five-sack season, and how miserable he was, and he said that to crawl out of a quagmire like that there was just one thing to do. "First of all, you've got to love the game," Strahan told Holmes. "You can't come out here and be mad and hate football because your situation is not good. Find what it is that makes you play, find what makes you love it, and that will make it easier." Holmes would go on to have three solo tackles against St. Louis, a sack of Kurt Warner, and he deflected a pass that landed in the arms of Sehorn, who returned it 31 yards for a score that gave the Giants a 17–0 lead. In the minutes prior to the contest Strahan spoke to the team and guaranteed in a fiery speech that they would win the game. The Giants did.

Against Atlanta in the sixth game of the season, disaster struck, illustrating yet again the frailty of even a giant's body. In the first half of that game, defensive lineman Hamilton tore his Achilles' tendon and Strahan suffered severe back spasms. With both men sidelined, only Frank Ferrara, Lance Legree, Cornelius Griffin, and Dwight Johnson were left to play the defensive line.

In the bowels of Giants Stadium, in the trainer's room, Strahan and Hamilton were at one point lying next to each other when Hamilton, in intense pain, leaned over to Strahan and said, "You know there are only four of us left." Strahan was shocked. "There are only four D-linemen left?"

"Yeah," said Hamilton.

Strahan next immediately requested painkilling injections for his back, received them, and returned to the field, where he played the second half in pass rushing situations only. The following day his back was so pained and stiff that he could barely walk.

In October there was another poignant moment that exemplified Strahan's toughness and what is the best aspect of his game, his relentlessness. In the Giants' first contest against Philadelphia, Strahan went against tackle Jon Runyan, whom Strahan has embarrassed over the years. Runyan clearly felt pressured to do whatever it took to slow Strahan. On one play early in the second quarter Strahan grabbed Runyan by the jersey and bull-rushed him, driving the 6-foot-7, 330-pound player backwards. As Runyan scampered to stay balanced, he was shoved with such velocity he looked like a two-year-old on roller skates. Runyan smacked Strahan in the face as he fell backwards, and when Strahan attempted to stomp over Runyan to sack quarterback Donovan McNabb, Runyan leg-whipped Strahan, tripping him. Strahan had to leave the game with an intense pain in his leg but missed just a few plays before returning—and continuing to charge up the field, hard.

Several days later Strahan was watching film with some of his defensive teammates, who were sitting toward the back of the room. Still fuming over the Giants' defense giving up 299 rushing yards to McNabb's Eagles, Strahan was in no mood for joking. At one point during the film session some of his defensive teammates began giggling at the Giants' missed tackles. Strahan's blood pressure shot up like it was fuel-injected. "What the fuck are you guys laughing at?" he turned and said. "You think this shit is funny?" There was silence, and then, a few minutes later, unbelievably, there was more laughing at the poor tackling form of some Giants players. Strahan had heard enough. This time he stood and started yelling, "YOU GUYS NEED TO SHUT THE FUCK UP! WE JUST GOT OUR ASSES KICKED! SOME OF YOU MOTHERFUCKERS ARE THE REASON THEY KICKED THE CRAP OUT OF US. JUST SHUT THE FUCK UP!" There wasn't a peep the rest of the session.

Few players were as physically abused during games as Strahan throughout the 2002 season, one year removed from setting the sack record, which put a fat target on his back. Still, he was there, play after play, series after series, game after game. One offensive lineman admitted to me, the week his team was scheduled to play Strahan, that he was told by an offensive coach: "If you have to kick Strahan in the balls to block him, do it."

Against Tennessee on December 1, Strahan sacked quarterback Steve McNair, which gave him ten consecutive games with at least half a sack—tying a league record—but in that game Strahan was held several times. In another contest an offensive lineman grabbed Strahan by the shoulders and pulled him to the ground while simultaneously one of the running backs rammed his shoulder pads and helmet into the back of Strahan's legs. The player was trying to seriously injure Strahan. No penalty was called. Going into the game against Washington in December, with three weeks remaining in the season, Strahan had eleven sacks, which tied him for fourth in the NFL behind Simeon Rice, Jason Taylor, and Hugh Douglas. Strahan was having an excellent year, yet the abuse he was taking, and the lack of protection from officials, caused him to crack temporarily. One Redskins player, Wilbert Brown, knocked Strahan down from behind; then, as Strahan lay on the ground, Brown dived on his back and threw an elbow at Strahan's head. Strahan responded by shoving Brown, drawing a delay-of-game penalty. Strahan then angrily pointed his finger at an official and vented to coaches on the sideline. After the game, with reporters, Strahan was direct—and entertaining. "The official was looking the other way," said Strahan. "Just like they've been looking the other way the whole season. But if you want to be an idiot like [Brown was], you'll be treated like one. [Brown] isn't good enough to be in the league for too long anyway. I don't even know his name. But I do know his number. I've got to defend myself. Guys who play like that, well, it eventually comes back to haunt you. Guys who do stupid stuff make it easier for players to get hurt." Fassel defended Strahan: "Michael was getting held all over the place, and the frustration level was really rising in him. He was getting hit from behind. He was getting held. And he wasn't getting any calls. Michael's been as well behaved as any guy we've had on our team. He's got the patience of Job when you realize how he's being held. He's a marked guy. And at some point a competitor like him is going to snap."

Off the field Strahan's relationships with many members of the local media were at least steady, though not chummy. *Newsday* wrote in an article on December 19, "Strahan . . . has a well-earned reputation for moodiness but has spent most of this season in a good one. Considering his stature as a player and his dominant personality, that is not an insignificant factor in keeping the entire locker room in a good mood." The notion that one player's temperament can change an entire team's mood is, of course, harebrained. After all, there are over 50 men on an NFL team during the regular season. What is Strahan—a telepath? He now projects his feelings into the minds of everyone around him? Silly, yes, but at least Strahan wasn't expending his energy fighting with some of the local writers. The same could be said about his dealings with

Giants management. A détente had been reached there as well. For the moment.

Coming into the 2002 season, following Strahan's banner year, I felt that if Strahan got just ten sacks, it would be a tremendous accomplishment for him. He finished with eleven. Considering the amount of physical abuse he received, and how fat a target he was for opposing offenses, it was a nice achievement, and people around the league felt the same way: Strahan was voted in December to his fifth Pro Bowl in six years.

The Giants finished the year on a painful note with an embarrassing loss to San Francisco in the first round of the playoffs. New York's defense allowed a 24-point comeback, the second-largest in postseason history, and the Giants' defense was skewered by fans and the press, and deservedly so. Chris Russo, part of the popular *Mike and the Mad Dog* radio show on WFAN in New York, said during a broadcast following the loss that the Giants were a "terrible big game defense." He laid much of the blame for the painful defeat at the feet of Strahan, who had just two tackles while going against former teammate Scott Gragg, a player Strahan used to abuse in Giants practices like a low-end rental car. "We gave the game away," Strahan told reporters. "We can't blame anyone but ourselves."

Strahan is at times controversial and stubborn, but he is mostly kind and intelligent, a player who, perhaps most important, sees the big picture. Strahan is . . . himself.

4

THE OUTSIDER

Steven Thompson

4

SECRET SOCIETY

He remembers the evening well because it was the night he decided, the night that convinced him, more than any other in his life, that he would never publicly discuss with any teammate or friend—no matter how close they were or how open-minded they seemed—that he was a gay man. Steven Thompson was a respected National Football League veteran on that night—still is. Though Thompson is not a superstar, he is a player hard-core fans would know, and someone whose teammates, oblivious to his true sexual orientation, have publicly claimed commands respect in the locker room. And of course, Thompson is not his real name.

Thompson remembers that evening because it crystallized something for him: that his sport is not even close to ready for an active player to announce that he is gay. Thompson knows that all the plays he has made and the injuries he has fought through would mean nothing after such a pronouncement, and that all the hugs he has given teammates would suddenly take on a new meaning in the minds of those players.

Not to mention that there is little doubt Thompson would be run out of the sport and be subject to public ridicule. Or worse: it is not out of the question to Thompson that an openly gay man in the NFL would risk physical violence off the field—from gay-bashing fans—or even on the field. Bounties have been put on players during games for less.

The night Thompson says changed everything for him was on a Friday in San Francisco. I believe that he tells this story at some risk, because if the men he speaks of remember the incident, Thompson could be outing himself. He insists, however, that the teammates at the center of this ugly tale won't have retained the information, because there are so many sordid stories of gay-bashing in the sport that it is difficult for anyone to keep track of them all. Thompson's team flight had landed that afternoon to play the 49ers on Sunday. No team dinner was scheduled until the next day, so after a short position meeting in which coaches quickly recapped some previously discussed strategies—in the NFL constant repetition is a way of life—Thompson and three friends on the team decided to go to dinner at a San Francisco restaurant.

One of the three teammates was the backup quarterback, a man Thompson says he did not know well but always thought seemed nice enough, despite what Thompson felt was too much bragging about his conquests of women. The second was an offensive lineman Thompson had befriended a few years earlier. He was from a small town in the Midwest, extremely religious, and if there was steak on the menu when they went out to dinner, he usually gulped down two porterhouses like they were garden salads. The third man Thompson considered a close friend. He was the team's starting linebacker, a solid player, and an educated man with a family who Thompson says was one of the few married teammates who did not cheat on his wife. Thompson had been to his home and played with his children.

Once they were seated at the restaurant, the evening began normally. Other patrons stared at the men, because of their physical size, and they were used to that; a person gawking was something they had come to expect. A few came to the table and asked for autographs.

Several tables away a group of four men were waiting for someone to take their order. They were obviously two gay couples, as they were occasionally holding hands.

The two couples were seated behind Thompson, he says, and he did not see them until two of his teammates, sitting across from him, made a nodding motion and moved their eyes in the direction of the gay men.

Thompson says he slowly and casually turned his head and saw what had captured his friends' attention.

"When you're a closet gay guy and a situation like this comes up, your skin begins to crawl," says Thompson. "Because I've been around players when they start talking about 'faggot this' and 'faggot that.' You just bite your tongue and hope all that hate talk ends.

"So I just sit there and wait for this scene to explode into that type of childish crap, you know. I started to try and guess who would make the first comment." Thompson says he thought it would have been the beefy offensive lineman. "It was wrong, because I was stereotyping, just like teammates I've known have done with gay people," Thompson says. "But he was a Midwest guy who was very religious, so I thought he would declare a 'those gay guys should burn in hell' type of thing. But I was wrong, and I was surprised how wrong I was."

Thompson says his close friend made the first comment, doing so only seconds after their group saw the gay diners.

"Somebody should kill those fucking faggots," Thompson remembers his friend saying.

"This is a guy who I always thought of as one of the most open-minded people I had ever met," Thompson says. "Then he blurts that shit out."

From there it became an expletive-laced, gay-bashing free-for-all, Thompson says.

"Why do those motherfuckers have to hold hands in public?" Thompson says his friend asked the table, keeping his voice to just above a whisper.

"We *are* in Fagville," replied the quarterback.

Thompson explains: "That's how I've heard some teammates refer to the city of San Francisco. That or Fag City." In April 2001 Chicago Cubs pitcher Julian Tavarez referred to San Francisco fans as "faggots." Major League Baseball later reprimanded Tavarez.

Thompson says he remained quiet as the slurs were spewed. Suddenly, that sickening feeling in his stomach, eerily familiar, was back, the one that made him feel like a coward for not speaking up and telling his friends he was gay and to close their mouths.

Thompson says the comments grew nastier and continued sporadically throughout the nearly two-hour dinner. They ended only when Thompson told the group they were getting too loud. Since teammates always tell Thompson he is a prude and too polite, none of them suspected this was a gay man tiring of the obnoxiousness; they thought this was just the considerate Thompson wanting to quiet his rowdy and increasingly drunk friends.

Thompson had heard this type of talk before. NFL locker rooms are full of anti-gay banter, as when someone who does not play with pain is called a "faggot." What Thompson says made this scene different from others he had witnessed—in the locker room, on the field, in social settings—was the reaction of his friend. There had been a time when Thompson thought he could reveal his secret to him and he would be understanding. Instead, that dinner made Thompson realize how naive he was.

"It was a stupid thought," Thompson says. "Now I know doing something like that would end everything. There would be no more endorsements, my friendships on the team would end, and I would be ostracized. Eventually I'd be run out of the league. If [his friend] was thinking that way, a guy I thought was the nicest person I had ever met, then what would some of these other guys think?

"Part of me already knew that," he says, "I guess I was hoping I was wrong."

||

No active NFL player has ever publicly declared he is gay. The reason is simple: any such pronouncement would finish the player in football. Even what Thompson is doing now, in speaking with me for this book, is groundbreaking, despite his anonymity in print.

Thompson was told that by granting this interview, he risked being discovered, though the chances were slim. Still, why do it? "I'm not brave. I'm gutless, really," he says. "I won't be discovered because, though I know people will play a guessing game, I'm one player out of thousands, and it will be impossible for people to discover who I am. But by talking about this, I can make it better for the gay player who does have more guts than I do and will come out while still playing. It will happen one day."

How can doing this interview make it better for a future gay professional football player? he is asked.

"The more you talk about the issue," he says, "the easier the idea of a gay football player becomes. The less we become monsters. The less the whole issue is taboo."

II

Of all the professional sports in America, perhaps the world, football is the most violent. And no venue for playing the game tests the mental and physical skills of a human being like the NFL. Players are asked to go on the field with broken bones, torn ligaments, concussions, and worse. To play through pain, and to win, requires a bond that few outside of the sport can understand. NFL players tell stories of how they become closer to the men in the locker room than they do to their own families.

A gay man simply could not exist in such an environment, straight players maintain, because it would disrupt the closeness of the locker room. Some players believe this might apply to all male professional sports. John Salley, the former Detroit Pistons basketball player, told HBO: "John Rocker would be accepted, you know, into the NAACP [before] a gay guy on a team." That might explain why of the 6,582 men competing in the Sydney Olympics, just two were out of the closet, and why, as of 2003, there is not a single openly gay male in American professional team sports.

Said a Baltimore Ravens player who did not want his name used: "If there was an out-of-the-closet homo on the team, everyone would be worried about if he was looking at you or wanted to fuck with you. The locker room would fall apart."

Ralph Cindrich, an NFL agent, has conducted several surveys of highly rated NFL rookies on a number of topics, and in one of the studies extensive questions were asked of the players on the topic of gay football players. Some of the survey results are good news. Sixty-three

percent of the total respondents said that it did not matter to them what
the sexual preference of any teammate was, 76.4 percent said they
would be comfortable playing football next to a gay teammate, and 58.1
percent said they would be comfortable having a gay teammate use the
locker next to theirs. The bad news is that 50 percent of the players who
responded to the survey said they had no problem calling gay men "faggots" or similar derogatory names, 16 percent said that if a gay man
propositioned him he would react with a physical assault, and 10 percent
agreed that the individuals who killed Matthew Shepard, the gay college student in Wyoming, should be punished less harshly if Shepard
had propositioned his killers.

There are other examples of the difficulties an openly gay NFL
player would face. One NFC coach who asked not to be identified says
that his team had a chance to sign a free agent player who was, in the
words of the coach, "a damn good player." The coach would not identify
the player.

The team was prepared to offer the player a contract until a background check performed by the franchise's security personnel revealed
that the player was gay. The coach would not say how his team knew, but
several NFL team officials said in interviews that a handful of current
NFL franchises have security officials who monitor gay bars to see if any
players use them. The gay bar spies spotted this then–free agent and told
the team. The coach believes his team is one of only a few that knew the
player was gay.

The coach says that only he, the general manager, and the team
owner knew of the player's sexual orientation. After extensive discussions, they decided not to offer him a contract. "Basically, this player was
not being covert about it," the coach says. "It was pretty well known, I
was told by our security people, that he was very visible at these gay
bars, and we were worried that it would get out, end up on ESPN, ruin
the guy, and then just like that there goes all that money you invested."

Another NFL coach, told of the team's decision not to sign the gay
player and asked for his opinion, has a different take. "Basically, if he
kept the fact that he was gay quiet and didn't flaunt it, and he was good,
I'd sign him," this coach says. "But he'd have to stay in the closet, and
he'd have to be real good to counter the risk of signing him."

As for the then–free agent player, another team signed him, and he is still in the NFL, the coach says. He believes the player's current team does not know he is gay, and the coach has no intentions, then or now, of informing the team. "I have no regrets about how we handled the situation," the coach says. "Call me prejudiced or whatever, but I have to look out for the morale of the team, and a known gay man could destroy it."

Others in the NFL strongly disagree that an openly gay NFL player would face a wave of bigotry. A Pro Bowl quarterback says he would have no problem playing with an openly gay man. "I play with wife beaters and drug abusers," he says. "Why would I have a problem playing with a gay man?"

An NFC general manager said that the presence of gay players would not be a controversial issue to today's NFL players because this generation is more open-minded than previous ones. "These kids today are more accepting of things that are considered out of the mainstream," the general manager says. But some examples illustrate that the NFL, as well as sports in general, remains an extremely homophobic environment. A gay player in the All-American Girls Professional Baseball League, Josephine D'Angelo, was kicked out after she cut her hair short, a violation of an agreement that players would keep the appearance of womanly heterosexuality. The track community was stunned in the summer of 2002 when Derrick Peterson, an indoor track champion, declared to *Genre* magazine that he was gay. He suddenly reversed course, however, following a myriad of interview requests, and denied that he was. Originally Peterson said that he liked "men and women" and that he was "definitely not heterosexual." As part of his retraction, Peterson claimed he was going through some sort of experimental phase when he was first questioned for the magazine story. Peterson expounded on his comments to the website letsrun.com, stating that he flat-out lied to the publication. Why? "I was upset that people of color were not getting equal representation in the 'alternative sexuality' areas," he wrote. Huh? It is less likely that Peterson was pushing for affirmative action in the alternative lifestyles arena and more likely that he changed his story for fear of the repercussions of admitting he was gay.

All these issues and stories explain why gay NFL players dare not enter the sporting mainstream. They would be alienated by many team-mates, team executives and coaches might decide not to sign them to lucrative contracts, advertisers might stay away, and some fans would blast them. The only visible and vocal support for a gay NFL player would come from many members of the news media. While I have long believed that a significant number of sports journalists are much more conservative in their political views, and racially insensitive, than they seem, most sportswriters would back a gay player. Some would do so because it is the right thing to do, while others would follow suit simply to appear more liberal-minded than they truly are.

Sports have always led social change. When Jackie Robinson became the first black man to enter Major League Baseball, he helped transform the hardened racial attitudes of many Americans, not just of baseball fans. The same thing could happen with a gay athlete, but, as Thompson says, somewhat debatably, "It will be much, much more difficult, because gays are the last group people are allowed to hate."

▌▌

There have been moments when Dave Kopay, a former NFL running back known as "Psych" because of his incredibly violent intensity on the field, begins choking on tears when he thinks of a former teammate. "I know this isn't politically correct," he has said, "but I wish I had outed Jerry Smith. He might be alive today."

A little-known running back who had played for five teams in his career between 1964 and 1972, Kopay decided in 1975 to use a newspaper interview with the now-defunct *Washington Star* to announce that he was gay. Kopay made his statement three years after retiring from the sport.

Smith was Kopay's teammate on the Washington Redskins and close friend. While Kopay had decided he had lived his secret life long enough, Smith would never acknowledge his homosexuality outside of gay bars. Kopay feels that the only way Smith could have broken out of his self-destructive tendencies, which included alcohol abuse, drugs, and anonymous sex—all contributing to his death from AIDS in 1986—would have been to publicly disrupt his secret life. Shame played a part in Smith's death as well, explains Kopay, who adds that Smith's liaisons with other men included NFL players.

Smith, a wide receiver, scored 60 touchdowns over 13 seasons. Many on the Redskins team knew that Smith was gay, Kopay says, but they tolerated it because he was such a good player. That attitude seems to back the thinking of a minority of NFL executives and coaches today who maintain that a gay player could play in the NFL only if he doesn't, in the words of one coach, "flaunt" that he is gay.

Since Kopay, there have been few NFL players who came out after retiring, only three, in fact, if Thompson is included. In 1992 Roy Simmons, a guard for the New York Giants and the Washington Redskins from 1979 to 1983, revealed that he was gay during an appearance on *The Phil Donahue Show.*

When I first heard in November 2002 of Esera Tuaolo's closeted NFL life, I had interviewed Thompson a number of times over several years, and their stories, with a few differences, sounded strikingly similar. Hiding. Using women as a kind of special-effects makeup, props to create a false character. Self-hatred. Hearing numerous anti-gay jokes in the locker room. The fear that teammates or fans, or both, would physically attack them. It was downright bizarre.

Thompson had never heard of Tuaolo, who was mainly a backup on several NFL teams, but he says Tuaolo's story proves what he has been saying all along—that there is a society of gay players out there. Most of them are hidden, living secret or double lives, and the only time those of us on the outside know they are there, he says, is when these players choose to reveal themselves or are discovered by spies on NFL teams hunting them out.

Thompson's pseudo-coming out to me was somewhat accidental. We met at a charity function. That's about all I can say without revealing too much of his identity. I tried for some time to get him to tell his story to me for the *New York Times*, but he felt that neither newspaper nor television media would be able to properly relay his tale. ("I start telling this painful story about being a gay player, then *boom*, it's break time, and suddenly there's Carrot Top doing an AT&T commercial," he joked.) When I decided to write an NFL book and to devote a chapter of it to him, in essence calling Thompson's bluff, he reluctantly concurred, but only after a list of written demands were agreed to so as to protect his identity.

Tuaolo's coming out was different—it was completely orchestrated. Joe Somodi, a gay filmmaker, attempted but failed to raise money for a documentary that would follow Tuaolo's coming-out process. The two men approached HBO, which declined interest, but HBO's *Real Sports* was interested and aired the segment. After that Tuaolo went on a media binge, making appearances across the media spectrum, from ESPN to the pages of the *Minneapolis Star Tribune*.

But I had a difficult time tracking down Tuaolo. He at first did not return my repeated phone calls, and when I did get him on the telephone, he said he did not have time to talk and would call back. He never did. Both Thompson and I found this to be a strange reaction. Thompson asked me so many questions about Tuaolo that you would think Thompson was doing his own chapter on gay NFL players. Since there are so few known members of that rather exclusive club, I thought Tuaolo would be just as curious about this other gay NFL player—and Tuaolo knew what I was calling about because his West Hollywood publicist, Howard Bragman, said he had informed Tuaolo—as Thompson was about him. When longtime black NFL assistant coaches told me about the pioneer days for black assistants in the NFL when there were only a handful of them, they constantly spoke to and supported one another, and when a new one came into the league, the others always welcomed him. Yet Tuaolo showed as much interest in talking about Thompson as a dieting supermodel does in a piece of double-chocolate cake. Maybe Tuaolo was simply tired of talking about the subject. He had done a string of interviews, including the *New York Times*, *Real Sports*, *Inside the NFL*, *SportsCenter*, ABC's *20/20*, *Donahue*, *Good Morning, America*, and *The Advocate*. Or maybe, like many people of all races, creeds, and sexual orientations, Tuaolo wanted the spotlight to himself. Maybe he wanted to be The Only Gay Player. I don't know.

While Thompson grew up middle-class, Tuaolo, who has been called brave, friendly, and engaging by the press, was the youngest of eight children struggling on a small banana farm near Honolulu. He was a superb athlete and played football at Oregon State. As a rookie for the Green Bay Packers, he had two noticeable achievements: 30 solo tackles and one singing of the national anthem at Lambeau Field.

Tuaolo told the *New York Times* that he never suspected there were other gay players in the NFL. Thompson believes Tuaolo purposely blocked out what must have been obvious clues. "When I go to a charity function like a golf outing," Thompson says, "I can tell who the gay players are." Kopay told the newspaper that Tuaolo's "gaydar must have gone dead."

Tuaolo told the *Times*: "I knew when I was young that I was attracted to men. But once I could give a name to it I backed off. I had girlfriends as a cover-up and I made sure I was seen leaving strip clubs. I drank a lot."

"I was always anxious," he continued, "always in pain. I was afraid if I was too much of a star I'd be exposed. Once you learn the system, you can do just enough to make the team. That's pretty sad. I didn't want to call attention to myself. If I had a sack, I'd have a sleepless night, wondering if now they would catch me."

||

Thompson says he knows there are other gay NFL players—because he has dated one—and he says he is an acquaintance of a handful of others. He declined to name any of the players. In fact, Thompson claims there is a secret society of some 100 to 200 gay and bisexual NFL players, insisting there are at least several gay players on each team, maybe more. I dispute his numbers. If there were that many, at least several of them would have been outed. Wouldn't someone have sold his story, particularly a marginal player, to a supermarket tabloid? "Remember, in all likelihood a gay football player is going to be as careful as I am," Thompson says. "If you are dating an executive at a Fortune 500 company, do you think that executive is going to go running to tell people? No. Because he knows if he does, he is done. In a strange way the homophobia of our society hurts and helps. It hurts because you deny who you are, but it helps you keep your secret because both partners are afraid of being discovered and labeled as sexual deviants."

Even an unsubstantiated rumor of being gay or bisexual can hurt a person in professional football. In the early 1990s an NFL head coach was questioned after police found him in his car on the side of the road with a passenger. A rumor that the passenger was a man dressed as a woman became so widespread—and believed, both on the team and around the league—that the coach was forced to address the matter privately with beat writers. He explained that police did question him, but that the person in the car with him was a woman he was having an affair with. Unfortunately for the coach, few believed his explanation, including many of the players on his team who were told of the tale. Several players said the incident weakened the coach's position in the locker room because of their subsequent belief that the coach was bisexual.

Also, former Oakland Raiders and St. Louis Rams defensive end Alberto White—eccentric is one way to describe him, so judge his following claims in that context—maintains that several players propositioned him for oral sex while he was with the Rams. Even more strange is that White says he was kicked off the Rams—and blackballed by the NFL—after alerting management because the team did not want the fact that there were gay players on the team to become public.

"I should not have to grant sexual favors to have a career in football," White told me in a tape-recorded interview.

Is White credible? Team officials on both the Raiders and the Rams describe White as someone with a nasty temper who was released by both teams because of constant conflicts with the coaching staffs, and that is the only reason. (White also once went on a profanity-laced tirade against the media covering the Rams.) At one point White attempted to sue the NFL for sexual harassment but was unable to find an attorney to take his case, he says.

The problem with the theory that there are hundreds of gay or bisexual players is that there simply is little evidence of this. There are just snippets here and there, rumors and gossip, pieces of a puzzle with no larger place for them to fit. And I am not swayed by the argument that because 3 to 10 percent of the general population is gay, according to experts, it automatically follows that 3 to 10 percent of the NFL is gay. If that were true, there would be somewhere between 50 and 169 gay men in the NFL, using an NFL 53-man roster multiplied by 32 teams.

Thompson explains the lack of concrete evidence by using himself as proof. He is gay, and no one will ever know it, except a select few, and he has managed this feat by a playing a cloak-and-dagger game to hide that part of his life, as Tuaolo allegedly did. But does that mean, because there is one Thompson, or five of him, or ten, or fifty, that there are hundreds?

Thompson says his therapist has told him that "it's up to you" about coming out, "but my advice is say nothing about this to anyone until after you retire." Thompson will not identify his counselor, but at least one other sports psychologist, Dr. Bruce Ogilvie, has also advised major league athletes to stay closeted, a warning soaked in common sense. So what if dozens or hundreds of other NFL players are getting the same advice? Thompson reasons that could at least partially explain the gay NFL silence.

Sports psychologist Kevin Elko said his advice to a gay player would be to "first come to terms with his sexuality. Don't be ashamed of it. Then seek others in the sport like yourself. We know there are gay players in football, just statistically speaking. So seek out support, and from the rumors I hear, the gays in football know who the other gay players are."

"I do feel alone," Thompson says, "and sometimes like a coward. I get frustrated and angry, but I also know that now is not the time for me to call a team meeting and say, 'What's up, everybody? I'm gay.' Now is not the time, and unfortunately that moment will not come in my lifetime.

"Basically, it comes down to, I love playing football more than I love myself and my sense of pride and well-being," he says. "I've heard players say, 'I know football is wrecking my body, and 20 years from now I'm going to be disfigured and walking like a fucking chimpanzee, but I don't care, I love the game.' I used to think that stuff was crazy. I know keeping this secret is eating me up inside. But right now I don't care. I love this game so much I won't do anything to jeopardize it."

II

Thompson has been able to keep his secret because he has learned how to blend in. He lies to teammates about going on dates with women, he goes to bars with fellow players and pretends to gawk over attractive women, and in the past, early in his career, he says he did have sex with women, then would recount those experiences in what he calls "the mandatory football thing, where guys sit in the locker room and talk about all the women they fucked."

"I've never felt a serious connection with a woman," Thompson says. "You can't understand what I'm talking about unless you're gay."

Thompson tries by explaining it this way: "A white person can hang out with black people all his life and think he knows what it is like to be black. But a white person isn't followed when he goes into a store, and a white person isn't called the 'N' word. There is a level that even the most open-minded white person cannot reach in trying to identify with blacks. With gays it's the same thing. There are things that I'll talk about that straight people can't understand."

Except for his physical stature, there is little about Thompson's appearance that would make him stick out in a crowd, and that has helped him stay underground, he says. He goes to gay bars only a few times a year, limiting his exposure, and it was in these bars that he discovered there were others in the NFL just like him.

"I've been to gay bars in New York, and after being there for five minutes I'll see an NFL player," he says. "Same thing in some other big cities." This is something I might not have believed if I had not seen gay NFL players in bars and at gay parties myself while doing research for this book. (A quick aside: at an ethics and sports media conference in Rhode Island in the summer of 2001, Dave Lohse, who works in the communications department at the University of North Carolina and is gay, said that from his experience black football players have the toughest time coming out of the closet. Lohse described being at a gay bar and bumping into a black North Carolina football alumnus, who was terrified that Lohse was also present and had recognized him.)

The only long-term relationship Thompson has had as a gay man was with an NFL player he met at a gay bar on the East Coast. "Some of these places have a great mix of people," Thompson says. "In one corner you'll see people in drag, and in another there will be businessmen wearing nice suits. I was attracted to him because he dressed conservatively like I did. We hit it off right away.

"It was funny, because I sort of recognized him, and he recognized me," Thompson says, "and there was that awkward moment of, 'You play ball.' You're so used to keeping that part of your life a secret that when you have to talk about it, you become very uncomfortable at first."

Thompson said he and the other NFL player, whom he refuses to identify, dated just over a year. "It was very intense and very weird because we rarely saw each other; it was a long-distance relationship," he says. "We communicated mainly through the Internet because he didn't want me to call him. I thought it was because he was overly para-noid. A lot of guys in the league, gay and straight, get paranoid on the telephone because they think the NFL monitors your calls." There is no evidence that the NFL electronically eavesdrops on its players, which would be illegal.

Sometimes they would not see each other for weeks or months, and when they did meet, they would do so on off days, usually Tuesdays, and at an airport hotel, the reservation in one of their names. They would never enter the hotel together.

It was in the midst of this relationship that Thompson, who until then thought there were only a few others like him in the league, says he discovered how wrong he was. The player told Thompson he had been in relationships at various points of his career with four other NFL players. "There are more of us out there than you think," Thompson says he was told. Thompson combined that fact with the gay players he would see at clubs and house parties and figured the gay underground in football was much bigger than he or many others thought.

The relationship ended, Thompson says, when he began pressing the player on why he could not call him more often. (I joked with Thompson that he sounded like some of my ex-girlfriends.) Thompson already knew the answer. Early in the relationship he had looked up the player's biographical information in the team's media guide and saw that he was married to a woman. Thompson never confronted the player, and the player never brought it up. "I think it was just unspoken," Thompson says, "but after a while I felt he owed me an explanation."

The player did come clean, Thompson says, and soon after that the relationship was over. Thompson felt that the player had probably repeated this behavior a number of times—getting into a gay relationship, feeling guilt over his marriage to a woman, and then ending the gay union.

"In a strange way I felt better after that relationship," Thompson says, "because I had met someone who was more confused than I was."

||

Thompson says the first time he knew he was gay was around his sophomore year in high school. "It is more like a gradual awakening," he says. "From my conversation with other gay people I think this is common. It is not that you suddenly have these feelings; it is more that you stop denying them to yourself. You face yourself and stop wincing or stop hoping that you change."

Thompson did not come from an overly religious family, but his father and mother both openly made anti-gay remarks throughout his high school years, which, Thompson says, "pushed me further and further into the closet." What compounds the problem is that he has been a top athlete most of his life, playing a number of sports, centering on football late in high school. "Sports is overly macho," says Thompson, "and that works against being honest about your sexuality."

"I went to my junior and senior proms," Thompson says, "with probably two of the most beautiful girls in school. I always played up that whole macho athlete thing. I was a bad actor, but in high school no one notices."

Once he was at college, the act continued. Thompson went to a top Division I school, and by his senior year he was a star player. "I overcompensated for being gay by having sex with a lot of women," he says. "But I did not have one long-term relationship with a woman in college. I always ended things before they got serious because I knew I was gay and that's not what I wanted, a woman. Basically I was using women as props."

||

It is Thompson's second year in the NFL, and he is in a classroom surrounded by teammates, sitting in the back of the room, listening to his position coach ramble on about strategies. Thompson always picked up this part of football quickly, he explains. He often stayed home on Friday and Saturday nights to study the playbook instead of going out with friends, especially when he was a rookie. There was little the coach was saying that he did not already know.

Toward the last part of the season Thompson's team was making a playoff push, and all that week there was the prerequisite screaming from coaches and extra hitting in practice that always seemed to walk hand in hand with a big contest. The classroom was no different, but despite the extra intensity in game plan sessions, Thompson, like a lot of players do, started to fall asleep. He began to slump a little in his chair when something the coach said woke him up like he had been slapped in the face.

The coach began talking about one player on the upcoming team. Some of the news the coach had relayed before, but not this. "This guy is a fairy," Thompson claims the coach said. "He's soft, real soft, and some of you guys know what I'm talking about." There was a murmur, and a few players, mainly some of the longtime veterans, began to chuckle. "He gets hit, he folds up like a bitch," the coach said. "So smack him around and he'll give up. Just don't bend over when you're near him." More laughter, this time louder.

Thompson was not shocked by the harsh talk about the player. He had heard such language again and again, going back to his high school days. It is as much a part of football as first downs and tackles.

It was the specificity of the coach's language—"*Some of you guys know what I'm talking about...don't bend over*"—that had caught Thompson's attention. He later cautiously asked a teammate who had befriended him, and had been in the league for over a decade, what the coach was talking about. The player took Thompson's question as that of a young guy who needed schooling.

"It's just kind of known that the guy coach was talking about is a gay guy," Thompson says he was told.

Recounting the story, Thompson laughs. "I wanted to call the player and ask him, 'Hey, are you gay? Let's talk.'"

Later that week, on the day of the game, Thompson noticed the player getting more than his fair share of late hits and cheap shots.

There were some kicks to the stomach, and one of his teammates spit on the player, all without the game officials noticing. While officials do catch some of that extracurricular activity, it is not uncommon for them to miss a number of such acts. They simply cannot see everything. Indeed, what fans often do not know is that these types of tactics happen often in professional football, especially when coaches identify a player as someone who could rack up lots of offensive yardage or defensive tackles. (When television cameras caught Denver linebacker Bill Romanowski spitting on San Francisco wide receiver J. J. Stokes during a 1997 Monday night game, it caused a national stir, but that type of incident has happened hundreds of times before.)

This situation was different, Thompson says, because of something that happened after Thompson helped the player off the ground. One of Thompson's teammates who, Thompson says, played with such aggression it was like he had "rabies," yelled at him for assisting the player.

"Don't help that fag up," Thompson says his teammate screamed.

When the player heard the comment, as he walked away, he yelled back, "Fuck you."

Thompson is asked if he ever assisted the player again that game.

"No, not really," Thompson says.

||

In the May 2001 issue of *Out* magazine, the nation's largest-circulation gay publication, editor Brendan Lemon set the sports world abuzz when he opened his column with the following words: "For the past year and a half, I have been having an affair with a pro baseball player from a major-league East Coast franchise, not his team's biggest star but a very recognizable media figure all the same."

The article set off the predictable response. Baseball writers and fans began a guessing game as to who the player was, and Lemon was criticized by the news media for partially outing his partner. There were even some who insinuated that Lemon had made the entire thing up (an accusation that might be leveled at me as well).

But a smart question was posed amid the noise: Is baseball ready for an openly gay player?

The only openly gay former baseball player doesn't believe the time is right. Billy Bean, the ex-outfielder who came out in 1999, four years after retiring, told *Sports Illustrated* after the Lemon article was published: "It would be very difficult for a player to come out today. This guy has to play in stadiums with 40,000 people. What's he going to hear if he strikes out? Overnight this guy's career will have nothing to do with his athletic ability. It's not a safe time to do it."

I do not believe I will see within the next ten years—probably much longer—an NFL player go beyond what Thompson has done, and that is, come out, minus the anonymity drape, in the midst of an NFL career. But here is what I believe *will* happen many years from now.

There will be a high-profile, extremely talented high school player who lives in a liberal part of the country, say, San Francisco or an East Coast multicultural city with a significant gay population, like New York. This player, unafraid of repercussions because he has a supportive family and school environment, tells a local newspaper he is gay. He does this his sophomore or junior year. By the time he is a senior he has become a national story and his sexual orientation is no longer hugely controversial, because he has done a hundred interviews about it, sitting down with Katie Couric for breakfast and Ted Koppel for a late-night chat. His town and then the country get to know him—he is likable and smart and handsome—and after a while the gay tattoo wears thin, even when he brings a young man to the senior prom. He begins to be just this great athlete who happens to be gay.

He finishes his high school career ranked by *USA Today* as the top prospect in the country. Colleges fall over themselves to recruit him. They tell the media repeatedly they don't care about his sexuality, they just see a great person and a great player.

This player then signs on with a top college program, like Stanford, leads his team to a national championship game, wins the Heisman Trophy, and is considered the top player in the nation. Again, stories about him being gay follow him throughout his college career—the lead of all the Heisman Trophy stories mention that he is the first out-of-the-closet gay man to capture the honor—but by now people have become used to seeing the great athlete with the movie star smile and magna cum laude pedigree.

The Cincinnati Bengals have the first selection in the draft—when aren't the sorry Bengals on the clock—and their head coach, Bill Parcells, who recently came out of retirement, again, says, "I could give a shit about what the guy does in the bedroom, he had just better show his ass up for practice on time." The Bengals select him number one, and sure, there are a few hateful letters from some fans, and a couple of players grumble about the sanctity of the locker room being violated by a gay man, but this player has been raised gay in the spotlight, right before our eyes, and America has grown used to him and likes him, and the reaction is, well, not much of one, because it just isn't that big a deal anymore.

||

The only known gay active NFL player, Steven Thompson, laughs heartily when asked if his sport is ready for an openly gay player right now.

"I'll answer that by saying this," he says. "I've had dreams about what if I did come out while still playing? What would the next day or next game be like? In one dream, after I come out, and try to play, I get shot in the chest by some fan in the stands.

"I'm lying there on the ground, bleeding to death," he continues, "and none of my teammates help me, because they think if they do they'll catch AIDS."

5

THE TEAM

The 5ᴬ Team

PHILADELPHIA STORY

. . . and the Worst Damn
Franchise in Football

The day that scared Joe Banner senseless was November 17, 2002. Banner, the president of the Philadelphia Eagles, was sitting comfortably in his box on the 400 level of Veterans Stadium that afternoon. The Eagles were in first place in the division, the Arizona Cardinals were on the field, which meant an almost automatic victory was at hand, and the 65,352 Eagles fans, who resemble those crazed, hatchet-wielding inmates from the Kurt Russell movie *Escape from New York*, were in full insult mode, screaming obscenities toward the Arizona bench. Even the in-stadium courthouse, put there because so many fights would break out among that angelic crowd, was empty. Yes, life was good. Banner was enjoying the moment, semi-relaxing for once, no salary cap figures prancing in his head, no agents ringing about contract extensions, no crises at hand. When the team's quarterback, Donovan McNabb, came limping toward the sideline, it was like someone had taken a razor blade to Banner's perfect canvas. A lump developed in his throat, and his stomach started to churn. That was McNabb, the team's backbone, hobbling, that was McNabb clutching his right leg, which was connected to the thighbone, which was connected to the hipbone, which was connected to his $115 million frame. The gorgeous day suddenly turned sour.

The phone rang.

It was a report from the sideline. McNabb had an ankle sprain, but he was going to continue playing. Banner breathed a little easier and sat more comfortably in his chair. After the game, in the bowels of the stadium, Banner walked into the trainer's room with owner Jeffrey Lurie and several others. On a large, elongated trainer's table was the outstretched quarterback, who had just received a precautionary X-ray. Everyone in the room began watching the Giants-Redskins game on television. At that point Banner still did not know how dire McNabb's situation was. Then running back Brian Mitchell trotted in to check up on McNabb.

"What's the deal?" Mitchell asked McNabb.

"It's broken," McNabb replied.

Banner was stunned. "I was hoping I had heard that wrong," he said. Banner immediately went looking for the team doctor, tracking him down like a bloodhound trailing the scent of an escaped bank robber. When Banner found him, the doctor held up the X-ray and trailed his finger along a long, thick line in McNabb's right fibula. "You don't have to be a doctor to see that break," he told Banner.

Andy Reid, the head coach, entered the room, and like Banner, he was unaware that McNabb did not have an ankle sprain after all—he had a fractured leg and would miss the remainder of the regular season, some two months. McNabb's father, Samuel, was also in the room, and everyone there had a blank look on his face. "Inside you have that empty feeling when you get bad news, like somebody sucked something out of you," said Banner later.

The organization attempted to stay upbeat, but a feeling of impending doom spread through the Eagles like a virus. The concerned Banner stayed at the team facility until 9:00 that night. When he put his children to bed after reading them a story, images of McNabb were still transfixed in his mind. Banner ate a piece of cake while watching the Raiders game on ESPN, fell asleep for a short while, then woke up, still disturbed by the injury to the team's star. Banner spent part of the following morning looking at several potential schools for his kids. His mind was still clouded. *What's going to happen to us,* he thought?

Coaches worry like this. Players do. But Banner is a salary cap guy. Since when does a numbers-cruncher get so emotionally involved?

The Eagles made a mistake in allowing McNabb to continue playing after first hurting his leg and not forcing him to get an X-ray earlier, during the game. McNabb had waved off the medical staff, insisting he was fine. "Hindsight is always perfect," Banner explains. "But if we had it all to do again, we would have had the X-ray done."

It is one of only a few missteps the Eagles organization has made in recent years. The other was a debilitating, brutal loss in the NFC championship game to the Buccaneers in 2003, a contest the Eagles should have won but failed to because the players were far too overconfident and the coaching game plan was much too conservative. Still, despite the occasional heart palpitation and faux pas, which every franchise, from the best to the worst, has suffered from time to time, if there is a model for how to build and run a football team—or any sports franchise for that matter—it is the Eagles. There are many reasons why. The owner, Lurie, is patient and resolute. The coach, Reid, is among the top five in ability. The Eagles have a brand-spanking-new $510 million stadium and a practice facility second to none. They have a young, talented quarterback locked up for his career and a comfortable salary cap situation. The team's .708 winning percentage over the past three seasons is the best in football.

The most profound reason for Philadelphia's status as the best NFL organization is the 50-year-old Banner. In a league that is overly image-conscious and has no shortage of plump egos quick to take the podium and claim credit for everything from the "West Coast" offense to the cure for measles, Banner is a refreshing, understated, and unlikely hero. He looks like a dentist, and on his really sexy days he resembles an accountant. But behind the nerdy bifocals and five-foot-five-inch frame is a formidable intellect whose persistence and cache of ideas transformed the Eagles from an average franchise into a top one. In the process, Banner has become the best team executive in all of professional football.

No other sport has such a complicated and formidable a foe as the NFL's salary cap system, a beast that has laid waste some of the best football franchises and their executives. The salary cap came into existence in 1994—the same year Lurie purchased the Eagles and brought Banner along for what would be a wild ride—and it is the NFL's strategic weapon in maintaining competitive balance. In baseball, excellence is determined by who spends the most money, and a club like the New York Yankees, with its big pockets, can simply buy a championship by spending obscene amounts of cash on free agents and its own players. Football is different. Each franchise works under a sort of ceiling—a cap—and exceeding it is punishable by fines or the possible loss of draft picks. The cap forces teams executives, especially men like Banner, to become capologists—to make smarter choices and be more disciplined. Overpay a player or show recklessness in signing free agents, and the cap will, as Banner says, "bite you in the ass and sink your team." When that happens, a season can be dead even before it starts.

Only a handful of teams manage the cap well. Bruce Allen, an executive with the Oakland Raiders, is another person who can juggle the salary cap's nuances. Other franchises have royally bungled it. The San Francisco 49ers' mismanagement of the salary cap throughout the mid-1990s—"salary cap purgatory" is how former 49ers coach Steve Mariucci described it—almost destroyed the proud franchise. The Washington Redskins, under owner Daniel Snyder, not known for his patience or long-term thinking, have made a series of poor free agent signings, including an aging Deion Sanders, the future Hall of Fame cornerback who had lost his speed when Snyder overpaid him. The Redskins' salary structure suffered for years afterwards because of Snyder's lack of foresight. In 2002 the salary cap was $71.1 million, and entering that season, the Eagles had $866,140 in what is called "ghost money"— cap dollars spent on players who are no longer on the roster. Such an amount is minuscule and a sign of wise cap management. Conversely, the Redskins had $11.5 million in ghost funds: 16 percent of their salary cap was being spent on men no longer playing on the team. That is terrible cap management, and it has hurt the product on the field. Also, the Eagles started that year with $15.7 million more in cap money to spend on players, either their own or free agents, than rival Washington. By December 2002 that number was still a hefty $14 million. The Redskins continued their irrational spending in the winter of 2003 by overpaying for average free agents like guard Randy Thomas. The Redskins handed Thomas a $7 million signing bonus, which is far too much money for someone who plays on the interior line, since those players are easily found. At one point the Redskins signed eight free agent players and traded for another, and many of those players were completely overpaid.

Pete Prisco of *CBS Sportsline* captured why Snyder is so sloppy when he wrote: "We hear owner Dan Snyder is the one who has done all the deals, the guy pulling the trigger. That could account for some of the overpaying; Snyder is the kind of owner who gets caught up in names and not production. If he would rely more on his personnel people instead of what he reads and hears, he would have a better team. Signing eight players is good for livening up a city like Washington, D.C., but the reality is that he'd have been better off waiting and being more selective."

Banner has been the antithesis of Snyder and the Redskins—disciplined, intellectual, and a student of the system. He and an assistant break down every player deal signed in the NFL. Every one. He originated the idea of the roster bonus as a way to ease salary cap pressure. When a team pays a player an exorbitant signing bonus and the player ends up a bust, the team releases him and the prorated portion of the signing bonus can accelerate into the current year's salary cap. That can put disastrous limits on a team's maneuverability in signing free agent players or members of its own squad. By creating the roster bonus, Banner started a system that allows a team the option of cutting that player and then siphoning his bonus and base salary back into the cap. This clever piece of maneuvering in NFL economics works for both the team and the player.

Banner's philosophy in building the Eagles has been simple, and while it was at first ridiculed by other team executives in football, many are now copying his strategies. Under Banner, the Eagles sign young, promising players to longer-term deals and resist the hypnotic temptation by grabbing for the short-term fix aging veterans, who tend to become financial albatrosses for years to come, the way Sanders was for Washington.

While Banner was earning his doctorate in caponomics, he was simultaneously pursuing the highly political objective of getting the Eagles a new stadium and practice facility. Banner doggedly worked the complex negotiations, mostly by himself, for a rocky three-year period from 1998 to 2001. The result was Lincoln Financial Field, which opened in 2003, and the team's NovaCare team headquarters, an 110,000-square-foot facility that resembles a presidential palace. (The only practice complex that rivals Philadelphia's is Cleveland's.) Banner engineered a 25-year, $65 million naming-rights agreement with the medical company NovaCare, the first naming-rights agreement for a franchise's headquarters in professional sports. The plush facility is a far cry from Veterans Stadium, one of the true historic dumps in the NFL (called a "shithole" by the Buccaneers' Sapp). The Eagles' weight room there was so run-down and cramped that when a visiting free agent player asked to see it, former coach Ray Rhodes would say, "You don't want to see that. Let me show you the rest of the complex."

Banner came to football by an unusual path. He was not a football lifer, as most people in his position are. In January 1993 Banner could not have been further from football, since he was vacationing in Hawaii after selling the retail clothing business that he and his father, Ralph, had owned. It was in the retail business that Banner honed his talents as a negotiator, skills he would later use when bargaining with agents over player contracts.

With his business sold and cash in his pocket, Banner could have stayed in Hawaii and sucked down fruity drinks in perpetuity. But he was bored. He wanted a challenge, and having always been a sports fan, the idea of getting in on the ground level of a franchise began at that moment. Banner remembered a chance meeting with George Young, the former general manager of the Giants, who told him the best way to break into the NFL was to foster a relationship with a potential owner. Banner just happened to know one—Jeffrey Lurie, an heir to a publishing and movie fortune whom Banner had grown up with in the Chestnut Hill suburb of Boston. After unsuccessfully pursuing the New England Patriots, Lurie purchased the Eagles and made Banner his trusted lieutenant.

When Lurie and Banner arrived in Philadelphia, the Eagles had a roster with talent, but the franchise's infrastructure was brittle and the team lacked direction. There was no computer system installed; there wasn't even voice-mail. The Eagles had a long-standing reputation for being cheap, and while Lurie would be accused of continuing that tradition (it depends on who you speak to), he did purchase a more spacious aircraft for team charters, quadruple the scouting staff, and add more bodies to the marketing department. Not counting players, the Eagles have nearly doubled the staff of the entire organization, from 65 employees in 1994 to an expected 150 once the new stadium is operational. While Lurie worked on the front office, Banner focused on the team itself, drawing a blueprint based on his eventual diagnosis that building the team slowly, through the draft, and treating the salary cap with respect instead of disdain was the right way to go. Banner went on to address many of the internal problems hampering the organization. One thing he began insisting on was that scouts gather more character information on college prospects, which was commonly done on other teams, but not the Eagles.

Lurie and Banner guided Philadelphia to two playoff appearances in four years, but those positive seasons were followed by 3–13 and 5–11 seasons in 1998 and 1999, respectively. Both men were ripped for being stingy, despite the large amount of money Lurie had put into the team to beef up its internal organs. Some of the greatest criticism came when Philadelphia had an opportunity to sign free agent quarterback Mark Brunell, at the time one of the more sought-after young throwers. The Eagles declined and were criticized by fans, but the organization was simply following Banner's design: watch the cap, don't hyperventilate over every sexy free agent who strolls down the block, and always think long-term.

Lurie and Banner also faced the animosity of the NFL establishment—owners, team executives, fans, and reporters—smirking at the two outsiders. Lurie and Banner weren't "football men." They were seen as two dorks with stopwatches, as football wanna-bes, as meddlers so far in over their heads they needed scuba gear. The agent Brad Blank, who has represented several Eagles players, says Lurie and Banner were viewed as "two guys who had no idea what they were doing." Talk radio gave Banner the nickname "the Rat." Philly is a brutal town, and when fans smell blood, they come on hard. Parcells, who made numerous trips there as coach of the Giants, once said of the town: "They call this the City of Brotherly Love, but it's really a banana republic." One incident demonstrates that Lurie and Banner were facing more than bad vibes and accusations from former employees that they were over-involved, which at times was true. But nothing excused this. A short time after Lurie took control of the Eagles, Banner was at a small table taking a break during what was a busy training camp day. Banner had his back to an Eagles assistant coach sitting nearby. Banner says he overheard the coach state to a group of friends: "The league has changed so much. It's only gone downhill since we started to get all these Jewish owners."

Banner and Lurie are both Jewish, and Banner obviously was not pleased. He confronted the coach, who promptly denied making the comment. "I heard you say it," Banner replied. The coach was told to pack his stuff and never come back.

||

Banner overcame the ill will that often accompanies a new regime to build a formidable franchise. He eliminated lengthy training camp hold-outs by draft picks, a plague on the Eagles for years. The team hired rotund and robust Reid as the head coach; he is nearly as exhaustive in his game preparations as Tampa Bay's Gruden, and he has the disciplined, intellectual feel that seems to now permeate the Eagles franchise. Hiring Reid was an inspired move, one Banner calls the best decision he and Lurie ever made, but it didn't always seem so obvious. There were eight teams looking for a head coach when Reid was available—and only the Eagles formally interviewed him for a head coaching decision.

Then came the drafting of McNabb, the Pro Bowl star thrower and the best player the team has had since Randall Cunningham and Reggie White. When they selected him in 1999, the move was so profoundly booed by Eagles fans gathered at the NFL's draft headquarters in New York that the ugly heckling scene that was broadcast nationally on ESPN became a part of Philadelphia lore.

Under Banner's reign, the Eagles have won at least eleven games for three consecutive seasons, something that had never before happened in the franchise's history. That is a good omen, because the core of the

Eagles' roster, the stable of young talent like McNabb, is locked up contractually for the long haul. Eighteen of the team's 22 starters are signed through 2003, and 15 are under contract through the 2004 season.

When I meet with Banner in his expansive office, he is wearing a white polo sweater and brown slacks, and he is warm and friendly. It takes only a short time, however, to see that behind his laid-back manner is the same competitive spark that is common among top players and coaches. He tells me: "People in the league are more positive toward me now. But it was tough at first. A lot of people in football initially thumbed their noses at us. I don't know if you ever truly forget how people treat you, or what they say about you. It motivated me, and I never doubted what we were doing. I think what gets me the most is how little other people in the NFL like to hand out credit." It is too ruthless a league for kind words to be tossed around like Halloween candy, yet there is no question that other front office personnel now respect what Banner has accomplished.

Evaluating what is the best franchise in football is not as difficult as picking the best coaches or players because there are fewer intangibles. It comes down to four simple elements:

1 Philosophy. There are two approaches to running a franchise. The first is to give the head coach the final say on all personnel matters, including the draft, and the other is the more traditional approach of having a general manager or team president work in conjunction with the head coach, but with the GM making the final decisions on personnel issues. The latter system is far more efficient. When coaches are given that much power, they tend to abuse it—not in a diabolical manner, but certainly in a short-term manner. Coaches think for the now and will draft for immediate needs instead of the longer term, spending lavishly on free agents and ignoring salary cap ramifications. They don't care about three or five or ten years into the future. But in running a franchise, the horizon is as important as what is directly in front of you.

When Mike Ditka coached the New Orleans Saints and had total control of the team, he traded his entire draft for running back Ricky Williams, which turned out to be a horrible decision. Williams became a bizarre malcontent with the Saints and was eventually traded to Miami. New Orleans was left without all of its vital picks once Ditka was fired—and a short time later they didn't have Williams either.

2 **Salary cap expertise.** It is startling how many teams still bungle the cap, failing to appreciate that having someone to manage it wisely is as important as coaching or drafting players.

3 **Facilities.** Because of the salary cap, popular free agent players are rarely offered significantly more money by one team than others. Contract offers are usually extremely close. Where a free agent decides to play can come down to such determining factors as whether the stadium has a grass playing field, which players believe is easier on their bodies, or the attractiveness of the team complex. Some facilities, such as Philadelphia's and Cleveland's, are striking. "I've had free agents come here, walk in the door, and their mouths drop," says Carmen Policy, president of the Browns. "It does make a difference."

4 **Tradition.** There is a reason why teams like the New York Giants, the Pittsburgh Steelers and the Green Bay Packers, among several others, have long, winning backgrounds. Their success can be traced to a single person or family from years ago, such as Vince Lombardi with the Packers, the Mara family with the Giants, or the Rooney family with the Steelers. They set a positive tone that lasts for years, and the correct way to run the franchise is handed down over a generation.

My top five franchises are: Philadelphia, the most well-rounded organization in the NFL despite what was a horrific performance in the conference championship game; Cleveland, which scores high in every category, especially tradition; the Giants, who, despite scoring weakly on facilities (the stadium was voted second-worst in the NFL by players following the 2002 season), have a splendid pairing in coach Fassel and the general manager Accorsi; Green Bay, whose only negative is that Mike Sherman, the coach, has final say on personnel matters (a mistake); and Pittsburgh, where the Rooney family has always been honorable and respectful of football tradition. Two franchises that just miss the top five: Tampa Bay, which traded two first-round and two second-round picks to get Gruden, who is worth it, but the deal will hurt the franchise for the immediate future since it will not be able to get top talent through the draft in the next few years; and Baltimore, whose owner, Art Modell, has made a commitment to running a diverse management structure in which blacks have a significant role. Modell is one of only a few NFL owners to do so. It should also be said that the Ravens also have the most gorgeous, fan-friendly home field in the NFL.

The Eagles have few flaws in their hierarchical structure, but the team must deal with several key issues on the field. As good as Reid is, he tends to become extremely tight in his play calling during big games. McNabb's talent is unmistakable. So is his weakness. He has yet to digest all of the intricacies of Reid's "West Coast" system, which relies heavily on feel and nuance, two aspects of McNabb's game that are average at best. Also, if the team does not draft a scary, explosive wide receiver, its offense will always be vulnerable to the league's top defenses, as it was against Tampa Bay.

||

Inside the NovaCare complex a quotation from Charles Lindbergh is stenciled in large letters on a wall: "The important thing is to start . . . to create a plan and then follow it step by step no matter how small or large each one by itself might seem." I find it a bit unusual to see a line from Lindbergh, who was accused of being an anti-Semite and Nazi sympathizer, stamped on a complex owned by a Jewish man, run by another, with black players and executives working throughout it. In 1941 Lindbergh claimed that the drive from "the British, the Jews, and the Roosevelt administration" for America to enter the war against Hitler stemmed from "the Jews' large ownership and influence in our motion pictures, our press, our radio, and our government." Lindbergh also accepted a medal from the head of the Nazi Luftwaffe, Hermann Goering.

However flawed the mind of the aviator, the point of the quotation is still sound. The Eagles became successful because of Banner's vision, his plan, his stubbornness, and his refusal to abandon his ideas, despite being mocked by people outside the franchise—and even some within it. For that fact alone, Banner deserves accolades.

Now Banner and the current Eagles regime face their sternest challenge. The team will have to convince an already cynical fan base that it can recover from the loss to Tampa Bay, as well as the loss of several critical free agent players, namely, defensive end Hugh Douglas, who left for Jacksonville in March 2003. The Eagles will feel immense pressure from fans, the news media, and themselves to abandon temporarily their principle of building patiently and wrestling the salary cap into submission and do what some of the more poorly run teams like Washington do, which is sign high-priced veterans for the short term. It is such a soothing, sexy thought. It is also wrong. The Eagles need to stay the course, and they will likely break through. Dear Iggles: take solace in what happened to San Francisco a decade ago. The 49ers lost the conference championship to Dallas in 1992 and 1993 but defeated the Cowboys in 1994 and went on to win the Super Bowl that season. With Banner at the helm, Philadelphia has a chance of traveling on a similar path. In a league that sometimes tries to discourage people with different thoughts and ideas, smacking them down like small dogs nibbling at heels, Banner has succeeded, demonstrating the resiliency of an aged offensive lineman. He need not abandon his principles now.

"Getting to the championship game twice in two years is a good achievement," Banner says. "But this game is more than that. We need to get to the ultimate goal. The Super Bowl is why we are all here. I feel very positive about where we are and where we're going. We're not in a crisis stage, but I do feel this is the first major test for Andy and this organization. How resilient are we going to be? I believe we will prove to be very resilient."

If only Banner could pass some of his wisdom on to the hierarchy of another team, a team that is the polar opposite of the Eagles, a team that does just about everything the gosh darn wrong way—oh, those Cincinnati Bengals.

||

This is a true story, and sad, and altogether funny, and it tells what it is like to be a Bengal. To be a Bengal is to be a sad sack. To be a Bengal is to be a laughingstock, a joke, and a cautionary tale from *Tales from the Crypt*, a how-to manual on how not to run a football franchise. This is a true story, and sad, and altogether funny, and tells what it is like to be a Bengal, and it begins with a former Bengals assistant coach and his son.

When the coach dragged himself home one night after a typically long day of meetings and practice, he headed for the basement of his house, where his son was watching television. As they spoke about how the son's day went, the coach noticed something wrong. His son was usually a cheery kid, but now he looked solemn, which worried the coach. He queried his son, who told him, without much prodding, that a group of kids at his school teased him about the Bengals' losing record, knowing that his father was on Cincinnati's staff. His son getting taunted was nothing new and not unexpected. The Bengals were mired in yet another losing streak, and it is common for the children of coaches and players on losing teams to be cruelly mocked for the lack of success their parents are having on the field. The teasing at times can be merciless, even cruel, but his son knew how to deal with it, so the coach was surprised that this round of tormenting had left the boy so sour.

"So what did the kids say this time?" asked the coach.

"They said the Bengals suck," his son replied.

"Well, you've heard worse than that," the coach said.

"Yeah."

"So why are you so upset?" the coach replied.

His son paused and muttered, "Because I agreed with them."

||

Jokes. Like the one about a white, powdery substance found on the Bengals' home field that the Bengals players avoided, panicking. After a detailed analysis it was discovered that the foreign material was . . . the goal line. Jokes. How can you tell when the Bengals are going to run the ball? The back leaves the huddle crying. J-o-k-e-s. What do you call a Cincinnati Bengal with a Super Bowl ring? A thief. Jokes, jokes, jokes. Why was Cincinnati's head coach angry when someone stole the team's playbook? Because he hadn't finished coloring it yet.

It wasn't always this way. The Bengals were once a proud, productive franchise, run by Hall-of-Famer Paul Brown. Condoleezza Rice, national security adviser and football super-fan, rooted for the Bengals once upon a time because she had so much respect for Brown. "He was a studious, smart man," she says. Brown had five winning seasons, but more important, he set a foundation for the franchise that would hold it upright for years. Cincinnati went to Super Bowl XVI in 1982, losing to San Francisco, and seven years later the Bengals played the 49ers again in the championship game, this time losing Super Bowl XXIII. The Bengals may have failed to win those title games, but at least they got there.

It is easy to trace where the problems began for the Bengals. When Brown, who was one of the NFL's greatest innovators, died in 1991 at the age of 82. That transition began the era of the ugliness—and the jokes. Mike Brown is a nice man, but he lacks the vision, passion, and skill that his father possessed. One of the main problems with the Bengals, as former Cincinnati quarterback Boomer Esiason has pointed out, "is the lack of culpability in the front office." That is because the Browns are a family affair. While there have been four head coaches, six offensive coordinators, five defensive coordinators in 13 years, and, entering the 2002 season, the 12th opening-day quarterback in the past 12 losing seasons, all culminating in a 55–137 record since the franchise last made the playoffs in 1990, the Brown family has remained gainfully employed. As a result, no one in the front office has been held accountable for the Bengals' misery. Brown's daughter, Katie Blackburn, the team's executive vice president, negotiates player contracts. Her husband, Troy Blackburn, runs the business side of the team. Mike Brown's brother, Pete, leads the personnel department. With all of this football inbreeding, no one can be fired. Especially considering that Mike Brown is not just the owner but the general manager, and as general manager, he has hired only 48 front-office employees. Houston has almost 150.

How bad have the Bengals been under Mike Brown's stewardship? While racking up 137 losses, Cincinnati has not made the playoffs or had a winning season since he took full control of the franchise. For a team not to make the playoffs in what is now the NFL's Age of Parity is not just an embarrassment but almost impossible—as unlikely as all of the universe's galaxies aligning themselves perfectly, or Daniel Snyder showing humility. More than any other sport, the NFL practically guarantees teams that they will make the playoffs every few years, especially after the NFL's postseason field expanded to 12 teams in 1990, which gave franchises better than a one-in-three chance of making the playoffs. While the Bengals have headed home every January since Brown took over, tails between their legs, the expansion Jacksonville Jaguars, for example, have earned postseason berths multiple times. In fact, the Bengals are the only NFL team other than the Houston Texans, which came into existence only in 2002, not to make the playoffs since the postseason field grew 13 seasons ago.

The Bengals have lost at least ten games a season a record nine times since 1991, including starts of 0–4, 0–6, 0–7, 0–8 (twice), and 0–10. With this kind of record, the Bengals have become regular fodder for Jay Leno. Theoretically, the losing should at least help Cincinnati get an influx of talent, since teams with the worst records have the highest draft picks, but even that hasn't gone right. Cincinnati has the smallest scouting operation in football with just two scouts, while most teams have around 15—Green Bay has 20, and Washington has 19. This scout shortage may be why many of Cincinnati's top draft picks, the ones that should have reinvigorated the franchise, have been complete busts. David Klingler, Dan Wilkinson, Ki-Jana Carter, Reinard Wilson, Akili Smith—they would all be a nice start for an all-bum team. The Bengals have picked in the top ten in ten of the past thirteen drafts but have almost nothing to show for it because of poor choices. So around and around the Bengals cycle goes: a lame, mom-and-pop front office with little ambition since there is no threat of being fired; a small scouting department because the team is cheap, which, in part, leads to bad draft choices; and, consequently, no influx of new talent. This is the Bengals two-step—two steps backward, no steps forward.

Last season fans became so fed up by Brown's leadership that some began appearing at games with T-shirts that read: DEAR MIKE, PLEASE TAKE MY NAME OFF THE STADIUM. LOVE, DAD.

||

Hall-of-Famer Anthony Muñoz, a former Bengals offensive lineman, says that, when he watches the Bengals, "I don't see the spark, and I don't see the fire in the players when they take the field." That is what constant losing does to a franchise. It drains the desire out of the body, the way a vampire pulls the plasma out of his victim. Bengals players believe they are going to lose before they take the field. The Bengals assistant coach says that, at times, "a blanket of depression covered not just me when we would lose, but my entire family. There were times my wife would cry so hard it was like our dog died."

After Cincinnati's 34–6 drubbing at the hands of San Diego in 2002, Chargers tight end Stephen Alexander crucified the Bengals to the team's website reporter. "Did you see them lying around?" Alexander remarked. "They didn't know if they wanted to play or go to the sideline, every single one of them, all of their front guys. The D-line and linebackers, they're on the ground, looking around, 'Nah, let's shut it down.' They were terrible." Loss number 12 in 2002 came mostly because coach Dick LeBeau made the decision—which he would later concede was unwise—to allow rookie kicker Travis Dorsch to make his debut as the team punter against Carolina. Dorsch had two of his low kicks returned for touchdowns, and another sailed only ten yards. The Bengals lost to the Panthers 52–31. LeBeau was fired following the 2002 season after the Bengals finished a franchise-worst 2–14.

"We're the laughingstock in this league, and I take it personal," Bengals fullback Lorenzo Neal says. "Every game we play, I'm hitting guys in the mouth. I'm frustrated, and guys aren't going to call me a bum. I refuse to be a bum, and I refuse to be a loser."

The cheapness of the team is one of the most disturbing aspects of its lack of success. The franchise takes in tens of millions from television revenue every year but does not properly invest it in the team. The Bengals have historically been so stingy that, according to players, management has been known to charge them several dollars for things like duct tape, which some players use to repair faulty equipment.

How do you fix the Bengals? Here are five solutions that would be a good start:

1 Brown must relinquish all daily control of the team. He's proven a miserable failure at running the franchise, in almost every way, and has had more than a decade to improve the Bengals. That's plenty of time to get the job done.

2 Hire Ron Wolf to become general manager. He reloaded the Green Bay Packers into perennial Super Bowl winners. The owner–general manager dual role simply does not work in modern football—look at Dallas and Jerry Jones.

3 Boost the number of bodies in the personnel department. It is no coincidence that the Bengals are terrible talent evaluators: they have the thinnest scouting department. The more eyes there are looking at players, the better the chances are of determining what kind of potential each player truly holds.

4 Give season ticket holders a onetime rebate equivalent to 50 percent of the value of their tickets. Bengals fans have been the most abused in all of sports. They deserve a reward for their loyalty.

5 Employ a top Madison Avenue publicity firm. Seriously. The Bengals have a battered image. They are being ridiculed not just in America but in other parts of the world. A British sportscaster in 2002 joked, "Next week the Bengals have a bye . . . where they are six-point underdogs." This public beating must change. So after one winning season—I know, easier said than done—the Bengals should employ a high-powered PR organization to change their image and continue the good feelings of a winning season.

There is hope. The team hired Marvin Lewis to coach the franchise in January 2003. He has the smarts and fundamental coaching skills required to deal with the mess that is the Bengals. However, since nothing else in the Bengals' problematic hierarchy has changed—Lewis says that Brown has handed over more control over the roster, but I'll believe that when I see it—I fear that Lewis will be sucked down the drain, joining a long line of head coaches before him who put on that Bengals hat and dreamed of turning the team around.

||

A guy and a dog walk into a bar. The dog is sporting a Bengals jersey. "Hey, no pets in here," the bartender yells. "You'll have to leave." The man begs him, "The game has been blacked out, sir. You guys have a satellite dish. Please let us watch. I promise we will be good." The bartender finally relents and tells the man and his dog they can have a seat. The game begins. The Bengals get the ball and immediately plow down the field; though stopped from scoring a touchdown, they successfully kick a field goal. The dog jumps up on the bar and begins celebrating, giving everyone high fives. "Great dog," says the bartender. "What does he do when the Bengals score a touchdown?" The man replies, "I don't know. I've only had him for a couple of years."

The Team

SPY GAMES

When Bill Parcells coached the New York Jets, he was viewed as one of the worst control freaks the league had seen in some time. One Jets player would discover just how much. During the 1999 season the player was at the team's practice facility in Hempstead, New York, and accidentally stumbled upon an unmarked room the size of a walk-in closet. The door was cracked open, and he peeked inside. He was stunned by what he saw. There was a bank of video screens, the player said, and on those screens were pictures of various portions of the complex, including a view of the locker room. Hello, Candid Camera. "A lot of things around here have knocked me for a loop, but this was one of the biggest," the player says. "My first thought was, 'Has the team been spying on us?'"

Word of the secret videotape system spread like wildfire through the locker room. Players searched for the tiny hidden cameras and eventually discovered some of them. Keyshawn Johnson, the sharp and flamboyant former Jets wide receiver who now plays in Tampa Bay, found some of the devices, several of which were also in the team's weight room. Johnson said that once, jokingly, he made an obscene gesture toward a camera he had located. He stood in front of it and raised his middle finger: no, he wasn't saying Parcells was number one.

Several player agents said the team told them Parcells installed the cameras after a rash of locker room thefts, but players on the team as well as their agents believe they were planted more to watch what the players were doing than the moves of any possible cat burglar.

The Jets' situation under Parcells illustrates a phenomenon that has been raging for several years but has recently reached an apex. Teams are keeping a close eye on their players and the complexes in which they work. Union leader Gene Upshaw once told me in an interview: "I think a lot of facilities have surveillance equipment throughout the complex and in the locker room. I believe this, and I've been told this by some teams. But the equipment is there for security, not so much for surveillance. I don't think most players are aware of it, and I know it's like Linda Tripp, but if a player follows the rules, he has nothing to worry about.

"When I'm in Denver, in a meeting with the players at the Broncos' facility, you see certain things in the room and know they're not lights. I know management is listening. When I'm in Cincinnati, I know owner Mike Brown is listening. I don't want to say how I know, but I know." (The Broncos and Bengals deny ever eavesdropping on Upshaw during union meetings with players.) "But when it comes to this issue of cameras around the players, it's not a big deal to me, because they are there for the security of our players, and obviously the safety of the players is a primary concern for me," Upshaw continued. "I'd rather err on the side of caution than have some nut come into the locker room and do something."

Does the NFL even spy on the media? In their book *Pros and Cons*, which details criminal acts by professional football players, authors Jeff Benedict and Don Yaeger write that one day a researcher working for them received a knock at his door. The researcher said it was a private detective, who handed a copy of the researcher's cable bill over to him. Benedict and Yaeger write that they believe the man was hired by the NFL to spy on them and that the flashing of the cable bill was an attempt to intimidate them by signaling that the NFL was looking over their backs.

Most players do not know they are being taped, and teams even keep the fact that they use this equipment from the league office, team officials have said. There are no NFL rules against videotaping players in the locker room.

Erosion of privacy has long been a concern for workers in other industries, as well as for the private organizations that safeguard citizen rights. The *New York Times* reported in September 2002 on a Security Industry Association estimate that at least 2 million closed-circuit television systems are in use in the United States. A survey of Manhattan in 1998 by the American Civil Liberties Union found 2,397 cameras fixed on places where people pass or gather, like stores and sidewalks. All but 270 were operated by private entities, the organization reported. CCS International, a company that provides security and monitoring services, calculated last year that the average person is recorded 73 to 75 times a day in New York City.

Now privacy has become an issue in professional football as well. More teams are using high-tech devices, such as tiny video cameras not much larger than a quarter, and hiding them in their complexes, those interviewed say. Some players explain that they agree that video spy equipment provides more security, but they raise questions about abuse. Are teams watching the private conversations that players are having with teammates or reporters? And how far away is the use of hidden microphones? Would teams listen in on a player's cell phone conversation with his agent? Players resent that level of privacy invasion.

Some of the NFL's snooping is warranted. During Super Bowl XXXVII, with the threat of terrorism a distinct possibility, the NFL employed a high-tech, $400,000 surveillance system of 52 cameras that covered every corner of Qualcomm Stadium. What made this video monitoring structure so different was that law enforcement officials were not required to monitor the cameras from a central location. Instead, they could plug monitors into cell phones, dial into the system, and see any part of the stadium they desired, which allowed for a faster response time.

Video cameras have been part of football for years. The San Francisco 49ers in the 1980s were among the first to tape team meetings so that a player who was ill and missed one could be given the tape and not fall behind. Teams now routinely tape practices—even warm-ups. One reason is to debunk the compensation claims players have filed asserting injuries when none existed.

Videotapes made from spy cameras mounted around the team's complex played a role in the bizarre case of former New Orleans wide receiver Albert Connell. Police accused Connell of stealing $863 from the locker of his teammate Deuce McAllister and $3,500 from McAllister's car in December 2001. Why, we might ask, would a player who had signed a five-year, $14 million contract that included a $2.5 million signing bonus steal what amounted, to him, as petty cash, from a teammate of all people? Joel Goldberg, a sports psychologist who has counseled players on the New York Giants, the New Jersey Nets, the Chicago Bears, and the Carolina Panthers, believes that when players steal from teammates, several complicated factors come into play. A significant number of athletes come from poor backgrounds or situations where family structure and discipline were lacking or nonexistent. The moral fiber of such athletes is not fully developed, and neither is their sense of guilt. Anything, even stealing from a teammate, can be rationalized, Goldberg explains. But why did the police believe they knew it was Connell committing the alleged theft? Bob Long, the Jefferson Parish assistant district attorney, said that his office watched a Saints team security tape that allegedly showed Connell stealing money from McAllister's locker. Connell repaid McAllister, who did not want to press charges, and escaped prosecution. Until that point most Saints players were unaware that a taping system even existed.

Upshaw cites another remarkable example of how one team used videotape from the locker room. A certain player, he says, filed a grievance against a team. (Upshaw would not identify the player or the team.) The core of the grievance came down to where the player was at a particular time. The player said he was not at the team's facility; the team said he was. To back its claim, the team used videotape of the player in the locker room taken at the very time he maintained he was not there, Upshaw says.

It was a videotaped union meeting that caused the NFL and the union a moment of embarrassment in the summer of 1999. The union recorded one of its annual gatherings in Hawaii; the tape later showed just how raucous these summits are. Cameras caught all of the bickering, infighting, and union politics. There was a union official offering to instruct players on how to beat the salary cap. There was a long debate about the implicit racism some union members believed was behind the league's plan to prohibit players from wearing bandannas. And there were candid discussions about substance abuse, including an assertion by one official that alcohol abuse was the biggest problem among players. Most startlingly, the union informed its membership that a significant number of players had failed drug tests that year but were not punished or suspended because of a secret agreement between the league and the union.

All of the proceedings at the union meeting were captured on more than 40 hours of videotape by a Florida company hired by the NFL Players Association to film the meetings. The intention was to create a promotional package that could be distributed to players and perhaps improve the union's standing with its constituents. After the videotaping was finished, however, the film company sued the players' association in a dispute about payment, and the union never took full control of the tapes. Thus, I was able to view them in their entirety.

The videotapes offer a rare glimpse into the inner workings of a major sports union. The biggest revelation from the videotape comes during a talk by Doug Allen, the union's assistant executive director, about the differences between the league's old drug policy and the new one that was to take effect in the months following that meeting. The tape shows Allen saying the union was informed by the NFL that a significant number of players had failed drug tests and faced suspensions. Allen goes on to say that because of a private agreement with the league office, the players would not be suspended. Instead, they would get a second chance under the new policy, which was more formidable. "I will tell you, there were a number of players who were notified of suspensions under the old policy, and those suspensions were held in abeyance until we got the new policy done," Allen says on the videotape. "We convinced them not to suspend those players." Allen goes on to say that "a number" of those players would have been suspended for one year. The league official who insisted on anonymity said there were 16 players who faced suspensions, from four games to one year, but were not suspended.

At the meeting Allen also informs the player representatives that there were a "dozen alcohol situations" from that year. He is no more

specific than that, but his words fall into the same portion of the meeting in which he discusses failed drug tests. On the tape Allen says,
"Frankly, the biggest problem we have with substance abuse is not marijuana, or cocaine, but alcohol." Privately, players and team officials have
claimed for years that alcohol abuse is far more of a problem than illicit
drug use. But no union or league official has ever made such a statement
publicly.

The tape ends with a dispute over the union being $51,000 over
budget. Players argue constantly and vehemently until one unidentified
player says, "Why can't we get past this . . . being $51,000 over budget?
Damn, $51,000? That's just two Pontiacs."

Conspiracy theories aside, if coaches or players do not like being
videotaped on a team's complex, can they sue the franchise? Little prevents a team from secretly recording the locker room or any other part of
the team's facility (except bathroom stalls). The sole federal law that
limits monitoring by an employer is the 1986 Electronic Communications Privacy Act, which prohibits eavesdropping on personal communications. Companies, however, can monitor all nonspoken personal
communications.

Which means that players will probably always have that electronic
eye, staring, watching them. Like Big Brother. Only richer.

||

From the electronic eye to plain, old-fashioned thievery. Some franchises routinely steal other teams' plays, and the latest strange yet ingen-
ious method in play pickpocketing is reading lips. This is a tactic some
coaches and scouts are increasingly employing to capture the other
team's signals and play calls and, in turn, anticipate what play is coming,
some NFL coaches say. To prevent lip reading, more coaches and assistants—when sending in plays to the quarterback or the defense using
the radio system that pipes plays into the players' helmets—are shielding their mouths when giving the call. "Stealing signals is an old art
form in the NFL," Lovie Smith, the St. Louis Rams' defensive coordinator, once told me. "But this newest thing is pretty unusual, and more

teams are trying it." The Giants' Fassel says: "There have been rumors that it has been happening. But if someone can pull it off, more power to them, because it seems extremely hard to do. I don't buy it is happening a lot. It's too difficult."

But if lip-reading thievery is rare, then why are so many who call plays from the sideline shielding their mouths when sending in the plays? Watch almost any televised game and you see the head coach or coordinator covering his mouth while sending in the play over the speaker system to the quarterback.

Some old-school forms of spying used simpler techniques. The Giants once claimed that opposing teams stuck assistant coaches in a hotel along Route 3 in New Jersey that overlooked their practice field so they could see the plays the Giants practiced.

Obviously, teams take such desperate measures to steal signals and audibles because doing so can give them a distinct tactical advantage. When Oakland and Tampa Bay met in Super Bowl XXXVII, Jon Gruden had just such an advantage. Rich Gannon, like many quarterbacks, comes to the line of scrimmage and may change the play several times, based on the defensive alignment, and instruct the offense on the new play by shouting a series of calls, or audibles. Gruden, who had designed the Raiders' offense, basically handed his defense a dictionary of what those calls meant. He told some of the Buccaneers: "I don't expect them to use the same audibles from when I was coaching there, but just in case they do, here you go." Gruden's overpreparation of his team paid off because Oakland actually changed little of its offense. Tampa Bay defensive players sometimes knew what play was coming because Gruden had practically handed his team Oakland's playbook, and Raiders coach Bill Callahan was too arrogant, or careless, to change the system prior to the biggest game of the team's life. Quarterback Gannon said that as he shouted a call after reaching the line of scrimmage, sometimes Buccaneers defenders would almost finish his sentences. "It would have been easier if Gruden wasn't" with the Buccaneers, said Oakland guard Frank Middleton following the 27-point championship loss. "We called a lot of audibles where it seemed like they knew them. Like they knew what was coming. It made a difference."

Lip reading takes spying to an entirely new level of sophistication. There are two ways this type of spying works. The first kind of lip reading happens during the game but is less reliable. Say, for example, the former Giants offensive coordinator Sean Payton, as he often did, is standing on the sideline and sends in the play to quarterback Kerry Collins, using a radio device that sends Payton's voice into Collins's helmet. As Payton is sending in the play, an opposing coach or scout, high up in the coaches' box and using high-powered binoculars, reads Payton's lips. Payton usually reads the play slowly so the quarterback can understand it, allowing the spy a legitimate chance to decipher the words. The spy makes a note of the play call, writes it down, and waits for the play to come again. It is not uncommon for a coach to use the same play call several times in a game and many more times in a season. When he sees the same play called, the spy in the sky radios down to the coaches on the sideline, who then tell players what is coming.

There is one problem, however, with this particular lip-reading system, as Fassel points out. "There's too much chaos during a game to pull something like that off on a continuing basis," he says. "Maybe a play or two gets stolen that way. Maybe. Because by the time an opposing coach reads lips, tells the coaches on the field what he thinks the other team is going to do, and that coach instructs the players, too much time has gone by." But it has happened, coaches insist, and sometimes very successfully.

The second scenario, coaches say, involves television and makes lip reading much easier. Networks often show extreme close-ups of coaches as they call plays. Opponents videotape the games and later read the lips of the few coaches who do not shield their mouths. There have also been instances when scouts videotape opposing coaches while standing on the opposing sideline or sitting in an upper deck box. They later review the tape, slowing it down to make it easier to understand the target's words, coaches say. The spy will then match the play called to what the defense did on the field and—presto—they have stolen a call. If the teams play again, the heisted information might be useful, although the same kind of game chaos that slows the first method also applies here. Nevertheless, one National Football Conference assistant coach says he has stolen several dozen plays from a total of five or six teams using all of these methods. "Cover your mouth," says the coach, who asks not to be identified, "and your plays are safe, but get careless and you're fair game."

Another coach who has stolen plays this way explains that a friend of his daughter's reads lips and he asks her, after videotaping a game, to translate what the coaches were saying.

Yes, coaches are that desperate to get an edge, any edge.

Stealing plays from an offense this way is much more difficult, however, than taking them from a defense. That is because most offensive plays have a lot more words. "I think defensive coaches like myself worry about this more than offenses," St. Louis's Smith says. "That's because of the verbiage. An offensive play might be 'Z right 20 Bingo, blah, blah, blah,' and go on for 10 or more words. It's hard to steal that play by reading lips because it's so long. It happens but it's hard."

"But most defensive calls are short," Smith adds. " 'Three-over' or something like that. That can be stolen kind of easy."

Smith says Rams coaches do not steal signals using the lip-reading method because "you want to get every edge, but really, in the end, how well does it work? In the end you're still guessing to a degree, and we don't want our players to guess, we want them to know," he says.

But Smith thinks that other teams have stolen signals this way. Fassel says a microphone extending from his headset protects him from potential thievery since it covers his mouth. (The NFL digitally encrypts the conversations coaches have with players to prevent electronic eavesdropping.) When he was coordinator, Payton, while reading from his play sheet (an oversized piece of laminated paper) and making the call on his headset to Collins, often used the sheet as a shield, hiding his mouth. Philadelphia's Reid shields his face on almost every call he makes in games. Other coaches say they cup their hands around their mouths, not to shield them from spies but to block out as much crowd noise as possible when calling in the play.

There are some coaches who worry about the new form of play stealing, but Fassel is not one of them. "If someone is that smart to pull this off, they should be curing cancer," he says, "not coaching football."

||

Denver coach Mike Shanahan is issuing a stern warning to a roomful of the NFL's best and brightest at the rookie symposium: they should never try to get away with anything they "shouldn't do," because they will be caught, no matter what team they're on, no matter where they are. The coach is always watching.

Many teams police their players as closely as possible because franchises want to protect their investments. A star NFL player, to a coach or owner, is like a stock or a retirement plan. He must be looked after constantly so that trouble can be headed off as quickly as possible.

"I'm telling you, as a head football coach, the head coach knows," Shanahan says to the rookies. "People will call him, tell him where you are at, what you're doing, how you're handling yourself. So just conduct yourself as a professional. Just think about all the time you've invested throughout your life for this opportunity.

"I tell guys during the season, if you're out the night before a game and I catch you, you're gone," Shanahan continues. "If we've got everybody working their butt off on the same pace and everybody gets a good night's sleep the night before the game, we've got a chance to be something special. But if we've got three or four guys that think that nightlife the night before the game or even during the week is more important than what's at hand, we may get to the playoffs, but we'll never be the champs."

Don't feel too sorry for the players, though. It turns out that some of them have been doing a bit of their own spying. A group of more than 100 Philadelphia cheerleaders filed a lawsuit last year against 29 NFL teams seeking punitive damages for "invasion of privacy, trespass, intentional infliction of emotional distress, gross negligence, failure to supervise, conspiracy, and outrageous conduct." They accuse players and others of spying through peepholes at Veterans Stadium while the Eagles cheerleaders showered and dressed. Players allegedly had been spying on the women as far back as the 1970s and up until as recently as two years ago. Only the Jacksonville Jaguars and Houston Texans, who have never played at Veterans Stadium, and the Eagles, whose locker room is in a different part of the stadium, were not named in the suit, which continues to plod through the Philadelphia court system.

According to the suit, the "ability to peer into the cheerleaders' locker room, and to view them in [various] states of undress, was considered one of the special 'perks' of being a visiting team of the Eagles." The suit continues: "It was common knowledge among virtually the entire National Football League—while at the same time a carefully guarded secret to be known only to the players and other team employees of the [visiting] teams—that these conditions existed."

Players told me in interviews that they would spy on the cheerleaders prior to games by peeking through holes scraped through painted-over windows and gaps between doors and by slipping mirrors under doors. Dallas Cowboys players said there were shoving matches to catch a glimpse of the naked women showering. The best vantage points from which to get a look were passed from team to team like perverted secrets. The only player to publicly admit spying on the women was Mike Wells, who was a member of the Detroit Lions when they played at Veterans Stadium in 1995 and 1996 and was with the Chicago Bears when they played Philadelphia in 2000. Wells bragged about "peeping practice" and added that "you can see into their shower room."

Suzette Walsh, a former captain of the cheerleading squad who is now a schoolteacher, says she felt "violated and degraded." Another cheerleader downplays the entire sordid story. Sharon Sweeney, a former cheerleading coach, tells of players and dancers looking in on each other. She recounts an incident in 1980 when a player was staring through a crack in a door when at that moment a dancer opened the same door to go peep into the players' locker room. The door slammed into the player's head, causing him to become woozy and miss part of the game. Sweeney says the spying was simply "boys being boys and girls being girls."

According to Michael McKenna, the lawyer representing the cheerleaders in their legal action against the NFL, one of the suit's female plaintiffs says a team owner, like the players, spied on the dancers through the peepholes. Why does this former Philadelphia cheerleader suspect this? The woman says she always wore underwear that had the days of the week printed on them, but she had to wear her Tuesday pair on Sunday because it was the only color that matched her game day uniform (and you thought being a cheerleader was simple). A visiting owner, the dancer claims, approached her during a game and remarked that he knew of her undergarment choices.

"Honey, it's Sunday," she claims the owner said, "not Tuesday."

The Team

5c

THE WONDERLIC

NOBODY IN FOOTBALL SHOULD BE CALLED A GENIUS.
A GENIUS IS A GUY LIKE NORMAN EINSTEIN.

> —*ESPN football analyst and former Washington Redskins*
> *quarterback Joe Theismann*

I WANT TO RUSH FOR 1,000 OR 1,500 YARDS,
WHICHEVER COMES FIRST.

> —*Former New Orleans Saints running back George Rogers*

The year was 1998, and Ryan Leaf was sitting in a comfortable back room at Madison Square Garden, a small group of family and friends clustered around him. Just a few hours before the beginning of the NFL draft, the buzz predicted the San Diego Chargers at the second overall spot would select Leaf, the powerful quarterback from Washington State. The Indianapolis Colts, picking first that year, would select Peyton Manning from Tennessee. The debate within the NFL and the news media had been fierce. Half of the league thought Manning would be better than Leaf; the other 50 percent expected the opposite.

I had spent the morning following Leaf for a story that was supposed to show a day in the life of a top draft selection: the nervousness, the anticipation, yadda, yadda. After just a few hours Leaf proved to be about as deep as a cup of coffee. (A scout once joked to me that Leaf was so dumb he watched the sofa while sitting on the TV.) That day Leaf's mind was everywhere except on what he was about to become and that was an NFL quarterback, the most prestigious position in all of professional sports. Instead of contemplating the grand turn his life was about to take, Leaf complained that he hated the food at the hotel and thought the media was "a pain in the ass." When I had interviewed Manning the previous day, one of the first things he had said was that he couldn't wait to get to the Colts' complex and start watching reel after reel of NFL defenses. He was serious. It's not fair to judge another human being after such short contact with him, but before that day I had been certain that Leaf would turn out to be the better player of the two. Those two afternoons spent with the players initiated some serious doubts.

Jonathan Niednagel, however, never had one.

Niednagel is a researcher who leads the Missouri-based Brain Type Institute and has dedicated more than three decades of his life to studying brain types. In the months leading up to the draft the Chargers were compiling their research on who would be the better player, Manning or Leaf. As part of the team's evaluation process, the franchise went to Niednagel, whose reputation for forecasting athletic stardom, and a bust or two, is remarkably accurate, even approaching legendary status. Niednagel bases his conclusions about a player on field observations and the way a player carries himself, as well as on his responses to specific questions. Niednagel then develops a brain type. An ESTP type—extroverted, sensing, thinking, perceiving—is ideal for a quarterback. Many of the great ones—Joe Montana, Brett Favre, Joe Namath, Troy Aikman, Phil Simms, Dan Marino, Jim Kelly, and John Unitas—fit that model. Niednagel thought Manning would be a superb player, and he told the Chargers in no uncertain terms that Leaf would melt under the pressure of being a franchise savior and turn into an unequivocal bust.

The Colts knew of Niednagel's prediction, and it played a small part in their selection of Manning. The Chargers wanted Leaf despite the brain expert's dire forecast. San Diego was sitting in the third spot but handed Arizona two first-round draft picks and two players in a trade to move from third to the second position. San Diego selected Leaf and gave him an $11.25 million signing bonus. Niednagel's prophecy would prove scarily accurate. Leaf was the biggest draft bust in NFL history, spending just two years with San Diego before the team was forced to release him, and not solely because of his ugly play on offense. His behavior off the field was equally as horrid. Leaf was once caught on camera screaming at a reporter. After unspectacular and brief stays with Tampa Bay, Dallas, and Seattle, Leaf last year retired from football, before his 25th birthday. He spends most of his days now playing golf.

There are FBI profilers who crack the criminal brain, and there are now a number of NFL profilers like Niednagel who probe the athlete mind in search of the perfect football machine.

The idea that NFL players are simple brutes with squirrel-sized brains has long been an ugly stereotype. It's simply and blatantly false. I've met too many players who, following their playing careers, went on to become judges, doctors, and scientists. What players do on the field also proves the dumb jock typecast to be false. Offenses and defenses have become so remarkably complicated that most players, especially at certain skill positions like quarterback, must be exceptionally sharp to fully grasp them. NFL players need smarts, and teams need to know what's going on in those highly paid heads. Many franchises are using sophisticated tests like Niednagel's to test the mental capacities of their players, but just as many still rely heavily on the old standby of intellectual and psychological probing: the Wonderlic Personnel Test.

The test measures general cognitive ability; since it has just 50 questions, the Wonderlic is basically a short version of an IQ test. Many people who take the Wonderlic don't complete it in the allotted 12 minutes. The median score is 21, which equates to an IQ of about 105. A score of 10 basically means that the applicant is literate. The average NFL prospect scores a 19. Quarterbacks and offensive linemen—who play positions that often require quick mental adjustments from play to play—often score the highest, averaging around 24–26. The belief in the NFL is that the closer a player is to the football, the higher his score.

Teams are not supposed to leak a player's results, but they always get out. Some of the quarterback scores include Brian Griese 39, Drew Bledsoe 37, Steve Young 33, John Elway 30, Troy Aikman 29, Tony Banks 26, Brett Favre 22, Scott Mitchell 19, Randall Cunningham 15, and Jeff George 10. Former Cincinnati player Pat McInally, a Harvard graduate, is the only NFL player to score a perfect 50. (Only one in about 29,500 people do.) Meanwhile, kicker Sebastian Janikowski scored a 9. (In its guide to interpreting the scores Wonderlic describes the job potential for anyone who finishes with a score of 12 or less this way: "Use very simple tools and equipment; repair furniture; assist electrician; simple carpentry; domestic work. 13% of the population score within this range." A person with this score is "unlikely to benefit from formalized training setting; successful using simple tools under consistent supervision." In Janikowski's case, a kicking tee can be described as a simple tool.)

The Wonderlic's use remains controversial. That's because a player's score does not always accurately predict intelligence or how successful his career will be. Dan Marino scored just a 16 and went on to a Hall of Fame career. Infamous busts like quarterbacks Rick Mirer and David Klingler had scores of 31 and 30, respectively. Still, despite the problems of career prediction, teams feel it is better to have more information on a college prospect than less, especially when it invests millions in a draft pick. The Giants have been among the leaders in using intellectual and psychological testing behind team psychologist Joel Goldberg, and the former general manager, George Young, once told me: "Going into a draft without some form of psychological testing on the prospects is like going into a gunfight with a knife."

Potential draft picks now study the Wonderlic the same way high school students prepare for the SAT. The Wonderlic company says copies of its tests are top-secret and difficult to get—but they are not. I was able to get a copy of one easily. NFL agents get them as well and have their football clients take the test repeatedly so they become accustomed to how it works.

Wonderlic sent me a sample test of 12 questions and gave me permission to reprint it. (The company forbade me from publishing the actual 50-question test.) The sample test questions are comparable to the real test questions, though the actual test is more difficult. The answers are on pages 299–300.

---

1 Assume the first statements are true. Is the final one:
1 true   2 false   3 not certain?
The boy plays baseball. All baseball players wear hats.
The boy wears a hat.

2 Paper sells for 21 cents per pad. What will 4 pads cost?

3 How many of the five pairs of items listed below are exact duplicates?

Nieman, K. M.	Neiman, K. M.
Thomas, G. K.	Thomas, C. K.
Hoff, J. P.	Hoff, J. P.
Pino, L. R.	Pina, L. R.
Warner, T.S.	Wanner, T. S.

4 PRESENT   RESERVE—Do these words . . .
1 have similar meanings   2 have contradictory meanings
3 mean neither the same nor the opposite?

5 A train travels 20 feet in 1/5 second. At this same speed, how many feet will it travel in 3 seconds?

6 When rope is selling at $.10 a foot, how many feet can you buy for 60 cents?

7 The ninth month of the year is
1 October   2 January   3 June
4 September   5 May

8 Which number in the following group of numbers represents the smallest amount?

7   .8   31   .33   2

9 In printing an article of 48,000 words, a printer decides to use two sizes of type. Using the larger type, a printed page contains 1,800 words. Using smaller type, a page contains 2,400 words. The article is allotted 21 full pages in a magazine. How many pages must be in smaller type?

10 Three individuals form a partnership and agree to divide the profits equally. X invests $9,000, Y invests $7,000, Z invests $4,000. If the profits are $4,800, how much less does X receive than if the profits were divided in proportion to the amount invested?

11 Assume the first two statements are true. Is the final one: 1 true   2 false   3 not certain?
Tom greeted Beth. Beth greeted Dawn.
Tom did not greet Dawn.

12 A boy is 17 years old and his sister is twice as old. When the boy is 23 years old, what will be the age of his sister?

My Wonderlic score? I took the real test and registered a respectable 38. Maybe the three glasses of wine I consumed beforehand boosted my brainpower.

6

THE LEAGUE

The 6 League

AN ANTIVIOLENCE PLAN

Irving Fryar's life used to be about adventures. Not the good kind, mind you. Not the kind where the family packs up the station wagon and heads for Yosemite. Nope. The bad kind. Where there are drugs and arrests for gun possession and fights outside bars and scuffles with the wife and all of the headline-grabbing nonsense that goes on and on until you are sitting in jail one night, as Fryar once was, asking yourself, "What am I doing with my life?" It was at that moment that the former New England wide receiver decided the answer to that question was, "Not much," and changed his course. Now he is a Pentecostal minister, preaching not just about God but also about making the right choices, about staying away from adventures.

Fryar spends a lot of time speaking to young NFL players; today there are 262 of them, all rookies, hanging on to his every word at the NFL's rookie symposium the way Fryar himself once hung on to a fingertip catch. This annual event, which costs the NFL about $750,000, teaches rookies about life in football and the mantra is, "Choices, decisions, consequences." What makes it effective—for the players who choose to heed the numerous warnings from the NFL—is the current and former players telling of their good and bad experiences. Now Fryar is talking about messages and choices and adventures. He begins with a warning, and his words—portions of which appeared in a *New York Times Magazine* article—are stunning.

"We're going to have some idiots come out of this room," Fryar says. "Those of you feeling good about yourselves, stop it. You ain't did nothing yet." Fryar goes on to his infamous list of acts of self-destruction that includes a drug habit since he was thirteen and four trips to prison. "The first time, I was stopped in New Jersey," he explains. "I was on my way to shoot somebody. Driving my BMW. I had guns in the trunk, and I got taken to jail. The second time, also guns. Third time was domestic abuse. Fourth time, it was guns again. No. Yeah, yeah, it was guns again. Things got so bad for me, I put a .44 magnum up to my head." Fryar obviously decided not to kill himself—but it was close.

"When I was a rookie," he says, "we didn't have anything like this. I had to learn it the hard way. Don't use me as an example of what you can get away with, brothers. Use me as an example of what you shouldn't do."

Fryar later asks the group a question. "Why do you guys wear your pants sagging, hanging down low on your butts?" There are a few mumbles and quizzical looks. No one knows where Fryar is headed with this particular query. A few players respond that it's just a cool thing to do. What's wrong with it?

"Do you guys know where it started?" Fryar says. "It started in prison."

The sense of shock is palpable. A number of young black men, including some in that very room, have been emulating convicts, and they didn't even know it.

Mike Haynes watches Fryar drop his bombshell on the rooks and smiles slyly. If there is anyone in football who appreciates people like Fryar, it is Haynes. That's because Haynes has one of the toughest jobs in the sport—keeping rich, young, attractive football players, a significant number of whom come from dysfunctional backgrounds, out of trouble.

Some would say it is a fool's mission, and indeed, the symposium will not save everyone. The following July a Buffalo Bills rookie, Rodney Wright, will be arrested on felony hit-and-run charges. But Haynes has nevertheless taken to the task like a general preparing for war. One of the main reasons football has prospered so much is that some of the smartest people in all of sports are running it: Commissioner Paul Tagliabue, union leader Gene Upshaw, NFL executive Harold Henderson, who has smoothed the way for labor peace and instituted some of the league's better proposals, and Gene Washington, the NFL's director of football operations. Haynes is quickly approaching that echelon of big brains. In 2002 he was hired away from the Callaway Golf Company to become the league's vice president for player and employee development. Tagliabue and Henderson liked how he thought out of the box.

Haynes has, to say the least, stepped into chaos.

Perhaps the greatest threat to the NFL's stability is the issue of players and off-field violence. The topic is, unfortunately, not new to football, or to sports in general, but what concerns me is the perception I pick up from NFL players when it comes to the ugly issue of domestic violence. There is a tone of entitlement emanating from some of them, especially the young players; they believe their stardom, in some twisted way, allows them to do what they will with their wives or partners.

In July 2002 Miami Dolphins linebacker Derrick Rodgers was told that his wife was seeing another man. Now, such talk might merit a serious conversation or two, or three, with the better half, but Rodgers evidently decided to do more than have a little chat. According to police, he stormed into a Miami Beach restaurant soon after he heard the news, allegedly picked up a metal chair, and slammed it into the head of the man he believed was having an affair with his wife. He followed that WWF move by punching and kicking his spouse in the midsection, witnesses told the police.

Those same witnesses also stated that Rodgers had prefaced his attack by saying to the man: "Do you know who I am?"

Do you know who I am?

Players are no longer afraid of repercussions, from either the courts or the NFL. They know a physical attack on a wife or girlfriend will probably fail to lead to a prison term because the woman, as often happens in domestic violence cases, may not seek to prosecute her attacker for a variety of reasons, some of which include the honeymoon period that typically follows an assault and the lack of an opportunity to discuss domestic violence in a safe environment. Numerous incidents of women claiming an attack did not happen when there is clearly evidence of one have led a number of communities to adopt victimless prosecutions and/or no-drop policies. (Interestingly, following Rodgers's alleged assault, his wife stated publicly that the entire ugly episode was simply a misunderstanding.) Even if the abused woman does not refuse to testify, most players are wealthy enough to hire a top-notch attorney who can work the system to keep them free.

Players, especially the highly talented ones, also understand that no matter what they do, short of a murder conviction, there will always be a job waiting for them in football. They've learned. They have watched this scenario play itself out a hundred times. They see it embodied in running back Lawrence Phillips.

While at the University of Nebraska, Phillips pled no contest to assault after being accused of dragging his girlfriend down a flight of stairs by her hair. Still, despite his violent outburst against a woman, in 1996 the St. Louis Rams drafted him in the first round with the sixth overall pick and later signed him to a three-year, $5.62 million contract. He celebrated their choice, during a probationary period for the assault, by getting arrested for driving drunk on a California highway. He was sentenced to 23 days in jail. One of the more disturbing scenes from Phillips's tenure in St. Louis was the picture of Coach Dick Vermeil picking up Phillips from prison and driving him home.

Phillips wasted no time demonstrating what one scout on the Washington Redskins once said to me: a thug is always a thug and you don't change him by giving a hug. Phillips went to counseling, courtesy of the Rams; the team attempted to treat him gingerly and respectfully, hoping that would shake him out of his errant ways. It didn't work. Phillips was arrested three times during his 19 months with the Rams. Miami picked him up later in the 1997 season. Then, just weeks after playing his first game as a Dolphin, he was released following an allegation he struck a woman in the face after she refused to dance with him in a Florida nightclub. Phillips pled no contest to misdemeanor battery and was sentenced to probation. But Phillips was handed more football job opportunities despite being a convict, including signing with NFL Europe, followed by a short stay with the San Francisco 49ers (he was released for refusing to practice), and then the Arena Football League. Recently Phillips was playing in the backfield of the Canadian Football League's Montreal Alouettes, wearing one wristband that said "fuck" and another that said "you." Then even the Alouettes had had enough of Phillips after he skipped two practices without an explanation. Following the second AWOL, they suspended him. (You know your career is down the tubes when a CFL team, so desperate for bodies it would play a dead man at running back, suspends you.) Chance after chance after chance. When it came to Phillips, teams were mesmerized by one "P" word—potential—while ignoring another—punk—that better described him.

The story of Tito Wooten might illustrate even more clearly the way teams, and the court system, make embarrassing compromises so a player can take the field despite accusations of abuse.

ǁ

I wrote the following article with Steve Strunsky that appeared in February 1998 in the *New York Times*.

> *The proceeding in Hasbrouck Heights Municipal Court last December 17 lasted mere minutes. Tito Wooten, a star defensive back for the New York Giants, was facing charges that he had choked, beaten, and bloodied his girlfriend, Akina Wilson. Wilson, who had told the police that she was pregnant when the December 7 incident occurred in a New Jersey hotel room, appeared in the courtroom alongside Wooten.*
>
> *In a move that prosecutors later conceded was unusual, Pasquale F. Gianetta, Wooten's lawyer, was allowed to speak on behalf of both the accuser and the accused. Gianetta told Judge Harry Chandless that Wilson wished to drop the charge. The prosecutor, Frederick Allen, despite a police report that stated that Wooten had pushed Wilson to the floor, punched her in the face, and "choked her by the neck with his hands," spoke briefly with Wilson and then agreed that the charges be dismissed. There was no mention of the fact that Wooten had twice before been arrested*

on charges of assaulting women. The idea of counseling was not brought up.

The judge instructed the couple to be "careful not to cause any similar conduct" and, in closing the hearing, remarked to Wooten, "Have a good game."

[Christine Hansen, executive director of the Miles Foundation, a Connecticut-based organization that provides domestic abuse services to the military community, said the judge's commentary resembles that of judges when a uniformed service member appears on similar matters in military court, particularly since the deployment of troops following the September 11, 2001, attacks.]

Wooten did have a good game four days later against the Dallas Cowboys, and earlier this month the Giants signed the fourth-year emerging defensive star to a long-term contract worth $8 million.

But the 26-year-old Wooten's arrest on charges of assaulting Akina Wilson was only the latest in a series of arrests and assorted other misconduct for a player living at the margins of accountability. And so in signing Wooten, a promising player but hardly a marquee performer, the Giants appear to have again demonstrated how much a professional sports franchise is willing to countenance—and gamble financially—in the name of talent.

The National Football League, like all professional sports, has always had its share of troubled, even criminally violent players. In the last five years, at least 37 current or recently retired NFL players have been arrested or accused of family violence crimes, from assault to kidnapping. Those incidents clearly contributed to the NFL's adopting a domestic violence policy last year for dealing with its players, although the policy leaves it to individual teams to impose any mandatory counseling.

Akina Wilson's life ended shortly after the December court hearing when she committed suicide at the age of 22. She was found dead on January 10 of carbon monoxide poisoning on the floor of Wooten's garage in West Paterson, New Jersey, his Mercedes 550 sedan idling alongside her. There is no way to say what led Wilson to kill herself, but friends and family said her final months were not easy, at least in part because of her volatile relationship with Wooten.

Wooten has been arrested five times over the last six years, once on charges of assaulting his wife, once on charges of beating another girlfriend, once on charges of stealing a car. Wooten, who was expelled from both the University of North Carolina and Northeast Louisiana University, has also been repeatedly fined by the Giants for violating team policies. Once, according to current and former team officials and an NFL executive, Wooten was found intoxicated and asleep behind the wheel of his car on the New Jersey Turnpike.

But Wooten, who has twice pleaded guilty to reduced charges, has wound up only paying modest fines. In New Jersey, prosecutors have twice agreed to dismiss the domestic violence cases—the women involved refusing to testify or asking to withdraw the charges. And both the Giants and the NFL, while saying that they have held to league policy, say that Wooten has never been disciplined beyond being ordered to seek occasional counseling.

Ernie Accorsi, who was recently named general manager of the Giants, said the decision to sign Wooten was approved by the club's owners, Wellington Mara and Robert Tisch.

"The organization tries to take great care in these situations," Accorsi said. "We made a decision based on the information we had."

Wooten declined to be interviewed for this article, but issued a statement through the Giants that read in part: "I've had a lot of pain and hurt in my life. A lot of people have to deal with those kinds of things in their lives. I've made mistakes. I've done things I'm not proud of. Again, like a lot of people, if I could change things in my life, I would, but I can't. I can only move forward."

Meanwhile, in Teaneck, New Jersey, Akina Wilson's parents are bitter—both about what they say was Wooten's abuse of their daughter and by the Giants' decision to reward him with a multimillion-dollar contract.

"I am not going to sit here and tell you my daughter was the *perfect child, but she was trying to improve her life," said Joyce Wilson, who said her daughter was anxious and confused about her immediate future. "When she met Tito Wooten, everything got worse for her. He may have been this big-time football player, but to me he was a coward who would beat up my daughter. I will always wonder why she put up with him and what made her feel like she had to die and what could have been done to help her."*

Tito Wooten was born in Goldsboro, North Carolina, in 1971. His mother, then only 14, left him to be raised by his grandmother, Callie Wooten. Wooten became a star football player at Goldsboro High School and went on to the University of North Carolina. Once there, though, he wound up declared academically ineligible by the end of his freshman year. He then wound up in jail.

On July 9, 1992, according to police and court documents, Wooten was arrested for allegedly stealing a 1988 Honda Accord. He was charged with felony larceny and jailed. He later reached a plea agreement and paid an undisclosed fine, but was expelled from the university.

Wooten next enrolled at Northeast Louisiana. But he was arrested on charges of assaulting his wife, Brenda. Wooten agreed to pay a fine, court records in Monroe, Louisiana, show. He was expelled and soon entered the 1994 NFL draft. The Giants selected Wooten in the fourth round. Wooten, despite a number of girlfriends, remains married to Brenda, though she does not live with him.

"Tito, if you ask me, is a good person," said Ed Zaunbrecher, the football coach at Northeast Louisiana. "I don't think he looks for trouble, but he is one of those guys who just seems to always be in trouble."

Wooten's troubles with the Giants, current and former coaches said, took myriad forms and often involved an inability to handle his finances. But he performed well on the field, becoming one of the team's most valued defensive players.

Wooten, according to records and the accounts of team officials and hotel managers, has lived a nomadic life as a member of the Giants. In four years with the team, he has had seven addresses in northern New Jersey and has spent parts of every season living in hotels around Giants Stadium in East Rutherford, New Jersey.

One reason for the repeated moves and the hotel stays appears to have been Wooten's problems managing his money. Despite making from $200,000 to $400,000 a year, Wooten has been sued at least twice for failure to pay his bills—once by a car leasing company, Blasko Auto Leasing, and once by Prime Hospitality, a firm seeking payment of a hotel bill. Once in 1996, Sam Calello, the manager of the Harmon Meadow Holiday Inn, filed a criminal complaint for theft of services against Wooten, dropping the charges once the player's agent paid the $2,000 bill.

His troubles, though, went beyond paying his bills. In November 1995, he missed a mandatory bed check before a game against the Arizona Cardinals, said a former coach. That year, having acquired the nickname Thug Life among his teammates, Wooten, with $1,000 in fines, led the team in violations of rules.

One night in the 1996 season, Wooten was found by the police inebriated and asleep behind the wheel of his car on the shoulder of the New Jersey Turnpike, say former team coaches and officials and an NFL executive familiar with Wooten's history. While officials with the police said no record of an incident existed, the former Giants officials said Wooten, whose driver's license was then suspended, was taken to a state police station house for the night and returned to Giants Stadium the next morning. No arrest was made, and the Giants did not discipline Wooten.

Meanwhile, Wooten was becoming more of a force on the field.

"We looked at Tito as someone who could have been one of the top three safeties in this league," said one of Wooten's former assistant coaches, who spoke on the condition of anonymity. "That's why he was able to get away with so many things."

The coach concluded: "Those are the facts of life. Anyone who says every player is treated equally, that's a lie."

The Giants, who often say they weigh personal character

very seriously in their personnel decisions, have made exceptions. Lawrence Taylor's troubled personal life did not prevent him from enjoying a long career with the team. And last year, the Giants signed Christian Peter, a defensive lineman with a history of violent problems with women, although they went to great lengths to portray Peter as rehabilitated.

Clearly, the Giants recognize they have taken a risk with Wooten. In one measure of concern, Wooten's agent, Ted Marchibroda Jr., has power of attorney. The contract also links $1.5 million of the $8 million to demands that Wooten remain chiefly in New Jersey throughout the year—working out under the supervision of team officials.

But Marchibroda said there was a fuller picture of Wooten. "As long as I've known Tito, he has been nothing but a good person," Marchibroda said. "He has a good heart." Marchibroda added, "He is one of those guys who does a lot of good things but doesn't talk about it."

Jim Fassel, who took over as the Giants' coach in 1997, said he was prepared to be tough with Wooten.

"We are not going to baby-sit Tito," Fassel said. "I just came into this guy's life. I know since I came here he has done what I have asked him to do. He has not been perfect, but he is trying to change his life."

Tito Wooten's most serious problems with the law have involved incidents or allegations of domestic violence—problems that began in college.

On April 27, 1994, according to police records, the police were called to a parking lot outside a Northeast Louisiana dormitory. Wooten and his wife, Brenda, were fighting.

The responding officers saw Wooten punching his wife in the face. Wooten, the records say, also struck one of the officers. Wooten was arrested on charges of battery of his wife, battery of a police officer, resisting arrest, and drunken and disorderly conduct. Larry Ellerman, the school's public safety director, said Wooten paid a fine and court costs after pleading guilty to assault-

ing the officer. Brenda Wooten did not ultimately press charges. Tito Wooten was expelled from the university.

Wooten's second arrest on charges of assaulting a woman came two years later. On August 18, 1996, the police in Hackensack, New Jersey, responded to a call of domestic violence. Lydia Urbina, a girlfriend, told the police that the 195-pound Wooten had grabbed her by the throat and thrown her over a couch, Deputy Chief Edward G. Koeser said.

Wooten was arrested, and Urbina and her family all sought and were granted a protection order against Wooten. But Urbina declined to testify against Wooten. George Geyer, Urbina's father, said in a recent interview that his family had feared for its safety. But he said that his daughter was currently involved with Wooten again and that "everything is fine now."

The hearing in Hackensack Municipal Court on dismissing the charges lasted barely minutes. The municipal prosecutor, Michael A. Gallucci, said the state wished to drop the charges. Wooten was ordered by Judge Louis Dinice to pay $200 in court costs. Gallucci did not return repeated telephone calls, and a spokeswoman for Judge Dinice said he would not comment.

Roughly a year later, early last December 8, Wooten was once more arrested, this time inside Room 294 of the Holiday Inn in Hasbrouck Heights, New Jersey.

Akina Wilson, who had told friends she was two months pregnant with Wooten's child, told the police that she had argued with Wooten when he tried to question her about where she had been that night. According to the police report, Wooten knocked her to the floor, punched her in the face, and choked her. The police report said Wilson was found with "obvious cuts on her hands" and blood under her nose.

Wilson signed a criminal complaint against Wooten and was granted an order of protection. However, the police, who state officials said were obligated to sign the complaint as well, did not. Chuck Davis, a spokesman for the New Jersey Attorney General's Office, said the police have to sign a complaint when there is evidence of abuse to protect victims from intimidation from their abusers.

According to family, friends, and hotel employees, the relationship between the football player and Wilson included frequent, often dangerously bitter fights. While Wooten rented a condominium in West Paterson, Wilson and Wooten often lived at the Hasbrouck Heights Holiday Inn Hotel in a room that the hotel manager said was paid for by the Giants.

John Thomas, Wilson's cousin, said that he often heard the two arguing viciously. Joyce Wilson said that she had urged her daughter to break off the relationship, but that Akina Wilson was "in awe of him because he was a football player." Randy Antiporda, a night manager at the Holiday Inn, said he frequently heard fighting and loud noises from inside the room, often with Wilson's voice being the loudest.

When the case against Wooten came to Hasbrouck Heights Municipal Court last December 17, the hearing again was brief.

Allen, the Hasbrouck Heights municipal prosecutor, said the police told him there were no serious injuries, despite the detailed reports that stated otherwise. Allen, in an interview, said there was "a gray area of what is signs of abuse." Judge Chandless in an interview said that he granted the dismissal in part because Akina Wilson had already agreed to withdraw the order of protection.

"What I really was concerned about was whether she really was injured and whether she really wanted to withdraw these charges," Allen said. "Whether she wanted to continue the relationship, I don't think that's any of my business. She seemed very self-assured."

Evan Stark, a professor of public administration at Rutgers University at Newark and the director of the domestic violence training project at Yale New Haven Hospital in Connecticut, said many New Jersey domestic violence cases wind up dismissed in much the same way.

"I've been in New Jersey courts and it's unbelievable to

watch," he said. "The judge asks, 'Is it okay now?' and the batterer is standing right next to her, and she says, 'Yes.'"

The NFL's policy on domestic violence demands that any player accused of a violent crime submit to counseling. A failure to do so can result in fines or suspensions. A conviction for such a crime can result in suspension, and a second conviction can result in being banned from the game.

Officials with the Giants said their team psychologist, Joel Goldberg, has helped coordinate some counseling for Wooten over the last two years, although they said it had not been continual and they could not describe its exact nature.

Joe Browne, a spokesman for the league, said confidentiality concerns prevented him from discussing how much counseling Wooten had received and whether it had met the spirit of the league's policy. Browne said the policy was "working well."

Akina Wilson's mother, disbelieving, read about Wooten's contract this month in the newspaper. Wooten, she said, had never telephoned after her daughter's death. He even refused, she said, to drop off her remaining belongings, choosing to simply turn them over to the police.

For Joyce Wilson, what Wooten said publicly after his arrest for assaulting Akina had been proven right.

"I've been here and I've been in trouble a couple of times," Wooten, talking of his Giants future, said shortly after his arrest. "They understand that sometimes I have a temper and can get a little bit out of control. But they tend to look at people as football players. They want to leave it up to me. I'm a grown man."

II

It is not solely the players themselves or the teams that make excuses for athlete batterers. Sometimes it is the media. A few days after the Wooten story was published, the *New York Post* was given access to Wooten by the public relations staff, and a more sympathetic story about Wooten was penned. The newspaper quoted Wooten as saying he was a "good person" and that the blood on Wilson was from a broken fingernail. The newspaper described Wooten as a player who "smiles and giggles often" and "likes cartoons."

The Giants eventually realized that their giggling, cartoon-loving woman-beater was not going to change his ways, and they finally released him in 1999. Now, at this point, shouldn't teams know to stay away from such a troubled player? Don't teams learn their lessons?

In this case, no. "It's all about talent," says former coach Jimmy Johnson, who himself has signed players with questionable backgrounds. "Sometimes those of us in the football business put blinders on." The Indianapolis Colts signed Wooten to a multimillion-dollar contract just a few short months after New York had decided to cut the cord. His stay in Indianapolis lasted less than a year. The Colts gave Wooten the boot in December 2000. First, they suspended him for four games following an incident in which he and a teammate went on an all-night partying spree in Atlantic City, New Jersey, the evening before a game at Philadelphia, and missed bed check, as well as a meeting the next morning. Wooten is now out of the league. His wife Brenda filed for divorce in 2002.

The attitude of some organizations is changing. There are franchises that are unwilling to draft scoundrels, or at the very least, that select them lower in the draft, where there is less financial risk. In 1998 wide receiver Randy Moss fell to the Minnesota Vikings with the 21st selection because of an off-field arrest record that included jail time for battery. His talent should have garnered him one of the top five slots.

In an attempt to avoid nasty surprises, the league checks the backgrounds of rookie prospects. Team scouts talk to dozens of people, asking all kinds of questions. How does he treat other people? Is he punctual? Confident? Polite? Belligerent? Some teams, like the Giants, take even more precautions. Through Career Consultants Inc., founded by Goldberg, they administer two psychological tests. One is a 434-question brain-strainer called the California Personality Inventory that asks questions like, "Do you want to harm animals?" and, "Which color do you like better—blue or pink?"

After testing the Giants' rookies for more than two decades, Goldberg has devised his own test. Six sample questions include:

1 How many of your friends and family have been convicted of a crime? Please explain.

2 The last time I was arrested was? Please explain.

3 I wish I was more disciplined in:

4 The three words that best describe me are:

5 If I did not play football, I would:

6 Tell me about your accomplishments:

While there is more information on players available to teams than ever before, some executives and coaches are still ignoring warning signs. In 1999, as coach of the Dolphins, Johnson, who had won two championships in Dallas, decided to draft running back Cecil Collins in the fifth round. Johnson ignored some problems: Collins had been kicked out of McNeese State for failing a drug test and was arrested twice for fondling women. It was predictable that Collins's tenure as a pro would be short, and it was, lasting less than one season. He was arrested for felony burglary after crawling through a female neighbor's window and watching her sleep. He is currently in jail.

Johnson explained his decision this way to the *Denver Post*: "We made a mistake there. But we needed a running back. Sometimes you can take a player with talent and bad character, or take a player with good character and no talent. You have to make a decision. I knew if it didn't work out my reputation could take a hit, but at that point in my career, I didn't care about my reputation."

Maybe Bill Parcells, the former Giants, Jets, New England, and current Dallas coach, put it best when he said, "If Charles Manson could play, someone would take him."

II

It is difficult to say—impossible actually—if modern NFL players are battering women more now than, say, 50 years ago. No one has tracked these types of cases until recently, so there is no benchmark. What can be said with certainty is that while NFL executives have taken the problem more seriously in the past few years—toughening, slightly, their antiviolence rules—the league has not caught up to the societal trend of prosecuting domestic violence offenders. More rigid state statutes, tougher penal codes, and the Federal Violence Against Women Act confirm that law enforcement has been going after these types of criminals. The harsher, more thorough laws are one of the reasons why in recent years there has been a decline in domestic violence cases among the general population, from 8 per 1,000 people over a decade ago to 3.1 per 1,000 now. Still, the tragedy of men committing violence against women remains a significant one. In 1995 alone 3 million women were battered, and according to a study conducted by the Boulder County Safehouse, a Colorado women's shelter, one-third of the women who are physically assaulted by their partners have endured 16 or more physical beatings before contacting police, half have experienced 6 or more assaults, and fewer than 10 percent dial 911 after the first incident of abuse.

The sports world has not escaped this troubling phenomenon. It seems as though not a week goes by without a professional athlete appearing on the police blotter for attacking his wife or girlfriend. Indeed, we've heard this anger-management song many times before. Here is just a recent, partial list of the lifestyles of the rich, athletic, and allegedly violent from the past few years: Al Unser Jr., Glenn Robinson, Scott Erickson, Jason Kidd, Mike Tyson, Christian Peter, Jim Brown, Riddick Bowe, Corey Dillon, John Daly, William Perry, José Canseco,

Michael Pittman, Darryl Strawberry, Rod Smith, Mario Bates, Mustafah Muhammad (the football player, not the boxer), Denard Walker, and Warren Moon.

Football players receive the most attention because their sport is considered the most violent. Many in the sport believe it is judged unfairly, and that the proliferation of media coverage gives the impression that NFL players commit more acts of domestic violence than others. Tagliabue says that, as a group, NFL players are better behaved than other members of society. "The overwhelming number of NFL players are good people and good citizens," Tagliabue says. "We are extremely proud of NFL players as a group. As a league, we need to have, and do have, a wide array of strong programs and policies not just to support our players, but also to hold them accountable to higher standards."

Tagliabue explains that, for example, of the 2,500 players who were in training camp in the summer of 2000, law enforcement officials investigated only 26 for various crimes, while just 11 were convicted. The NFL says that the number of players investigated and convicted of crimes has steadily declined in recent years.

"If the rest of society can do as well as we do in the NFL, America's crime problem will be well addressed," Tagliabue says.

Still, there are theories that exposure to long-term aggression can increase the risk of a person becoming more violent toward others, especially women. Few fans truly understand just how violent a player's world has been, and has become, with bigger, stronger men suffering from brutal collisions. "When you think about it, it is a strange thing that we do," Redskins linebacker Jessie Armstead says. "During a game we want to kill each other. Then we're told to shake hands and drive home safely. Then a week later we try to kill each other again."

How players deal with that weekly cycle, punctuated by three hours of cold-blooded fury, is an unnerving and largely unstudied chapter of life in the NFL. But it is apparent from interviews with hundreds of players, as well as team officials and psychologists, that a significant number of players are not able to leave that fury on the field. The up-and-down cycle of the NFL may affect a player's long-term mental health and cause strains in his personal relationships, leading to domestic violence.

"Football can take more years off a player's life than drug abuse," Chris Shannon, a sports therapist who has worked with dozens of NFL players, once told me. "I find that football players spend so much time gearing up for the violence, they have no energy left for anything else in their lives."

Psychologists who work with NFL players say that a lengthy football career may permanently change some players emotionally. John Hannah, the Hall of Fame guard who played for the New England Patriots from 1973 to 1985 and is now an investment banker, once told me that he still seeks counseling occasionally to help him cope with the absence of the adrenaline rush he would feel during his playing days more than 15 years ago. Hannah said that during one game he ran downfield, full speed, and crashed head-on into a defender. After the collision Hannah felt a ringing in his ears. When he attempted to take off his chinstrap, he could not, because the helmet was cracked almost in half.

And that is just the violence that fans and the media see. Often there is much more, a sort of second-by-second, play-by-play battle for physical and psychological supremacy that goes unnoticed by the public. There are bites that nobody sees, punches in the stomach that are lost amid the furious action, and illegal leg-whips that officials miss. One player said that he once urinated on an opponent on the field and that no one noticed except the other player, who responded with a swift kick to the groin on the next play.

Offensive lineman Jumbo Elliott remembers going against Bryan Cox prior to the linebacker's leaving the Chicago Bears and joining Elliott on the Jets. Elliott smashed hard into Cox on one play, sending him toppling backward. As they both fell, with the 300-pound Elliott on top, Cox punched Elliott in the ribs several times. When they hit the ground, Elliott grabbed Cox around the throat and, with his face inches away from Cox's, asked a simple question. "Do you know who's in control of this situation?"

It is difficult to walk away from that violence unscathed. Some players do, many do not. For the latter, the effects of experiencing such collisions can last months and years. Harry Carson, a Giants linebacker from 1976 to 1988, says he stayed wired for two months after the Giants won Super Bowl XXI. Another former player says he became addicted to the violence. Craving a physical pounding, he attacked his two Rottweilers, both weighing more than 125 pounds, hoping to instigate an attack. The dogs bit him on his hands and arms.

Hannah explains to me that he sometimes speaks with Vietnam veterans seeking advice, because football players can suffer the symptoms of post-traumatic stress disorder. "There are cases where the post-traumatic stress in players rivals that of men who have come back from wars," Shannon says.

And like soldiers who cannot manage day-to-day family relationships, football players may not be able to handle marital stress. That may be why divorce is a significant problem among players, according to a National Football League Players Association study. In the 1989 survey of former players, 50 percent of those who responded said playing in the NFL caused problems in their personal lives; that figure was 30 percent in 1970. About 33 percent of the respondents said they were divorced. Some therapists who work with NFL players believe the divorce rate in professional football is now over 60 percent, beating the national average by over 10 percent.

One reason for the high rate of separation, therapists say, is that players want to take the same risks in their personal lives as they do when they play. An extramarital affair may be a way to recapture the excitement of a blocked punt or a touchdown run.

"There are probably a lot of arguments between players and their wives," former NFL player Matt Millen, now the general manager of the Detroit Lions, once said to me in an interview. "It happened with my marriage. You have to be selfish, getting ready for a game that only a handful of people understand. It's tough on the people around you."

Millen retired in 1992, after playing for the Raiders, the 49ers, and the Redskins, but his playing days often come flashing back. Millen remembers that in 1998 he was playing a game in the family's swimming pool with his teenage son. When his son started to beat him in the game, Millen began to feel the competitive urges again. He started to pile up points against his son. Millen's wife suddenly yelled, "Matt!" "Dad," Millen's son told him, "you're sick."

II

Football is often compared to war. While the comparison is clearly wrongheaded, there is one link to examine when juxtaposing the two: domestic violence, which occurs with alarming regularity in both occupations, and its possible link to occupational violence.

When four women were killed by their soldier husbands during a six-week span in 2002 around the sprawling community of Fort Bragg, Georgia, home of the Army Special Forces Command, it highlighted the problem of domestic violence in the military. Christine Hansen, the executive director of the Miles Foundation, said the congressionally mandated Defense Task Force on domestic violence created in 1999 resulted from studies indicating that spouse abuse in the military increased to 25.6 per 1,000 soldiers in 1996, up from 18.6 six years earlier. Meanwhile, during that same time period, the overall number of abuse cases was declining slightly in the general population.

Psychologists and domestic abuse counselors say there are a number of theories as to why domestic violence rates are higher in the military, and three of them could also be applied to football.

1 **Power and control.** Hansen says that extensive Department of Defense studies show that prior to and following deployments there may be increased risks of domestic violence. Hansen believes the explanation stems from issues of power and control. A spouse may have become more independent and developed more resources on her own in the time that a soldier has been away, and when the soldier returns, he wants to reestablish the control he had prior to leaving.

In the NFL the football field is the place a player controls. Even during a loss the player still has a large degree of control because he is exerting his will on other players by tackling them or running by them or catching a pass on them. Following a game, is it plausible that an NFL player wants the same kind of controlled situation at home that an NFL game provides?

2 **Fear.** In the military, abusers may control their victims by manipulating their fear of consequences if they tell the truth about what is happening at home. Hansen says she hears such threats all the time. For example: "'You'll ruin my career. You won't have any money. You won't have a place to live. You and the children will be out on the street.'" Two congressionally mandated studies found that the primary barrier to reporting domestic violence in the military is fear of loss of benefits.

An NFL player's wife told me that following a 2002–2003 pre-season game, her husband, a player for an NFC East team, pushed her to the ground during an intense argument. When she threatened to call the police, the player's response, she says, was to remind her that she had no money of her own and his career was the only thing that "paid the bills." She claims her husband also said: "I'll get kicked out of the league and you won't have a roof over your head."

3 **Lack of prosecution.** Although exact statistics are not kept, experts believe that less than 5 percent of military domestic violence cases result in the initiation of court-martial charges.

In the year 2000 four NFL players were punished under the league's Personal Conduct Policy:

- *Mario Bates of the Detroit Lions was suspended for one game for pleading guilty to a single count of assault/domestic violence.*
- *Mustafah Muhammad of the Indianapolis Colts was suspended for two games after a conviction for one count of domestic battery. He was sentenced to a suspended one-year jail term, placed on one year's probation, and ordered to perform community service and participate in domestic violence counseling. When the case went to court, Muhammad's six-year-old stepson took the witness stand. The boy talked about hearing his mother screaming, then seeing Muhammad twisting her arm and shoving her against a windowsill. The boy went to his toy chest. He got a plastic bat. "I wanted to stop Daddy from hurting my mommy," the boy said. His mother was five months pregnant with the couple's second child.*

- *Denver Broncos wide receiver Rod Smith was charged with third-degree assault and harassment charges. In a deal with prosecutors, he pled guilty to a misdemeanor count of verbal harassment. The NFL fined him $25,000, but the fine was conditional: if he adhered to the terms of his two-year probation, it would be revoked. He did, and it was.*

- *Denard Walker of the Tennessee Titans was suspended by the NFL after pleading guilty to assault in a domestic violence incident and receiving a one-year period of probation and counseling. The league at first suspended Walker for two games but then reduced it to one after he appealed.*

These cases are all interesting because they prove, first, that players are not severely punished by the courts or the NFL for committing domestic crimes and second, that the players do not fear repercussions from the league. Indeed, what eventually got Wooten kicked out of football was missing a bed check—not his repeated violence against women. As of late 2002, just six players have been suspended for domestic violence—five for one game, one (Muhammad) for two games—since the league's more aggressive anticrime policy went into effect in 2000.

||

Richard Lapchick, the respected sports sociologist who helped found the Mentors in Violence Prevention program that works with college and professional teams, says that an average of 100 arrests for domestic violence involving collegiate and pro athletes have been reported each year for the past five years through 2002. Based on the tens of thousands of athletes in college and professional sports, that is a tiny percentage committing acts of domestic violence.

In the general population there are between 960,000 and 3 million annual cases of violence against women by their husbands or boyfriends nationwide, according to experts. As many as 3 percent of all men might be batterers. "There's no question there's a perception among the public, and even among athletes, that athletes are more inclined to be sexually violent than non-athletes," Lapchick has said. "I think it's a false perception."

Still, Lapchick explains that he would like to see a year's ban for a first offense and a permanent ban for a second when it comes to any athlete who is convicted of battering a girlfriend or wife. "It's really essential that batterers be banned from sports," he explains. "Not because there's a disproportionate number of athletes who are involved, but because they're such role models for kids. If kids see athletes get away with hurting a woman, then they might feel that it's okay for them, that they're going to get away with the same thing."

Many athletes are looked up to as heroes. Most people know who Barry Sanders is but cannot identify their U.S. senator. That is the power of sports, and that is why professional football players, the most high-profile of all athletes, should be held to higher standards.

||

It is also increasingly difficult to keep players from committing violent acts, including violence against women, because so many come from extremely dysfunctional backgrounds. Their histories are not excuses for them, but this is simply a fact. Kevin Elko, a sports psychologist who works with NFL and college teams, says that he has interviewed more than 2,000 troubled professional and college football players over the past ten years, and that about 89 percent of them came from divorced households, or households where they rarely, if ever, interacted with their fathers. That lack of initial structure, paired with the trappings of football, including constant pampering by everyone from agents to teams, may cause a player to develop an oversized sense of entitlement, Elko says.

"If I'm a player and I walk on the field and I say, 'This game belongs to me,' that would make me a great ballplayer," Elko says. "Then when I come off the field, I need to turn that emotion off, because if I don't, I can end up in legal trouble. Some players can't. They think everything belongs to them." Goldberg says, "When it comes to crime issues with some athletes, it's all about not getting caught. Not morals, or what's right, just seeing what they can get away with."

Which brings us back to an original point: How do you prevent a player from thinking, as I believe a significant number do, that if he attacks a woman, he can get away with it, then continue his playing career, as players like Phillips and Wooten and Collins and many others have done?

You make the NFL's policies tougher, scarier, bulletproof. Here is how to do it.

1 An initial conviction for violence against a woman, domestic or otherwise, or a plea bargain involving such a crime, would result in a *yearlong suspension without pay*. During the suspension the player would receive extensive counseling, the league would monitor his compliance with protective orders, and the player would also pay for counseling for the victim.

Seems excessive? Consider that a first-time steroid abuser in the NFL is suspended for four games.

2 An accused player who feels he has been wrongly convicted in court can appeal to *an independent arbitrator* agreed upon by the union and the league. The arbitrator would investigate, with expenses paid by taking 1 percent of the league's television revenues, which are $17.5 billion, and placing the money in an interest-bearing account, which would provide an arbitrator with a budget of millions per year, thus funding his or her expenses and investigative staff. The arbitrator would decide the player's administrative appeal, or in essence, his fate. Lastly, the arbitrator would have domestic violence training.

If the arbitrator upholds the court verdict, the player would be suspended. But if he uncovers evidence that convinces him the player should not have been convicted, then the league would have to pay the player treble damages for his pain and suffering. The NFL would take out full-page newspaper advertisements and television commercials in the player's NFL city reporting on the league's findings.

Lie detector tests would also be used to prevent the unthink-able: a couple faking an attack to collect money from the NFL. Such examinations are not infallible, but when combined with the skills of a competent investigator, lie detection testing can be an invaluable tool.

This second step is necessary because, even in domestic violence cases, the court system can make mistakes. Witnesses lie and evidence is tainted or fabricated. In the case of black players, America's courts have historically treated African American men more harshly and unfairly—O. J. Simpson aside.

3 A second conviction or guilty plea for domestic violence would result in a *lifetime ban from the sport.* The same appeals process would apply.

4 If a team signs a player with a previous conviction or suspension for domestic abuse, and the player is convicted a second time, *the team would face a $5 million fine and $5 million salary cap hit.* Hitting the teams in the pocketbook should require them to become more accountable. Too many still gamble on players with questionable backgrounds. These players tend not to be weeded out but to circulate throughout the leagues, like stale air in a house.

5 Develop a *hotline for victims of domestic violence.* An independent office such as the Miles Foundation would run it, and any accusations would be quietly investigated. The player's team would not be notified unless the investigators discovered evidence of abuse. People specifically trained in the field of intimate partner violence would operate the hotline and would also offer resources to victims, including shelter, support, referrals, and advocacy.

6 The NFL should *track the names of players under restraining orders.* Already, the league attempts to keep the identities on file, but the effort is not particularly organized. And police and the league do not coordinate.

These proposals are not suggested arrogantly. I know they will not solve all of the domestic violence issues. Particularly considering that within society overall there are a small number of sociopaths whom no rules or laws can intimidate (and some of these people can fool lie detector tests).

Also, these proposals would surely face legal challenges, including due process, equal protection under the law, and double jeopardy issues. Let these challenges come. Sports leagues are billion-dollar enterprises teeming with lawyers. It's time they took a tougher approach on this issue, even if it involves some peril to them.

Otherwise, there will continue to be more players like Derrick Rodgers, who was so bold in the face of consequences that he had the temerity, allegedly, to punch his wife in a crowded restaurant.

||

I asked three experts to respond to this chapter in general and also reply to my proposals. One is North Carolina–based attorney David Rudolf, the legal representative for former Carolina Panthers wide receiver Rae Carruth and one of the most skilled criminal defense attorneys in the country. The former NFL wideout Carruth was convicted in January 2001 of conspiracy to commit murder and two other charges, and acquitted of first-degree murder, in the shooting death of his pregnant girlfriend, Cherica Adams. Carruth was sentenced to 18 to 24 years in prison and has appealed his conviction. The second is Christine Hansen, who specializes in domestic violence issues. Last is Mitch Abrams, a respected sports psychologist who focuses on the management of emotional states that interfere with peak performance. He has been working with athletes, coaches, parents, and sports organizations for the past eight years and has developed effective programs in anger management and dating violence prevention for athletes of all ages.

Rudolf writes: "As the lawyer who represented Rae Carruth, I read this plan with a different perspective than most. I believed Rae was innocent and continue to believe that he had nothing to do with the death of Cherica Adams. But as we prepared for his trial and did research into the attitudes of prospective jurors towards football players charged with acts of violence towards women, it became clear that we, and the NFL, had a real image problem. The average person believed that professional football players were more likely to commit such acts solely because of their status as professional football players. And I think this perception affected the outcome of the trial (acquittal of murder, conviction for conspiracy to commit murder).

"Thus, I would turn this plan on its head. Rather than there being an NFL appeal from a conviction, an unworkable suggestion that would undermine the credibility of the league's efforts to address domestic violence and could produce bizarre results (like a player serving a prison sentence being found "innocent" by the NFL), I would suggest that there be a mechanism whereby the alleged victims of domestic violence could seek redress from the NFL, regardless of the outcome of the criminal case (or in lieu of bringing criminal charges at all)."

Hansen writes: "The military culture is considered a special population with characteristics such as residential mobility, deployments, financial insecurity, and fear of adverse career impact. The parallels between the military and sports cultures could occupy an entire volume. For example, the development of an employee assistance program to provide counseling and rehabilitation to violent offenders within the National Football League is similar to the programs within the Department of Defense and the service branches (Zero Tolerance Policy and Family Advocacy Program). The clinical or therapeutic approach to serial battering is evident within these approaches to intervention. Also, entitlement and power are evident in both cultures (star athlete with potential and good soldier, sailor, Marine, or Airman)."

Abrams writes: "American culture encourages aggression. From the NFL player to the woman on Wall Street working towards a promotion, our society reinforces aggressiveness without much regard for teaching skills that are necessary to manage the emotions that often accompany such behavior. Athletes tend to be the most popular people in school and often get preferential treatment. When this is engrained from such an early age, it is going to be very difficult to change. It is the main reason why so much attention is given to youth sport. Coaching seminars and parent workshops given by sport psychologists to educate adults on the effects of sport (both positive and negative) are crucial to avoid perpetuation of these tendencies that don't serve the athletes well over time."

||

Back at the symposium, and following the riveting speech by Irving Fryar, an HIV counselor, Sandra McDonald, is speaking to the rookies about sex and making safe choices. She takes a banana and then unfurls a condom over it. She shows photographs of people severely infected with gonorrhea and syphilis and herpes—oh, there is no fuzzy message here. And this is not a rated-G affair. But it gets the players talking, and the questions come firing at McDonald—pop, pop, pop.

"I've heard a lot of horror stories about women setting up guys," one rookie begins. "So, is it true that if a woman puts K-Y jelly in her vagina, it'll like, burn up the condom?"

The beginning of knowledge always starts with the answer—I do not know. That is why the symposium is so important. I have long believed it is one of the best ideas the NFL has ever had. Rookies, some of whom are from drastically depressed backgrounds, learn information that many others take for granted. How well the symposium actually works—specifically in helping to change the attitude of players toward domestic violence—we may not know for years.

THE GAME

7

The 7ᴬ Game

THE GREATEST

Passionate football fans have slugged it out when "debating" who are the best players of all time. Lists like these can become intensely personal. With luck, these choices will not lead to violence. The only rules for my fantasy team: no player can be used twice, and the nominee for best assistant coach ever cannot have been a head coach at any point in his professional career.

And remember—no punching allowed.

Quarterback: John Unitas—High Tops

Following his final game with the Baltimore Colts, John Unitas—he hated being called Johnny—was standing at his locker when the team's public relations director, Ernie Accorsi, approached him. He asked Unitas if he could have his uniform to send to the Hall of Fame.

"You can have everything but the high-top shoes," Unitas replied.

"Do I see a touch of sentiment?" Accorsi asked.

"Fuck no," the hardened Unitas said. "They're just great to cut the grass with."

II

Unitas's impact on football was the equivalent of Ted Williams's on baseball. Unitas was NFL royalty, the league's first larger-than-life thrower, known for his gruff exterior. But as Accorsi said, the lower on the totem pole a person was, the better Unitas treated him.

He was known for his trademark crew cuts, drooping shoulders, and black high-top shoes. Unitas did not look like a great athlete, but no quarterback combined the qualities of toughness, accuracy, and command of a game in the final minutes like he did. Unitas's grit was partly developed after his years of playing semiprofessional football for the Bloomfield Rams, where he was a quarterback and defensive back, earning $6 a game, while also working a construction job as a pile driver. The fields were barren—more glass than grass—and it was not uncommon for Unitas to have cuts all over his body after one of those contests.

His brilliance in Baltimore's classic overtime victory lasting 13 plays—or as they are known in football circles, "13 plays to glory"—over New York in the 1958 title game helped to catapult the NFL into the country's consciousness, to a spot where the sport has remained until this day. When Unitas retired in 1973 following one year in San Diego, he owned almost every passing record. Several still stand, but the most impressive is this one: Unitas threw at least one touchdown pass in 47 consecutive games. The next closest is Dan Marino with 30. Unitas was able to pick apart defenses at will because of his field vision and because he did something that no modern-era quarterback has done since Jim Kelly seven years ago and that Peyton Manning does to a lesser degree: call his own plays for an entire game. "One time when I was playing for the Redskins," says Hall of Fame linebacker Sam Huff, "I called nine different defenses. He beat all nine of them. I didn't want to call any more defenses because nothing worked against him."

His toughness was legendary. Unitas once stuffed mud up his nose during a game to stop massive bleeding. Some of those football injuries would lead to more debilitating ones later in his life. He died from a stroke in September 2002 at the age of 69.

When any discussion of the best pass throwers of all time arises, Unitas must be at the top of the list, followed closely by Joe Montana.

Unitas had some great players as teammates, like the Hall-of-Famer Raymond Berry, but Unitas was the cog that made the Colts machine roll, while Montana was a vital part of the San Francisco offensive system. Unitas won games often by himself; Montana had a lot of help from the greatest offensive system of all time.

Hall of Fame safety Larry Wilson said that Unitas "was one of the people who made this game what it is today. He had the best vision of any quarterback I've ever seen."

Running Back: Jim Brown—Troubled Genius

It's March 2002, and Jim Brown is on the telephone from Ventura County Jail in California, and the sense of irony does not escape him. Normally when Brown, a Hall of Fame running back, steps into a prison, he is counseling inmates, preparing them for the day their sentences will end and they attempt to become functioning members of society. Now Brown is not an adviser who will stay for a few hours, then depart. He is locked up in a cell the size of a walk-in closet. The teacher has become a prisoner.

His voice sounds tired, perhaps one effect of his 14-day hunger strike to protest what he calls an unfair sentence. A judge sentenced him to a six-month jail term after Brown refused to go to court-ordered counseling and perform community service resulting from a conviction for vandalizing the car of his wife, Monique, in 1999. Brown says he has consumed only water since he arrived at Ventura County Jail and that prison nurses plead with him to eat. They tell Brown that if he does not, he risks serious health problems. Brown refuses. "I have not eaten since I've been here," he says over the static-filled line, his first interview since going to jail.

"I'm fasting. I'm on a spiritual fast. That way I am setting the terms of my imprisonment."

What his hunger strike demonstrates is that even at 66 years old, Brown still possesses the qualities, in abundance, that made him one of the most important athletes of our time. Brown's hardened will shaped him into the best professional football player ever, and that same self-confidence off the field made him an unflinching symbol of black pride and self-reliance.

Those qualities have also helped him land in quicksand more than once. The former owner of the Cleveland Browns, Art Modell, once told me that he saw Brown do things on the field he did not think were physically possible, and off of it, "I helped Jim, very quietly, get out of more serious jams than anyone will ever know." Modell would not provide details. But the core of Brown's known problems has been his involvement in a number of incidents of violence against women.

Brown is not thinking about that right now. Asked to describe his cell, he says the only items in it are a bed, a toilet, and a small cardboard box that holds his personal belongings. Brown is in what prison officials call "administrative isolation," which means he must spend 23 hours a day in lockdown.

The man who once ran free on football fields and in political circles now spends all but one hour a day in his 6-by-14-foot cell.

"The prison's rationale for the 23-hour isolation is that they need to protect me because I'm a celebrity," Brown says. "But it's like being buried in a hole."

There are rules he must follow. Prisoners are required to remain fully clothed at all times. He is allowed a shower every two days. He must make up his bed. He must keep his cell clean.

Brown says that the few times he has interacted with other inmates, a group that includes violent criminals, they have been respectful. Many of them know of Brown's work getting troubled youths out of gangs. They leave him alone, in part because of that, but mainly because he is Jim Brown. He has more clout than the president inside these walls.

Brown was sentenced to jail on January 5, 2000, for misdemeanor vandalism after smashing the windows of his wife's car with a shovel. Judge Dale S. Fischer had originally sentenced Brown to a year of domestic violence counseling. She had also ordered him to spend 40 days on a work crew cleaning up streets or to put in 400 hours of community service, pay $1,800 in fines, and serve three years' probation.

Brown refused to go to counseling, saying he did not need it, and the notion of the proud Brown picking up garbage, well, that was never going to happen. So he went to prison. Brown contends that the judge was biased because he is a celebrity, but City Attorney Rocky Delgadillo said his office "pursued this case as we pursue any case."

Every superhero has a gross flaw; with Brown, it is his brutal treatment of women. Five times he has been accused of threatening or attacking women, and five times his accusers have refused to testify against him.

The filmmaker Spike Lee made an appreciative—but honest—documentary about Brown's life called *Jim Brown: All American*. The moving portrait of Brown captures how he became a new kind of black hero, but what gives the film depth is the fact that Lee does not shy away from Brown's problems with women.

One of the most infamous moments in Brown's life was in 1968, when he was accused of throwing Eva Marie Bohn-Chin, a German model, off a second-story balcony. Brown insists she jumped. Other accounts say she fell while trying to climb off after an argument. In her first interview on the subject, she says in the movie: "I was young, good-looking, a person who loved life. Why would I jump?"

Fischer called Brown's attack on his wife's car the worst case of vandalism she had ever seen. In the phone interview Brown does not talk about the incident. But he says he chose jail instead of complying with the probation requests because the judge's sentencing "was wrong, mean-spirited, and not justice. They offered me three deals," he says, "and I refused."

Brown is asked what he misses most about the outside world. He responds by telling a story from a few days before, when he called his wife from prison and asked her to glance into the backyard and see if the new grass Brown had planted before entering prison was growing.

"That's what I miss," he says. "Just being around my family and being at home."

After his release on July 3, 2002, Brown and his wife reconciled and now live together in Los Angeles.

||

Diane Pucin, a columnist for the *Los Angeles Times*, wrote that Brown is a despicable woman-beater, and in her world that is all he is, and all he will ever be. She ripped into several journalists (myself, Bob Costas from HBO, and Bob Ley from ESPN) for offering any sort of positive portrayal of Brown. I have often found in sports journalism that a significant number of white writers like Pucin rarely afford forceful black athletic men the luxury of being multidimensional the same way white athletes with problematic backgrounds are. John Daly, the white professional golfer, is often viewed as a happy-go-lucky goofball, despite an arrest for assault after allegedly hurling his wife against a wall, pulling her hair, and trashing their house. He later pled guilty to harassment and was placed on two years' probation, with a stipulation that he enroll in a domestic violence treatment program. During a practice round before the British Open he was quoted as telling spectators, "I see my ex-wife's face every time I whack the ball."

There are many other examples of this kind of hypocrisy. It is interesting to note that a few days after Pucin's column ran, another *Los Angeles Times* sports writer, J. A. Adande, spoke of Brown's complexity as a human being. Adande is black.

Brown is many things. He is a man who has saved the lives—literally—of hundreds of young black kids, pulling them out of gangs, sometimes by the throat, and transforming some of them into doctors, lawyers, and teachers. In that vein, Brown is a black hero, an American hero, with an activist background that can be traced back to 1960s Cleveland, where he helped found the Negro Industrial Economic Union to help black-owned businesses. Brown is the most physically sturdy, mentally tough, and versatile athlete the NFL has ever seen. He is also a man who refuses to see that he has an unforgivable violent streak when it comes to his intimate dealings with women. In other words, Brown possesses both heroic and troubling qualities, all wrapped in a truly human package.

Running Back: Gale Sayers—Light Speed

No player mastered the art of the wiggle like Sayers. Just when a swarm of tacklers would surround him—*whoosh*—he would squirm out of trouble. At times defenders were simply unable to tackle him. It is said that Sayers was so fast that he was never caught from behind. Sayers's rookie year in 1965 illustrated his all-around talent. He scored a rookie record 22 touchdowns—14 on the ground, six receiving, one on a kickoff return, and one on a punt return. That same season he scored six touchdowns in one game.

Sayers was the best all-purpose back in NFL history, despite playing just 68 career games because of several painful and debilitating knee injuries. It is frightening to consider how much Sayers would have shredded the record books had his career been longer.

Tight End: John Mackey—Runaway Train

Trying to tackle John Mackey was like roping a Kodiak bear. During his 1963 to 1972 career with the Baltimore Colts, Mackey had the speed to dart past defensive backs—and sometimes did—but he preferred running *over* them instead of *around* them. Interestingly, the 224-pound tight end was considered physically huge for his position. Now wide receivers like Terrell Owens, who tips the scale at about 220 pounds, are just as big, and tight ends routinely weigh 250 pounds or more.

Mackey revolutionized the position because, until him, no tight end had combined powerful blocking skills against ends and linebackers, soft, pass-catching hands, and good running skills. The Colts sometimes used Mackey on end-arounds. In 1966, six of his nine touchdowns came on plays of at least 50 yards—unheard-of production from the tight end position. Mackey was soft-spoken, but his game was loud—and historic.

Wide Receiver: Don Hutson—Back to the Future

To understand how far ahead of his time Don Hutson was, savor this statistic: Hutson caught 99 career touchdown passes in an era—his career lasted from 1935 to 1945—when offenses were stuck in the Pleistocene Age. Hutson's startling success was due to his speed. He ran the 100-yard dash in 9.4 seconds, and his quickness—he was a jet engine when wide receivers during that time period ran more like Model Ts—made him the centerpiece of the quick-strike Green Bay offense.

Hutson is one of only a handful of men who could play wide receiver in any decade and utterly dominate.

Wide Receiver: Jerry Rice—Work Ethic

It is 7:00 on a July morning in 1995, and the early-morning clouds of San Francisco have produced a hard, steady rain. Still, the thought of canceling the first half of the daily morning workout doesn't even enter the mind of Jerry Rice.

On this day five people have chosen to work out with him, to get a taste of one of the most legendary and rigorous workout routines in professional sports, one that normally lasts from four to five hours. Players like Detroit running back Barry Sanders and San Francisco Giant Barry Bonds have tried it. And with the exception of Sanders and a few others, most have left with bruised egos and sore bodies. Only a handful can actually finish it; even fewer return for more.

Tiny puddles begin to form on the track at Menlo College in Atherton, about 20 miles south of San Francisco, and the participants in Rice's workout—one of them a reporter—splash through them while doing 20 minutes of stretches and warm-ups. Leading the workout is Rice's trainer, Raymond Farris, who has worked with Rice for nine years and helped him become the hardest-working player in the league and arguably the best receiver ever in the National Football League.

After the warm-ups, the workout shifts to the football field, where Farris has set up a series of cones for the running exercises. The sprints are called "accelerators." One cone is set up 20 yards downfield, and the runners build up steam until they reach the cone. The group then sprints full speed for 60 yards until the next cone, which is the signal to downshift for 20 yards. Rice eventually does 14 of these, each one in perfect form, each one at 100 percent, with no rest in between. He often trains like a rookie fighting for a job—not a guy headed for the Hall of Fame.

Never mind that the San Francisco 49ers' training camp—which most players use to get in shape for the season—is still weeks away. While others pull hamstrings and throw up in the sizzling camp heat, Rice will be simply engaging in some fine-tuning. Never mind that his shoulder is still sore, the shoulder he separated during the 49ers' Super

Bowl blowout over the San Diego Chargers. Never mind that it still burns and won't be completely healed until September. For Rice, the satisfaction is not getting to the top. It is staying there.

The five who have initially joined Rice for the workout make up a smaller group than normal. The rain has kept others in their warm beds. Eventually, the group's jokester, Ricky Watters, shows up at about the seventh accelerator. By now, most of those in the group are beginning to breathe heavily. Rice does not. Before joining in, Watters, the former 49ers running back who joined Philadelphia as a free agent during the off-season, looks to the sky. It is 56 degrees, and the rain has picked up.

Watters has a what-the-heck-am-I-doing-here look on his face. "I wasn't going to come today because of the rain," he announces, "but I knew he'd be here." He points to Rice with humorous disdain. When the next sprint begins, Watters, fresh and cocky, bursts ahead of everyone. Out of nowhere comes Rice. He blows by Watters. At the finish line Watters asks: "Where did the thoroughbred come from?"

Farris laughs in a quiet moment away from the group. "Jerry takes it personal when people come out here and try to beat him," he says.

Rice wants to run more, but the group protests. The rain is now almost a downpour. He grudgingly gives in, settling for an abbreviated version of the outdoor portion of his normal workout. Usually the group will run for another hour or so, scampering up hills, sprinting through agility drills. They also do "pyramids," which are full-speed sprints for 100 yards, then 90 yards, then 80, all the way down to 20. Not today. As others begin walking back to their cars, Rice smacks a few golf balls with the clubs he packed in his bag. Those with him are ready to call 911. Rice is ready to hit the weights.

ll

From the time Rice trounced his early-morning workout partners in 1995, I was convinced Rice was the most impressive athlete I had ever seen live. (I never saw Jim Brown play.) All these years later, as Rice's career has wound down with the Oakland Raiders, that still remains true. And as he has for decades, Rice still runs those hills and hits the weight room with the same vigor he did as a youngster. That's what is striking about looking back at Rice—not much has changed.

Rice turned 40 on October 13, 2002, and during a recent training camp conversation he asks, jokingly, "Do I look too old?" Rice is pinching his waist, which is remarkably slim—about 32 inches—and has the fat content of a rice cake. He then says: "What's too old, anyway?" Good question. Rice finished the 2002 season with 92 catches for 1,211 yards and was the oldest player ever to start a Super Bowl game—in other words, it was another solid Rice year.

Rice's departure from the 49ers was bitter. Clearly, part of him will always be upset about being let go for salary cap reasons. Still, Rice thinks, in the end, his leaving was for the best. "I think it was a blessing in disguise, because I got a chance to start all over again with the Raiders," he explains. "And it was exciting, because the last four or five years with the 49ers, it was just miserable. I went to work and did my job, but I was always looking over my shoulder. You knew [my departure] was coming. But I came here, and it felt like being a rookie all over again."

One of the greatest misconceptions football fans have had of Rice is that he was a speedster. That urban legend gained momentum because Rice was usually so wide open when making a catch and, in his prime, a defender rarely caught him from behind. One scout told me that he timed Rice when the receiver came out of college and Rice never ran faster than a 4.6 40-yard dash. Now most young wide receivers routinely run 4.3 or faster.

What gave Rice the edge over any other receiver ever, as well as any other NFL player with the exception of Brown and Lawrence Taylor, who are, in my opinion, the top two NFL players, respectively, was that Rice used a combination of athleticism, precision, and work ethic better than almost any athlete in any sport. If a cornerback was faster than Rice, Rice's precise route running would give him the edge. If the cornerback was slower or smaller, Rice would overpower him, and the reason Rice was constantly able to beat double-teams—the true measure of a receiver's greatness—was that he used his smarts to find weakness in the coverage, usually by studying films days before the game started.

Mike Shanahan, the skilled Denver coach, tells a story that epitomizes Rice. When Shanahan joined the 49ers as an assistant coach in the early 1990s, Rice was already in his eighth season in football and owned the majority of receiving records. Still, Rice never coasted. Shanahan would see Rice at the team complex, in the off-season, at 8:00 A.M., catching passes from the team's equipment man since no quarterback was working out that early. Then later in the day Rice would sit for hours in the film room watching tape of the top ten receivers in each conference, looking for tips or tricks he might not have conjured up.

Shanahan asked Rice why he was working like a rookie with his career so established. Rice told him, "I want to make sure no one ever catches me. I want to be the best that ever played the game." It was as simple as that.

Offensive Tackle: Anthony Muñoz—Ferocious

My top five NFL players go like this: Jim Brown, Lawrence Taylor, Jerry Rice, John Unitas, and Reggie White. Muñoz is at six—but misses the top five by just a hair. Off the field, Muñoz is a charitable, generous person and outstanding father. On it, he was the meanest son of a bitch there was. Once Muñoz started a block, he finished it, pushing and wrestling until the defender was on his back, staring up at Muñoz like a turtle that had just been flipped. For being so large, standing at 6-foot-6, 278 pounds, he displayed astonishing quickness. It was that combination of toughness and skill that made him the best offensive lineman to ever play, and Muñoz is the biggest reason why the Cincinnati Bengals made two Super Bowl appearances in the 1980s.

Offensive Tackle: Forrest Gregg—Equilibrium

This position could only go to one of two players—the Giants' Roosevelt Brown, who played from 1953 to 1965, or Forrest Gregg, the Green Bay Packer whose career lasted from 1956 to 1971. Gregg gets the edge over Brown—barely—because of what the best football coach in history said of him. The hypercritical Vince Lombardi called Gregg "the finest player I ever coached." Gregg played on teams composed of superstars, plus Lombardi rarely served up such superlatives, which should put in perfect perspective just how good Gregg was.

Gregg had the footwork of a much smaller player and mastered the art of using balance and leverage to attack defenders, skills that helped him overcome his light frame. At 6-foot-4 and 249 pounds, he was not as physically strong as many of his opponents, but he outmaneuvered them, using his quick feet to reach a point of attack faster than the defender. But Gregg was more than a ballet dancer in shoulder pads. Gregg was tough, playing in 187 straight games and winning five consecutive NFL championships and two Super Bowls.

Guard: John Hannah—Blunt Force Trauma

When Hannah pulled on sweeps, it was like a bulldozer demolishing a row of tents. He crashed into linemen with a controlled but ruthless abandon. Hannah instilled fear into players like few men in football could and was the focus of the New England Patriots running game that rushed for a record 3,165 yards in 1978. Behind Hannah the Patriots made an appearance in Super Bowl XX.

Guard: Gene Upshaw—Union Label

Upshaw's ascension from bone-crushing player to union leader shocks no one who has known him. He was a manager on the field—offensive team captain in just his third year in football in 1969—as well as off of it. When a fellow Raider, or any other player in the sport, needed advice, Upshaw was always welcoming. He is one of the few players capable of dominating his opponents while simultaneously staying immensely popular, which allowed him to become executive director of the union. Perhaps this quote from the legendary Raiders owner Al Davis, which appeared in *The Sporting News*, sums up Upshaw best: "Any time you come into an organization as a rookie, you start all but one game for the next fifteen years, your team goes to the Super Bowl in your first year and then two more times, you play with some of the greatest players who ever played the game and you rise above at least 95 percent of them—you've accomplished something remarkable."

Center: Mike Webster—Aftershocks

Mike Webster was the kind of football player who treated pain as if it were an insignificant pest. As a member of the Pittsburgh Steelers from 1974 to 1988, he played the frenetic and extremely violent position of center. Teammates considered him indestructible.

Known as "Iron Mike" because he played six straight seasons without missing an offensive down, Webster endured numerous shots to the head, sustaining multiple concussions, but seldom took a game off. When Webster died last year at age 50, in the coronary care unit of a Pittsburgh hospital, much of the focus was on his mental state, which a psychologist said resembled that of a punch-drunk boxer because of his years of punishing hits. Webster had become a prime example of the mental and physical deterioration that repeated head trauma can produce over the long term in a National Football League veteran.

"Late in Mike's life, his thinking was completely disorganized," Fred Krieg, a clinical psychologist who examined Webster several years ago, said shortly after Webster died. "He was having a difficult time performing the simplest of tasks."

While the damage to his mental capacities was significant—and, of course, sad—Webster's death also exposed what may be an even greater health risk to NFL players, in particular offensive linemen like Webster: heart disease.

After the players' union expressed concerns that some of its members were dying prematurely, the National Institute for Occupational Safety and Health studied the medical records of more than 7,000 NFL players who had played in the league between 1959 and 1988. The study found that offensive and defensive linemen had a 52 percent greater risk of dying from heart disease than the general population; it also determined that linemen had three times the risk of dying from heart disease as other football players. The cause of Webster's death was a heart attack, according to the Steelers and his son Garrett.

Webster, who won four Super Bowls in his first six seasons with the Steelers, suffered from brain damage that was not diagnosed until well after he retired in 1991. Krieg says his examinations of Webster over a nine-month period in 1998 revealed that Webster had sustained damage to the frontal lobe of his brain because of the hits he took on the field.

In 1999 Webster was charged with forging a prescription for Ritalin, a drug used to treat hyperactivity in children. Krieg says Ritalin had been prescribed for Webster because it increases the flow of serotonin to the frontal lobe of the brain, which improves attention span. Krieg says Webster had lost his "executive functions"; his memory was faulty, and sometimes he could not remember basic details of his life, a result of dementia. Webster sometimes lived in his car or occasionally slept in bus or train stations. When he died, he had been living with his son Garrett, a high school senior who is himself a football lineman.

‖

The depressing, final years of Webster's life should not overshadow what was an iridescent career. Webster gets the nod over Miami's Dwight Stephenson because he won four rings in a six-year period. He was a winner on a team of winners. I hope Webster's life will serve as a cautionary tale to today's players and to league and union officials: no one should downplay or ignore the potentially devastating health problems NFL players face.

Defensive End: Deacon Jones—Sack Attack

Jones, who spent most of his career with the Los Angeles Rams, from 1961–1971, is the father of the prototypical pass rusher. Every great modern defensive end who followed Jones—from Reggie White to Bruce Smith to Charles Haley to Michael Strahan—owes his career to him. Jones originated the word "sack" and was so overpowering that offenses began to triple-team him, the first player to force such a strategy. Jones used the head slap as a brutal weapon; he sometimes knocked a lineman into a state of wooziness. (The NFL later banned the move.)

For 14 years Jones dominated the league with his physical ability, handling himself with a sparkling cockiness and sense of humor.

Defensive End: Reggie White—Minister of Defense

The sole weakness in Reggie White was his mouth, which sometimes spewed antigay remarks over the course of his career and in the years following his retirement after the 1998 season. On the field there has never been a defensive lineman with White's combination of muscle, speed, and athleticism. When I watched White play, I would swear the 290-pound player moved with the speed of a running back or wideout.

White could choose his poison. He had the power to plow through linemen and the swiftness to edge around them. At the height of his career, when he played on the Buddy Ryan–coached Philadelphia Eagles, no single offensive lineman could block White. His statistics are eye-popping, especially his NFL-record 192 career sacks. Once, in 1987, he had 21 sacks, just one shy of Mark Gastineau's season record, and he did it in a strike-shortened season composed of only 12 contests.

Despite his occasional venom toward gays, White was one of football's best citizens. White was a leader when it came to helping the oppressed and poor, often doing so with little fanfare. His passion buoyed his faith: he was a licensed Baptist minister. White inspired not just the teams he played for but many times entire communities.

Defensive Tackle: Joe Greene—Steel Curtain

The first pick of the Chuck Noll coaching regime came in 1969 when he plucked Greene out of North Texas State. Noll put Greene on the Steelers' defensive line and built an entire team—indeed, an entire era—around the most hostile player football has ever seen. Greene went to ten Pro Bowls in 13 years and four Super Bowls in six years. He put the stuffing in run stuffer. Many games typify his dominance, but one stands out. In December 1972, against Houston, Greene bruised that offensive line for five sacks, added a blocked field goal, and forced and recovered a fumble.

Away from the game Greene was quick to laugh and had a bright personality, which showed in one of the more famous television commercials of all time—Greene's piece of acting stardom featuring a Coke and a smile. On the football field the only time defenders smiled when facing Greene was at the game's conclusion, when Mean Joe wasn't thrashing them anymore.

Defensive Tackle: Bob Lilly—Mr. Cowboy

Lilly and Greene actually had similar physical playing styles; either man could blow up a perfectly good running game. Lilly was a relentless student of the sport who absorbed a defense's workings by watching game film. He also constantly worked to improve his technique. Lilly was the first Dallas Hall-of-Famer and its best player ever.

Linebacker: Lawrence Taylor—Self-Destruct

The former Giants linebacker Lawrence Taylor, considered by many to be one of the greatest players of all time, was voted into the Pro Football Hall of Fame in 1999 in his first year of eligibility. It's indicative of the notoriety he gained on and off the field that despite a stellar career, many voters felt his history of drug abuse should have kept him out.

The Giants' number-one draft pick out of North Carolina in 1981, Taylor has been arrested three times since his retirement and recently spent time in a drug rehabilitation clinic. Voters worried it would send a bad message if he was enshrined in the Hall of Fame. Taylor didn't help his cause when, in a conference call with the news media in late 1998, he seemed arrogant and unapologetic to some voters. In the end, however, Taylor's remarkable accomplishments on the field, as well as public pleas from the Giants' owner Wellington Mara, Commissioner Paul Tagliabue, and several football writers, proved to be the determining factors. Taylor needed 29 of 36 votes; the final tally was not released, but it was believed that there were at least five members who voted against him.

The voting committee was made up of news media representatives from all 30 NFL cities, plus five at-large members and the president of the Pro Football Writers of America. Normally, in their private meeting to determine the entrants, the committee introduces a nominee and spends six to eight minutes discussing him. When Taylor's name was introduced, several voters said, the committee argued for some 35 minutes and then had to move on to other candidates because the discussion involving Taylor became too contentious.

While the other entrants gave speeches and answered questions after their names were announced, Taylor did neither, instead releasing a statement through the Giants. "I am humbled by being elected to the Pro Football Hall of Fame," Taylor's statement read. "As I have said, I feel like it is the ultimate reward for playing the game that I love so much and gave so much. I appreciate the debate and the consideration that was given my nomination. Ultimately, this honor has to do with how I played the game. Obviously the majority of the committee felt the same way.

"It doesn't always come across, but I do appreciate the well-wishes and concerns of my family, my friends, and my former teammates. It means a great deal to me. It truly does." Taylor added: "I want to thank my coaches, especially Bill Parcells, my teammates, and the Giants' ownership, especially Mr. Mara. I would not be receiving this honor if it weren't for them."

Taylor dominated football for most of his career, which lasted from 1981 to 1993. He went to ten Pro Bowls, was a three-time defensive player of the year, and was named the league's most valuable player in 1986. He had 132.5 career sacks.

He is one of the few who changed the way a position is played. Using a combination of power, speed, and ferociousness, Taylor terrorized offensive lines. Coach Joe Gibbs of the Washington Redskins used an "H-back" player—a hybrid of a tight end and an offensive lineman—almost specifically to counter Taylor, because linemen were too slow to block him. Eric Dickerson recalls facing Taylor during his rookie season in 1983. On one play in that game, Dickerson says, the Rams' coaching staff instructed him not only to block Taylor but also to hit him low and cut him down. "I really didn't want to do that, but I did," Dickerson says. "When he got up, he looked at me and said, 'Don't you ever cut me again.' I said, 'Okay.' "

But Taylor's destruction of offenses on the field was matched by his self-destructive nature off it. He tested positive for cocaine use in 1988 and was suspended for four games. The incidents that put his Hall of Fame nod in jeopardy came once his playing days ended. Taylor was most recently arrested in 1998 for purchasing $50 worth of crack cocaine from an undercover police officer in a St. Petersburg Beach, Florida, hotel room. There were 15 crack pipes in the room, the police said. Taylor claims he was set up. He later changed his plea from innocent to no-contest, choosing not to fight the charges.

Soon after the Florida arrest, Taylor entered a drug rehabilitation clinic in New Jersey, with Mara paying about $7,000 for the visit.

"When the Giants' organization retired my jersey," he says, "I said this then and I'll say it now: there has always been and will be a Lawrence Taylor, but without the fans, there would have never been an LT."

||

The fact that there was even a debate about Taylor's Hall of Fame qualifications demonstrates just how self-destructive he was. If Taylor is not in the Hall of Fame, there should be no Hall of Fame. They should burn the building down. But some of the things he did away from the game were so ugly and distasteful that his nomination gave voters understandable pause. What kind of person are we choosing? What kind of message does that send? I would have voted Taylor in regardless because these are football players and the Hall is an evaluation of football careers—not how many times they went to church or fed soup to the homeless.

The thing that one always wonders about with Taylor is what his career would have been like had he taken care of himself. Taylor abused alcohol and drugs and rarely worked out in the weight room, yet his impact in football was the equivalent of Chubby Checker or Little Richard in music. He changed the sport and spawned a generation of LT wanna-bes. The phrase "he could be the next Taylor" became a common, albeit ridiculous, refrain when a college linebacker with seemingly

LT-like qualities was drafted. No one—not even remotely—has come close to the real deal.

Linebacker: Ray Lewis—The Best Player in Football

It was a warm Saturday night in September 2001 when Baltimore's Ray Lewis, the leader of a middle linebacker renaissance not seen in the National Football League since the days of the single-bar face mask, terrorized his first New York running back of the preseason. When the Jets' Curtis Martin caught a screen pass and began to scramble left, Lewis, in pursuit from the opposite side of the field, evaded two blockers and caught Martin from behind.

That play is one that maybe two middle linebackers in the league have the speed to make, and Lewis does it so often that it is almost taken for granted. Martin is not a burner, but he is fast enough, and Lewis made him look as if he were running in slow motion. Lewis likes harassing New York runners. He did it in Super Bowl XXXV against the Giants by dropping the quick Tiki Barber from behind on another spectacular play, one that defined that game and put Lewis's abilities in neonlike headlines. Lewis was at it again in the Ravens' 38–9 preseason triumph over the Giants on August 31, 2001, when he displayed another side of his on-field persona: the fiery trash-talker.

Lewis began taunting the Giants at the coin toss. The Giants won and chose to receive the ball.

"I don't know why you're taking the ball," Giants players claimed Lewis said, "because that just means I'm going to knock out Dayne faster."

Ron Dayne, the Giants' running back, was never knocked out, but Lewis made his usual assortment of eye-popping plays: hitting hard up the middle, making heart-stopping blitzes, covering fast running backs out of the backfield without help, and displaying his uncanny ability to squeeze his muscular 243-pound frame into running lanes to stop a play cold.

"When I'm on the field, I'm going to let you know that I'm about to make this play," Lewis says. "I'm going to let you know that your running back isn't going to be as productive as you want him to be today. I'm going to let you know, with confidence, and then go do it. People don't like that, especially offensive linemen, where you take their running back, who they block for, and take him out of the game."

For much of football history, the middle linebacker was the most glamorous and most feared position on defense, and second only to the quarterback in overall team fame. The position was made exceptionally popular by a nonpareil group from the late 1950s until about 1970, considered the golden age of middle linebackers. The group featured the player who is considered by many to be the best middle linebacker of all time, Chicago's Dick Butkus, a talented, brutal player who intimidated teams with his hard hits and menacing scowl.

But after Butkus retired, the middle linebacker became less of a factor as teams went from a four-man defensive line front with three linebackers—a scheme that allowed the middle linebacker to be the star—to a 3–4 alignment of three linemen and four linebackers. In the 3–4 defenses, popularized in the 1980s, outside linebackers like Taylor grabbed the glory and importance from the middle linebackers.

Now, as often happens in football, a cycle is repeating itself. The 4–3 is once again the preferred defense, and middle linebackers, like old movie stars making a triumphant return to the screen after a long absence, are again dominating football. As Butkus did, many in this group use intimidation as part of their game, trying to get inside the minds of opposing players with trash talk and aggressive moves. But unlike Butkus and others of his generation—like the Giants' Sam Huff, Joe Schmidt from Detroit, and Ray Nitschke from Green Bay—today's middle linebackers are faster, stronger, and more athletic.

"All players today are stronger and faster," says the Ravens' Modell, who has been a team owner for more than four decades. "That especially goes for the middle linebackers, I think. Today's middle linebackers are excellent and compare with any era."

No one exemplifies the comeback of the middle linebacker better than Lewis, a confident, one-man wrecking machine who is not only considered the best at his position but is also quickly being thought of as the best ever.

"Ray Lewis stands alone," says the Giants' general manager, Ernie

Accorsi, a student of football history. "I've never seen anybody better than him for flying around and disrupting an offense."

Lewis rarely watched middle linebackers while growing up in Lakeland, Florida, and playing at the University of Miami. He modeled himself after playmakers like Taylor and the former San Francisco defensive back Ronnie Lott.

Once the Ravens' coaching staff saw Lewis's athleticism firsthand, they began to devise ways to capitalize on it. The former defensive coordinator, Marvin Lewis, decided to funnel the entire defense through Lewis and give him the freedom to roam the field.

"Traditional linebackers are supposed to hit linemen and beat up fullbacks," Ray Lewis says. "There's a time to do that, but middle linebackers should be allowed to make the plays, and Marvin lets me do that."

The Ravens' winning scheme was simple. They used big defensive linemen—Tony Siragusa at 340 pounds and Sam Adams at 330—to occupy offensive linemen so Lewis could make the tackles. Teams have tried to slow Lewis, but he is too quick for fullbacks to block, and if an offense sends too many linemen after Lewis, his teammates are free to make tackles. Lewis maintains that some offensive players, frustrated that they cannot block him legitimately, have resorted to doing things like twisting his ankles as he lies on the bottom of a pile after a play. But even that has not stopped him.

Much of his game is built not just on the physical but also on the mental. There is no question he has a chip on his shoulder. Lewis was accused in the killings of two men following a 1999 Super Bowl party outside an Atlanta nightclub. The murder charges were dropped, and Lewis eventually pleaded guilty to misdemeanor obstruction of justice and was fined $250,000 by Commissioner Paul Tagliabue.

In some ways Lewis is still vilified, despite being cleared of the killings in court. After winning the Super Bowl most valuable player award last season, Lewis was ignored by Disney, which picked quarterback Trent Dilfer to promote Disney World, despite a track record of selecting 11 of the previous 14 MVPs. Lewis was also not on the cover of the postchampionship Wheaties box, and Siragusa appeared on the cover of the NFL's *Record and Fact Book*, another usual perk for a Super Bowl

MVP. "I'm a good player on the field and a good person off of it," Lewis says. "I can't help what other people think about me."

There is no question that Lewis, who shed 15 pounds in the 2001 off-season to get his body fat down to 3 percent, making him even faster, is the key to a defense that was one of the speediest and most athletic ever. In 2000 Baltimore set an NFL record for fewest points allowed in a 16-game season with 165 by holding four opponents scoreless and not allowing more than a single touchdown in 11 games. In the team's play-off victory at Tennessee, two of the team's three touchdowns came from the defense, including Lewis's 50-yard interception return.

"What I'm trying to do is change the position, the way it is played," Lewis says. "That's what I want my legacy to be. I want to be the best middle linebacker to ever play the game, and I believe I can be.

"I think any legacy that was ever created was over a period of time," he adds. "When people look at that guy and say, 'Wow. He's done it one year, two years, three years, four years, five.' And that's my thing. Every time I step on the field I feel I can get better. Every time I step on the field with my teammates I feel like I can make them play at a higher level because of the way I play. Not to be boastful, but the only way to slow me down is throw deep balls."

Lewis says that while he has tremendous respect for past greats who played middle linebacker, he also believes "only a couple could play today. Nowadays the speed factor is almost out of control. You have running backs literally running 4.2 and 4.3 in the 40. And coaches tell you, 'Cover him.' I mean, do you really think Dick Butkus could cover Marshall Faulk one-on-one?"

It is a controversial statement, but Lewis is so good, he can get away with saying it. Why? He explains it well.

"Because I back up my talk with play," he says.

||

Much has changed for Lewis since Baltimore won Super Bowl XXXV. Coordinator Marvin Lewis traveled an hour south on Interstate 95 to coach Washington's defense, and then moved on to a head coaching position in Cincinnati. Because of the salary cap, the Ravens were thoroughly dismantled, picked apart like a slice of pizza in a college dorm. Lewis no longer has his two globe-sized tackles to clear the lanes for him in Adams and Siragusa, who were let go because they were considered old and expendable. In all, the Ravens lost a dozen starters from that Super Bowl winner, and the Baltimore team switched from the four-man front, which afforded Lewis more protection from his defensive tackles. Now the Ravens play the 3–4 defense, forcing him to work harder for his on-field miracles. What is also different about Lewis is the size of his wallet. In August 2002, he signed a seven-year, $50 million contract extension, which included a then-record $19 million signing bonus. Middle linebackers don't normally see those types of contracts— quarterbacks do. But the deal demonstrated that Lewis shatters any mold or stereotype.

What has not changed is my opinion that he is the best player in the sport now. The argument is definitely debatable. Marshall Faulk from St. Louis, who is reminiscent of Eric Dickerson, and Brett Favre, who possesses the strongest arm and most guts of any thrower in NFL history, are the only two players on the level of Lewis. What puts Lewis a shade above those two is what Joe Gibbs once called the "disruption ability." He was referring to Lawrence Taylor when he used this phrase, but it equally applies to Lewis. Because football is such a team-centered sport, it is difficult for just one player to cause chaos, to single-handedly wreck the other team's plans from play to play, series to series, game to game. Faulk does it, Favre does it. But Lewis does it better than both, and better than any other player in football. I have seen Lewis cause such problems that an offense has a difficult time running the most basic of plays. That is true disruption ability.

One game in the September 2002 regular season typified how great a player Lewis is. On *Monday Night Football*, when Baltimore played the Denver Broncos, Lewis had 11 tackles, one interception, and a key, crushing block on a 107-yard Ravens touchdown return following a missed Denver field goal—*in the first half.* Analyst John Madden called it the most dominant two quarters of regular-season football for a defender since Taylor. All those numbers were racked up despite going against a Mike Shanahan offense, which can be difficult to decipher or disrupt. Lewis would miss the last half of the season with an injured shoulder, but his absence did not deflate my opinion that he is the best player in football.

There is also a strange phenomenon at work when it comes to the perception of Lewis as a player. Because of his involvement in the murder trial and subsequent admission that he lied to police, news media and fans have downgraded his abilities. Lewis is a perfect example of what the NFL constantly tells its incoming players at the annual rookie symposium: your conduct off the field can negatively affect your image on it. Even though Taylor was the best defensive player ever, there was still that intense debate among Hall of Fame voters, most of whom were members of the news media, over whether Taylor's often sordid and troubled life should prevent him from becoming a member. Lewis's legacy may also be tainted in the same way.

And it is not just stained by TV talking heads or print writers. In the months following the murder trial Lewis found himself a target of some ugly taunts from fans. During a preseason scrimmage in August 2000 against the Washington Redskins, Lewis was doing what he always does: hitting hard, running fast, and simply dominating. Suddenly the voice of a fan wearing a Redskins jersey rose over the clang of banging shoulder pads. Other voices joined in. They yelled to Lewis, "We know you did it."

When asked about the taunts, Lewis responds, "They don't play in between the lines. I do. You know what? Guys who yell that stuff aren't fans; they're jerks. I can't let them bother me."

Some of the criticism Lewis receives is more than fair and justified. He lied to the police in a murder investigation. That was a horrendous mistake.

Other criticism is not. I have heard numerous members of the football media and also fans criticize or mock Lewis for his pregame gyrations (his dances look like someone put a firecracker in his jock strap). Some media types state flatly, and somewhat ridiculously, that they will never like Lewis as a player because of them. His jigs never bothered me, though. As a black man who has played sports my entire life, I know that celebrations, dances, a little trash talking, are often part of the game when black people play it. (I never danced because I had no rhythm.) It is all part of having fun and keeping things loose. Other

media members seem personally affronted when Lewis and other athletes celebrate in this manner, thus Lewis loses style points, when in fact
that part of his personality should have nothing to do with evaluating
his abilities.

I once asked Lewis what he thought people would remember him
most for: being a great middle linebacker or wearing that orange jump-
suit and handcuffs in court, facing a life sentence for murder. Lewis
paused for a moment and said, "Probably both."

Linebacker: Dick Butkus—Wrecking Machine

Dick Butkus was nasty. When he hit somebody, it always seemed personal, like the player had stolen Butkus's lunch money—as well as his
momma's. The best way to describe Butkus is that he resembled the Tas-
manian Devil from those Warner Bros. cartoons. When Butkus took the
field, anything and everything was simply destroyed. He was an orgy of
violence.

Opponents both hated and respected him. Butkus wanted to be the
best, and he didn't just talk about it. He lived it. And Butkus had a quality many greats demonstrate: a dedication to his profession that bor-
dered on mania.

Cornerback: Mike Haynes—Blanket Coverage

The first thing you notice when meeting Mike Haynes is that he looks as
if his playing days ended yesterday, not 13 years ago, when he played his
last game for the Oakland Raiders after a seven-year career in New England. He is lean and fit. If the Giants get into a spot this season and
need another cornerback in a pinch, they should give Haynes a call.

Haynes is also smart. His IQ, not his looks, attracted the NFL.
Tagliabue hired Haynes recently to oversee player development for the
NFL. He was previously an executive at the Callaway Golf Company.
Haynes will need that sharpness in the coming years because he just
stepped into one of the toughest jobs in football.

As the NFL's vice president for player and employee development,
Haynes is responsible for the career development of the game's players

during and beyond professional football. That is quite a mouthful. Actually, it is a fancy way of saying that Haynes's main job is trying to keep players out of trouble. Financial trouble, legal trouble, even trouble that cannot be easily categorized. Sure, the program helps players finish their college education, and it also provides internships at top corporations, but Haynes's primary duty is preventing the NFL's more than 2,000 players from ending up as the subject of an ugly headline.

"Young players especially need to be educated about the kind of dramatic lifestyle change they are going to endure when they enter the NFL," he says. "They need resources and a place to turn to for advice. Players have to ask questions, and that's what we're here for."

One of the hot issues in football now, and one Haynes plans to spend an inordinate amount of time on, is getting players to take more control of their finances. Despite years of caution by the league and individual teams, there are still horror stories of players losing millions to scam artists or their own financial representatives and agents.

Players make delicious targets. According to NFL Players Association salary figures, the average yearly income of a professional football player has doubled in the last 10 years to $1.1 million. Such paychecks attract financial advisers to players like ants to sugar. Some of these advisers are good at their jobs, while others are just plain crooks. The union says that in the past three years about 78 players have been cheated out of some $42 million by agents, business partners, and financial advisers.

Perhaps the most obscene case is that of the former agent Tank Black, who was sentenced to five years in federal prison for taking part in a bogus investment scheme that cost dozens of players $14 million. Black swindled one player, Jacksonville running back Fred Taylor, out of his entire $5 million signing bonus. Washington Redskins wide receiver Jacquez Green was taken for $500,000.

"It gets me angry when I think about it," Green says. "I mean, when you set up your portfolio, you count on certain money being there when you retire. I'm not a real big spender, because you just don't know how long you're going to play in this league. I've already played five years, and I wasn't sure I'd last that long when I started out."

What Haynes says he wants to do is spread the word to players that they need to do extensive checks on potential money handlers before forking over their cash. "That is something that we can do for them," he says. "They need to understand that when it comes to their money, they have to be smart. Don't trust anyone just because they say they know what they're doing."

The NFL's security arm will perform background checks on financial advisers at a player's request. The checks usually consist of a public record search for criminal or civil filings.

The NFL considers the symposium so crucial for rookies that players who skip it without a legitimate excuse are fined. One of the speakers on a recent player-conduct panel was Jets safety Damien Robinson, who was arrested for carrying an assault weapon in the trunk of his car while entering Giants Stadium before a game.

"When you're young, you think you know everything," Haynes says. "What the symposium tries to do is have veterans that have been there say, 'No, you don't. Here are some things that will help.'"

II

As a player from 1976 to 1989, he was the thinking man's cornerback. Haynes was relentless in his film study and rehearsed his on-field moves and countermoves based on what he expected his opponent to do. That is why he seldom fell for fakes the way less studious cornerbacks did. Haynes made the Pro Bowl nine times and had 46 career interceptions. Like another great corner, Deion Sanders, when Haynes picked off a pass, he was an electrifying runner.

Cornerback: Deion Sanders—Prime Time

Few in the NFL were fond of Deion Sanders's act. Sanders was flashy and arrogant, and he could rub an opponent's face in the dirt, high-stepping into the end zone after yet another brilliant interception return. But behind the glossy exterior was a devious, cutthroat, and highly clever competitor who would bait receivers and quarterbacks into making game-wrecking mistakes.

The biggest criticism of Sanders was that he could not tackle well, and that was true. I remember one game when Sanders was with the Dallas Cowboys and New York Giants quarterback Dave Brown ran him over. No, tackling wasn't his thing. But that's what linebackers are for. Sanders was a pure cover guy, never giving a wide receiver a millimeter of breathing room, often taking an offense's best weapon completely out of the game. Coordinators, in maybe the greatest compliment to Sanders, sometimes didn't run a pass play his way an entire game, and Sanders excelled in one-on-one coverage without the liberal bump-and-run rules other great corners from past eras used to their advantage.

Safety: Ken Houston—Ballhawk

Houston was an athletic blend of reliability and skill, a durable package who played in 183 consecutive games. His 49 career interceptions were enough to put him in the Hall of Fame, but Houston took back nine of those for touchdowns, including four in the 1971 season. Houston was the premier strong safety of the 1970s.

Safety: Rod Woodson—Fearless

These words from Hall of Fame tight end Ozzie Newsome on Woodson typify the player completely. Newsome told *The Sporting News:* "The biggest thing about Rod Woodson, when the game was on the line and you were flirting with him, you were flirting with danger. That's the best way to describe him. He is a very tough guy. He is not a guy who wears an 'S' on his jersey and struts around. But he is tough. You don't have to question whether you want him in your foxhole or not." Woodson has spent most of his career at cornerback but has also played safety, where his guts and skill make him perfect to play the position.

Punter: Ray Guy; Kicker: Morten Andersen—Boomtown

Guy was the greatest punter of his era, possessing a strong leg that was also capable of pinpoint accuracy. In 1975 he led the NFL with an average of 43.8 yards per attempt. Andersen has been to seven Pro Bowls, the most of any kicker in history, and is one of only three players to ever surpass the 2,000-point plateau.

Punt Returner: Marshall Faulk—Shifting Gears

Having an all-star team without Faulk is like making a mob movie without De Niro. But there is a problem. Faulk can't be placed ahead of Brown or Sayers, and as superb an athlete as Faulk is, he can't play linebacker. There is also the self-imposed rule that a player cannot be used twice—or Neon Deion might go here. So what's an author to do? Put Faulk at punt returner, where his shifty moves, quickness, and power would make him the most dangerous punt return man ever.

Kick Returner: Bob Hayes—Rocket Man

Dallas drafted Hayes in 1965 using a seventh-round pick. The team hoped the Olympic track and field star would be able to turn his speed into a football commodity. It was a long shot that paid off. Hayes's speed as a wide receiver scared defenses so thoroughly that coaches used zone coverage to blanket him instead of man-to-man schemes. In other words, Hayes's swiftness forced an evolution in football. Hayes finished his 11-year career with 71 touchdown catches and a 20-yard average per catch. He is still the only athlete to win both an Olympic gold medal and a Super Bowl ring.

Fans: The Buffalo Bills

The psychotic devotees of the Cleveland Browns, the most vociferous, the most passionate, of any fans in any sport, should win the honor of best fans hands down, or better yet, paws down. (Okay. Green Bay Packers fans are pretty darn good too, but it's easy to root for a team when it constantly wins.) Two recent incidents, however, have sent the Dawg Pound to the back of the pack, where the Philadelphia Eagles fans are caged. (Speaking of Eagles fans, Michael Strahan describes them perfectly. Veterans Stadium in Philadelphia, he says, is "a hellhole. But I like it. It's the only place where you can pull up on the bus and you've got a whole family—grandmother, grandfather, kids, grandkids—flicking you off.") In October 2002, while Browns fans' own quarterback, Tim Couch, was slumped on the field, writhing in pain after a series of hits had left him beaten to a pulp, Browns fans cheered, which is one of the more despicable things fans can do. The year before that lowly incident, it was Browns fans who hurled hundreds of plastic beer bottles at fleeing officials after a controversial call.

At the top are Bills fans, perennially dedicated, mostly well behaved, who come to the games and pack the stadium even when that upstate New York weather is brutal and ugly, and more important, even after the Bills suffered through *four* painful Super Bowl losses. It's easy to be a fan of a team that wins a billion championships, like the Packers, but difficult to stay in love with a franchise that falls in the championship on four occasions. I've seen fans at Bills games when the temperatures were hitting well below zero and the wind gusts could chip off pieces of your soul. And at least one Buffalo fan would be shirtless, a cold beer in his mitts. Or hers.

Game Official: Referee Jerry Markbreit

It's a close call between two men. Hugh "Shorty" Ray held the position of supervisor of officials from 1938 to 1952. Ray streamlined many of the league's rules to speed game tempo, and he was among the first NFL executives to focus on player safety. The other candidate is Jerry Markbreit, who has worked four Super Bowls, the only referee to do so. Markbreit gets the spot because he has been a part of football in more modern times, when the speed of players has made the sport more difficult to officiate.

Assistant Coach: Jimmy Raye—History

New York Jets head coach Herman Edwards learned one of his first lessons about loyalty some eight years ago. He was the defensive backs coach for the Kansas City Chiefs—a very good one, by all accounts— when Marty Schottenheimer, then the coach, called Edwards into his office and fired him.

Schottenheimer and Edwards had bumped heads repeatedly over how to coach the position, but the firing still shocked and angered a number of other assistants on the staff, especially after Schottenheimer replaced Edwards with Kurt Schottenheimer, his own brother. Some of the coaches were so furious that they went to Schottenheimer and protested. One of the strongest objections came from Jimmy Raye, the offensive coordinator. "I was disappointed in what happened because I didn't deserve to be fired," Edwards recalls. "But I'm going to stick with what I believe in. Jimmy is the same way. Jimmy went to Marty and said, 'This isn't right.'"

Edwards never forgot what Raye did and hired him as a senior offensive assistant for the Jets after staff members of the Washington Redskins, where Raye was again offensive coordinator for Schottenheimer, were released at the end of the 2001 season. Edwards and Raye initially became close when they were in Kansas City and on slow days during the off-season would hit the links. In between golf swings and chitchat Raye would talk of the past, of football history, and Edwards listened closely, soaking up Raye's words like a sponge. What Edwards discovered was that Raye was not simply talking about history; Raye was talking about himself, his career, and his experiences. Edwards realized Raye *was* history, and indeed, Raye had dedicated his life to the sport as much as anyone, despite facing ugly racism, both as a player and as a coach.

Raye's résumé is not filled with NFL championships, his fingers do not sport gaudy Super Bowl rings, and there are certainly a number of great assistant coaches in football's long history—such as Fritz Shurmur, who coached 24 years as an assistant—who also deserve the honor of the best assistant of all time. Raye's greatness is embodied in many different ways, like persistence—27 years coaching in the pros—and not walking away from the game when it occasionally treated him so poorly. In a way this is a lifetime achievement award.

There are few people who have had Raye's football life experience. He was one of the first black quarterbacks to lead a Division I-A school, doing so for three seasons at Michigan State. Under Raye, the Spartans won two Big Ten titles and a 1966 Rose Bowl berth. Raye also played in the "Battle of the Century" game against Notre Dame in 1966, which ended in a 10–10 tie. Raye's credentials as a quarterback were so impeccable that he should have been an automatic to play in the NFL, but discrimination blocked him. Raye entered the league in the late 1960s, when coaches and personnel men believed that blacks were intellectually incapable of playing quarterback and blacks were routinely switched from passers to other positions, usually defensive back, as Raye was in 1969 by Philadelphia. Frustrated by his lack of opportunities to play quarterback, he decided to become a coach. As a graduate assistant at Michigan State in 1973, Raye coached a walk-on player named Tyrone Willingham, a high school quarterback, who would go on to earn a scholarship and, decades later, become the first black head coach of Notre Dame. After Raye went to coach in the pros, his stints as an assistant included San Francisco, Detroit, Atlanta, the Los Angeles Rams, Tampa Bay, New England, Kansas City, Washington, and now the New York Jets.

Raye rarely got to work with the best of the best when it came to players. It seemed he was always putting out some fire or working on the staff of some stale, rebuilding franchise. Look at the sorry lineup of coach-killing quarterbacks Raye has had to work with in his career: Marc Wilson, Tony Banks, Jeff George, Steve Grogan, Vinny Testaverde, and Elvis Grbac, just to name a few. But during the 1990s, when Raye was with the Chiefs, where he spent the seasons from 1992 to 2000, Kansas City went 102–58, the best regular-season record for the decade behind San Francisco (113–47) and Buffalo (103–57).

Raye is approaching 60 years old. In a league that worships youth, Raye knows his window to become a head coach is rapidly closing. He deserved that opportunity years ago, and one reason he never received it, without question, is the color of his skin. There are legions of men like Raye who have been discriminated against but plod on, because they are devoted to what they do. "There isn't a nicer man, or a coach who has paid more dues," analyst Brent Musberger said of Raye during the telecast of New York's 2002 season playoff victory over Indianapolis. The passion of men like Raye overrides any bitterness, though in the end, if Raye does not get the opportunity to become a head coach, a part of him will always wonder why. "The only thing I would ever regret in my career is if I was denied a head coaching opportunity because of my race," Raye says. "That would truly sadden me."

Head Coach: Vince Lombardi—Perfection

The beginning of a story that appeared in the *Chicago Tribune* typifies how Lombardi's career changed the course of many lives, and not just those within the sport.

> *The late Vince Lombardi began his NFL head-coaching career with the Green Bay Packers in 1959. That same autumn future horse trainer D. Wayne Lukas went back to the University of Wisconsin to get his master's degree after two years as a teacher and basketball coach at tiny Blair High School in northwest Wisconsin.*
>
> *Over the next eight years, while Lukas was in graduate school, studying physical education and working as Wisconsin's assistant freshman basketball coach, and then as a teacher and coach at LaCrosse Logan High School, he became one of Lombardi's most fervent disciples. When Lombardi had a speaking engagement, Lukas would hit the highways and byways of Wisconsin to hear him, and took every word to heart.*
>
> *"I'd drive 80 miles, 120 miles, 150 miles to hear Vince speak," Lukas remembered. "He was very visible and very accessible. I bought into everything he said—the work ethic, what it takes to be No. 1, the whole nine yards. He was my role model. He still is my role model."*

There have been books written about the Lombardi years. His career has been examined and talked about in the detailed and reverential terms usually ascribed to American presidents. Lombardi had a 105–35–6 coaching record in ten years, including five NFL titles and victories in Super Bowls I and II. His influence, however, as illustrated by the story on Lukas, one of the greatest horse trainers of all time, grew beyond football. Lombardi's insistence on dedication and perfection was the standard for all NFL coaches who followed.

My only rap on Lombardi: his acid coaching style, his scream-fests, would not have worked with the modern, independent player. Can you imagine a guy like Terrell Owens being coached by Lombardi? Or Ricky

Williams, who thought Mike Ditka was too tough on him? Today's players would tune out Lombardi like he was a bad oboe in the Philadelphia
Symphony.

General Manager: Tex Schramm—Innovations

It was 1970, and prior to the Baltimore Colts' game against Dallas, Ernie
Accorsi, staring at the players from both teams as they took the field,
noticed a dramatic difference between them. The Colts players were, in
the words of Accorsi, "tubby and squishy-faced," while the Dallas players "were these six-four, six-five, square-jawed, physical specimens."
Accorsi turned to a friend and said of the Cowboys, "You're seeing the
future of football right there."

The transformation of the Cowboys into one of the top organizations in sports was mainly due to Tex Schramm. His greatest gift to football was the invention of a sophisticated scouting system—the first
ever—that emphasized faster, more athletic players over slower ones
who were heavy but not muscular. The Schramm System, started in the
1960s, would help the Cowboys dominate football for decades, and every
NFL team eventually copied it.

"I'm wincing when I say this because I hate the Cowboys," Accorsi
admits. "But there was no real scouting system until Schramm came
along. Don't let anyone tell you differently. He was the best innovator in
our sport."

Among his many remarkable contributions, Schramm invented the
play clock, was the father of the television instant replay, conceived of
putting microphones on referees, and headed the competition committee in its formative years. Much of the look of football today is owed to
Schramm.

When Jerry Jones fired Schramm in 1989, it led to years of bitterness between the two men. When Schramm was inducted into the Hall
of Fame in 1991, Jones had prevented him from being inducted into the
Cowboys' Ring of Honor. That changed in April 2003, when Jones
finally came to his senses and Schramm, at the age of 82 and in failing
health, was given his proper place in the Ring.

Owner: Wellington Mara—Caring Hand

A few months after the 1993 season, the Giants readied a room for a news conference to announce the release of their longtime quarterback Phil Simms. In the back of the crowded room sat Wellington Mara, the owner, with tears in his eyes. That says a lot. Mara is a man who rarely shows his emotions publicly; indeed, it has been his steady hands that have helped to craft one of the best franchises in professional sports.

Afterward Mara was asked for his thoughts on the Giants' controversial decision to let go of Simms. Instead of trying to sweet-talk his away around a delicate issue, he addressed it head-on and voiced his extreme displeasure at the move. "I was convinced it was a mistake at the time, but I went along with it," Mara said four years later. "I was not happy about it at all."

Ann Mara, his wife of more than 40 years, said: "I have rarely seen him so distraught. He felt close to Phil and was very upset. That was probably one of the saddest days of his life. He thinks the team let Phil go too early."

The story illustrates only one side of Wellington Mara, but it may be the side that in 1997 put him into the Pro Football Hall of Fame, joining his father, Tim. His service to the NFL, which began in the 1920s, brought him to Canton's entrance. His knowledge of the game opened that door. And his great skill as an organizer and his ability to hire high-quality men and coaches ushered him into the room.

Mara's greatest asset, however, is none of those things. It is his ability to combine competitiveness on the football field with compassion off of it. Mara has an intense desire to win, but unlike others in the sometimes-nasty world of sports, he has never lost his ability to care about the people who work for him. People like Simms. "I know of no owner since I've been in the NFL that equals Well's contributions, his fairness, his decency," says Art Modell.

Mara's affection for Simms was a result of his becoming close to the quarterback as a person and not seeing him as just property. Mara's loyalty to coaches, players, and employees is legendary. On numerous occasions he has extended a helping hand to Lawrence Taylor, trying to pull

Taylor from the quicksand of drug use once his playing days ended in 1993. He could have just ignored Taylor or merely sent him Christmas cards, but Mara has remained an integral part of Taylor's life. "That's something that is really personal and should not be discussed publicly," Mara says when asked about his relationship with Taylor.

"He has helped a million players," Ann Mara says, "and you may never know who they are because he won't talk about it."

When Modell had two heart bypass operations in the 1980s, Mara flew to the hospital to be by his side. He has helped former coaches get new jobs. He has friends in every city the team travels to, and Mara always takes one or two to dinner. Those who know him say he is impeccably honest. "The man is incapable of telling an untruth," Modell says. "Honest," says Ann Mara, "and doesn't curse. I'm not allowed to say 'damn' around the house."

Mara has been able to do something that few can accomplish: he has earned the respect of almost everyone around him without fostering the jealousy that sometimes accompanies success. The football business is like any other business—or life, for that matter—in that when people achieve a certain level of success, they sometimes become targets. But Mara is so well respected, Modell says, that when he speaks at owners' meetings, "you can hear a pin drop."

"A couple of years ago during an owners' meeting, I remember someone—I'm not going to mention his name—said something critical of Well," says Dan Rooney, the Pittsburgh Steelers owner and another Hall-of-Famer. "He stood up and said to Well, 'The only reason you like this proposal is because you can get the votes.' So I said, 'That should tell you something right there. He can get the votes because he is so respected.'"

So Mara has remained strong-willed, true to his word and values, without compromising himself. In other words, Mara has proved to be a great leader of the NFL and the Giants, choosing smart managers and people around him. And as the Super Bowl rings and accolades rolled in, he did not change what had got him there. He never lost his compassion.

You may think that now that he has made the Hall of Fame at age 80, he will relax. Play a little golf, stay away from the office, and let his son, John, completely run the show. "He has given John some of the reins, but he won't retire," Ann Mara says. "I don't think that will ever happen."

II

After Lawrence Taylor's second arrest in three years in October 1998 for crack cocaine possession, Taylor checked himself into a rehab clinic. But Taylor was broke. How did he pay for it? Mara quietly footed the bill. The only way I discovered that he had done so was through friends of Taylor's—Mara was incensed that I learned about it. In fact, Mara had paid for several such stints for Taylor, never asking the linebacker for a penny back of the tens of thousands of dollars he spent on his rehab.

What makes Mara special is loyalty—loyalty to his players, his coaches, his team, but most of all, the NFL. George Halas, the Chicago coach and owner, is the only other owner, with the possible exception of the Rooney ownership family, who approaches Mara's impact. Halas is the sole person associated with professional football throughout its first 50 years, and he carried the league practically on his back. Mara did something just as important, if not more so. Along the way, while work-ing as a ball boy, secretary, vice president, president, and then co-CEO of the Giants, Mara took it upon his own slim shoulders to make certain that the NFL did not disintegrate into what baseball has become, which is several distinct entities, all looking out for themselves. Mara was the biggest proponent of revenue sharing, and it is his presence alone that has kept more egocentric owners like Danny Snyder from having a more destructive influence on the sport.

What I have also always liked about Mara is his bluntness. He is direct and honest and rarely shies away from answering a question. When I once asked Mara if he had ever met Snyder, he responded, "Yes, we've met. I wouldn't use the word *charming* with him, but he's been fine." Mara was the first owner to publicly criticize Snyder: "I don't agree with a lot of what he has done, and I don't want to get specific about what I don't like," he said. "He is entitled to do what he wants, because he paid $800 million for the team. A lot of us old fogies wish we had made as much money as he has at that age. But I wonder if he is the type of person who will only look out for himself, instead of the well-being of the entire league."

When asked if he thought Snyder was a younger version of Jerry Jones, Mara joked, "Please don't say that." Then, with a serious tone, Mara said: "Let's hope he doesn't become an older Jerry Jones. That would be unfortunate. But I think he's headed in that direction."

For Mara, it is about looking out for the league first, something he has always done better than almost anyone in its history.

Commissioner: Paul Tagliabue—Multitasking

It is August 2001, and Paul Tagliabue is at 13,000 feet, in a slick Hawker 800 corporate jet traveling 500 miles an hour. His seat is comfortable leather, and there is enough room, barely, for his six-foot-five frame to stretch out. Tagliabue should be relaxed, but there is concern on his face, and it has nothing to do with the turbulence shaking the plane as it leaves Teterboro Airport in Bergen County, New Jersey, for Albany, the site of the Giants' training camp.

Tagliabue is the commissioner of the National Football League, and in his eleven years at the helm he has developed into a successful and respected leader. The NFL has never been more vibrant, and owners say much of the credit should go to him. Yet these are stressful days for Tagliabue and the NFL. On August 1 Minnesota Vikings offensive lineman Korey Stringer died of heatstroke, his death rocking the sport and making teams reexamine their practice of training players in extreme summer heat, something the league has done for almost a century without a fatality. Tagliabue is also dealing with the referees' contract, which has expired; he says that replacement referees could be used.

Tagliabue began the summer with an intense training camp tour: 5 teams, 400 players, and 1,000 miles in 60 hours, arriving back in New Jersey late Tuesday night after visiting the Giants, the Cleveland Browns, the Buffalo Bills, the Washington Redskins, and the Pittsburgh Steelers. He uses these trips to become familiar with coaches and players, and they with him. He visits various training camps each preseason.

The trip was planned months before, but it took on a new urgency following Stringer's death. Rather than cancel his plans, Tagliabue felt he needed to be in the field to address players' concerns about heat-related health risks. As it turns out, few players believe they are in danger. While Tagliabue made his training camp visits, he says that as tragic as Stringer's death was, making any significant changes in the training camp regimens would be alarmist. "This has saddened everyone, to be sure," he says. "But the worst thing we can do now is throw everything out and start over again."

Yet there is something that does make Tagliabue nervous, as well as trainers and team physicians, and that is players' use of nutritional supplements, which can cause dehydration and thus pose a health risk to players as they practice in the heat. Last December the NFL's adviser on anabolic steroids, John Lombardo, warned players in a one-page memo about the stimulant ephedra, which is often used in weight-loss supplements. Lombardo wrote that ephedra could "contribute to a number of dangerous, even fatal, medical conditions." Tagliabue says the league is considering adding ephedra—and other drugs used in supplements the NFL considers dangerous—to the banned substance list, meaning that if players consume these products, they will face a fine and possible suspension. "We're definitely headed in that direction," he says.

When Tagliabue arrives at the Giants' cafeteria on the SUNY-Albany campus, he grabs a plate of salad and meets with the Giants' coach Jim Fassel, and they talk football for more than an hour. At their table—in fact at every table—is an explanatory chart on how players should stay hydrated. The chart, which was there before Stringer's death, states that supplements "may be counter-productive to hydration goals."

Tagliabue, after talking with Fassel, mingles with the few players who are left in the cafeteria. One is wide receiver Amani Toomer, who tells the commissioner that in the playoff game against Philadelphia last season someone threw hot soup on him, burning his leg.

"What should I do about that?" Toomer asks.

Tagliabue smiles assuringly. "Let us look into it," he says.

On these trips he is queried about everything, from the normal to the bizarre. If he cannot answer the question immediately, he always follows up, with either a note or a phone call from him or someone in the NFL office.

The questions are just beginning in Albany. At 7:30 P.M. he speaks to the team in the Giants' huge meeting room, every player listening intently to the commissioner. One of the things Tagliabue says is: "Don't screw up off the field. Act like you're Tiger Woods, responsible for how your sport is seen by the public." Then, a few minutes later, linebacker Dhani Jones asks Tagliabue if there are any current studies on heat exhaustion. "The biggest issue in that area are supplements," Tagliabue says. "Some are pretty dangerous." Quarterback Kerry Collins then asks for details about the league's new apparel deal with Reebok, and cornerback Jason Sehorn, who likes to wear Nike, politely argues with Tagliabue about players having a choice in what they wear. "I was warned Jason likes to debate," Tagliabue says later.

On Monday morning, despite a 5:00 A.M. wake-up call, Tagliabue is fresh and talkative. On the plane to Cleveland he studies the Browns' roster and comes across the name Tre Johnson. It rings a bell. He turned to the veteran public relations man Greg Aiello in the next seat. "Didn't I suspend him?" Tagliabue says. Aiello says yes, then the catchall mind of Tagliabue kicks in, remembering that Johnson was disciplined for accidentally striking an official in the head while he was engaged in a fight with another player. "I guess I had better stay away from him," Tagliabue says with a smile.

By 9:00 A.M. he is at the Browns' practice facility, one of the most luxurious in the league. He is accompanied by a prestigious group of NFL executives: George Young, the former Giants general manager and senior vice president for football operations; Cedric Jones, director of consumer products, on-field operations, and the coaches' club; and Ed Reynolds, the assistant director of football operations, as well as Aiello.

Players are still breathing hard from practice when Tagliabue begins to address them on the field, and like the Giants, players on the Browns listen to every word. He tells them to stay hydrated and that the league has long been careful about heat exhaustion. Afterward head coach Butch Davis excuses seven players for the 40-minute drive to Warren, Ohio, the site of Stringer's funeral service, and they thank Tagliabue as they jog off the field. Tagliabue attended a memorial service for Stringer in Minnesota the previous week. "Sometimes because the league office is in New York, there is a feeling among teams that franchises like the Giants and Jets receive favoritism," Carmen Policy, the Browns' team president, says. "These visits by Paul prove that notion is totally false."

Policy then introduces Tagliabue to Johnson. "I already know the commissioner," the 326-pound offensive lineman says sheepishly. "He suspended me."

Several hours later Tagliabue, after another plane ride, after another van ride, and after another shirt change—he has gone from a Giants polo shirt to a Browns one to a Bills one—is in Pittsford, New York, the site of Buffalo's training camp. Tagliabue's message has not changed: conduct yourselves like professionals off the field, and both honor and learn from Stringer's death.

There are more questions about the new Reebok agreement than there are about Stringer. One player gets into an intense five-minute exchange with Jones and Reynolds about why he dislikes the Reebok deal. In fact, out of the 400 players Tagliabue will eventually speak to, only two players ask questions about what the league plans to do to prevent another death like Stringer's. About a half-dozen query him about Reebok. Why so few questions from players about such a serious subject? Many players say that, to them, heat-related issues are on the bottom of the list when it comes to their concerns. "From the time you play football at ten years old to now, a football player always knows how to deal with playing in heat," Pittsburgh quarterback Kent Graham says. "We don't worry about it much because we know how to handle it."

By Tuesday the NFL group accompanying Tagliabue is beginning to drag, but he does not, displaying the energy so many owners say is noticeable the instant they see him. Tagliabue inherited his work ethic from his father, Charles, a 6-foot-4, 275-pound owner of a Jersey City construction business who worked 15-hour days. Tagliabue's intellect matches his energy level, which makes him well suited to handle one of the most complicated and challenging jobs in sports.

Tagliabue says one owner told him: "It is like being the father of 32 children, some of whom are not potty-trained."

On the final morning of the trip, another hot day, following another shirt change, this time into one sporting the Redskins logo, Tagliabue meets his energy match, the Redskins' owner Snyder, who excitedly tells Tagliabue how pleased he is with the team's training camp. In the background coach Marty Schottenheimer can be heard yelling as players go through their drills: "Make sure you get some fluid in your tank!"

Before lunch Tagliabue meets with the Redskins players—again, no questions about Stringer. Then he meets with Schottenheimer and his assistants. The coaches say they think the league office should take a harsher stance against supplements. Tagliabue tells them that could happen. Later in the afternoon Tagliabue is in Latrobe, Pennsylvania, on the practice field with the Pittsburgh owner, Dan Rooney, and they are both baking in the 96-degree heat.

Tagliabue keeps his post-practice talk brief, realizing the players, gathered around him in the middle of the field, are extremely hot. Still, despite their discomfort, they listen closely to Tagliabue while nibbling on Popsicles handed out by the trainers. By 8:00 that night Tagliabue is in the back of the corporate jet, his feet propped up on the seat before him, cruising at 25,000 feet. He has spent the last two and a half days in towns like Carlisle, Pennsylvania, and slept in hotels like the Del Monte Lodge. And while others with him can barely keep their eyes open, Tagliabue, 60, is wide awake, telling funny air travel horror stories.

As the plane nears Teterboro and home, a thunderstorm rages a short distance away. Lightning dances across the sky, and the collective blood pressure inside the plane rises ever so slightly. Tagliabue lightens the mood. "Tell the pilot to land the plane now," he says. "I don't care if it's on a lake."

The plane lands in New Jersey just fine—on a runway—and Tagliabue declares, "Boy, what a trip."

||

The league would go on to ban the use of ephedra, the first major professional sports league to do so, and it was yet another example of one of Tagliabue's strengths—getting things done quickly, forcefully. Prior to that trip, like many members of the media, I believed Tagliabue was too stiff, too much the Georgetown lawyer, using too many words like "de facto," and too little the passionate commissioner. After spending time with Tagliabue on his trip for those few days, it became clear he was not that at all. Indeed, Tagliabue is a creative and scholarly force, a consensus builder with passion who has a truly thankless job: keeping the NFL on top.

Some people will say I am an utter fool to select Tagliabue over two other men. Former commissioner Bert Bell forged the modern image of the commissioner, and he set the outline for what the next commissioner, Pete Rozelle, would complete. Rozelle, thought of by many as the best commissioner in any sport ever, negotiated the NFL's first leaguewide television contract, which has been the lifeblood of NFL success. Many football observers and owners would rank Rozelle first, because of a myriad of accomplishments, Bell second, and Tagliabue third. The reason for Tagliabue's bronze medal, in the minds of some, is well described by a commissioner of another sport: "Paul fell into the prosperity that other commissioners built."

That's definitely a debatable point. But there are two reasons why I believe Tagliabue deserves the top spot. First, not to degrade Rozelle, but the fact is, owners like Mara, Modell, and others had more to do with negotiating the television agreement than Rozelle did, and truthfully, Unitas was the bridge between the old and new NFL. He had more to do with the explosion of football's popularity than the three commissioners combined.

Second, no commissioner, in any sport, at any time, has had to deal with the complications of today's football landscape that Tagliabue does. Here is just a brief list: free agency; the salary cap; players using dangerous performance-enhancing drugs like ephedra and human growth hormone; threatened lawsuits over the lack of black head coaches; labor disputes with game officials; more attention than ever on player violence and domestic abuse; saturated media coverage that holds a magnifying glass to every move of the NFL and its entities; the fear of terrorism; an increasing number of physically debilitated players; an exponential rise in the number of players suing their team doctors; far more powerful player agents; strong competition from other sports leagues (in the Bell and Rozelle periods, the NBA was barely a blip on the radar screen); rapid expansion; more self-centered owners; serial contract breakers like Parcells; a football union that is far more powerful than it has ever been;

and players who increasingly care little about authority, even the authority of the commissioner's office.

The NFL has a level of complexity to it, a depth, that Rozelle or Bell could not have imagined. Those two men were the pioneers of the office of football commissioner. Tagliabue's efforts are continuing that grand tradition—and in many ways surpassing it.

The Game 7^B

THE 40 COMMANDMENTS OF CZAR FREEMAN

On a hot and humid day in the summer of 2002, the former congressman and University of Oklahoma football player J. C. Watts, who also had a stint at quarterback in the Canadian Football League, decided to see if he still had a little somethin' left in the tank from his playing days. So Watts joined the Washington Redskins defensive backs for a few wind sprints after a training camp practice.

Watts was only 44 years old at the time. Presumably all of his mental faculties remained intact, so it is a mystery why he would attempt such a feat. After all, these are NFL players with world-class speed, not a bunch of scrubs at the YMCA playing six-on-six.

Off Watts went, and after only a few runs, off went his hamstring, bunching up like a twisted rubber band. Watts had a severe pull and actually needed help off the field. It definitely was not the kind of photo op that politicians usually look for.

Watts's act of silliness, however, was thoroughly outdone by Stuart Scott's act of outright stupidity. The ESPN anchor, a former high school football player, was preparing to do a three-part series on going through an NFL minicamp. Scott lined up for a drill in which footballs are caught from a high-velocity pass-throwing machine. When the ball came firing out, it moved too quickly for Scott's eyes to track and—*booyah!*—it smacked him in the left eye, splitting his cornea and lens. Scott needed surgery and missed two months of work before making a recovery. Momma always said stop horsing around or someone would lose an eye.

The lesson from both of these examples? Stay off the field, people. It's over. You're done. Leave the professional stuff to the professionals, please.

What Watts and Scott did was every fan's dream—spending a little time with NFL types in their environment. Better yet, hard-core fans have other wants, like a desire to lay down the law. Be commissioner. Straighten out football's flaws. Dictate. Yeah. What the sport needs is a good, old-fashioned czar who would kick NFL butt and ask questions later. What did you say? You would like to nominate me for the position? I humbly accept. Thus, the Starfleet commander/supreme football being hereby lists his 40 commandments to fine-tune football. More after I gobble up this press box hot dog.

1 Al Davis, files too many damn lawsuits. He's clogged up every court in California. He is sometimes a bit paranoid. Davis has often wondered why the media does not treat his organization with more respect. It's because, under his orders, he treats many reporters like they are a week-old cup of half-eaten yogurt. He meddles with his coaches too much, is mule stubborn, and his poor treatment of former great Raider Marcus Allen has been a disgrace. But the czar feels that Davis, despite his flaws, deserves respect. He is a pioneer, a Hall-of-Famer, one of the game's great, historic minds. He is one of the only owners who appointed a top woman executive in Amy Trask, as smart a person as there is in football. He hired the first Latino man, Tom Flores, to become a head coach in the NFL, and then the first black man, Art Shell, in the same capacity. Davis also serves as something else: he is a human check-and-balance for a league that sometimes is too full of itself.

2 Meanwhile, the czar has filed a restraining order against Jerry Jones. He is prohibited from going within 100 feet of a television camera until he makes a decent draft pick.

3 John Madden shall use only one "boom" per broadcast.

4 All grudges against Art Modell are hereby forgiven, and he is granted immediate entrance into the Hall of Fame. A lifetime of remarkable football accomplishments should not be wiped out by one mistake, as severe as it was.

5 The Super Bowl will never be played in a cold-weather city, as has been discussed by the NFL. It's unfair to fans who shell out thousands of dollars to watch a game while sitting in the stands during a blizzard. If the championship is played in New York or Washington, D.C., in January, then all media, owners, and NFL executives will be required to watch from the stands with the fans. If that happened, there would never be a cold-weather, outdoor game again.

6 Celebrations are allowed back into football games, but only after touchdowns. All gyrations, dances, twirls, shakes, bumps, and grinds are encouraged. The players who have the most original group celebration will receive a $1,000 bonus from the team, and it will not count against the salary cap. One addendum: no throat-slash gestures. Any player who does is suspended for one game.

7 The NFL will put a 100-year moratorium on expansion. The talent in the league is too thin as it is. Look at what rapid expansion did to baseball. It almost ruined it. The NFL is everywhere it needs to be, and unless a market opens up on Mars, no further expansion is needed. The czar will allow an NFL team to be put back in Los Angeles, but only if O.J. finds the real killer.

8 Perennially sorry franchises shall be punished. If the Cincinnati Bengals finish with one of their typical 3–13 seasons, they will be banished to the CFL for one year. If they fire another head coach, they must replace him with Anna Nicole Smith. I know this discipline is harsh, but too bad. I'm the king of the NFL now. Another losing season by the Detroit Lions, and they will be forced to play the Mean Machine.

9 The Pro Bowl all-star game shall be played each year in the city that had the team with the worst league record. That way fans there will get to see some real football.

10 Game officials shall be given a freakin' break. Immediately. Do you know how hard a job it is to officiate such a fast, violent game?

11 Danny Snyder, short in stature and long in tantrums, shall no longer fire employees en masse. He will no longer pull coaches into a room and berate them, as he did with Norv Turner before firing him. You bad boy, Danny. He will no longer use his pudgy media hit man, Karl Swanson, to swat at those pesky newspaper guys who dare write the truth about Danny Boy. Danny will use lit cigars only for their prescribed purpose. (Danny knows what the czar is referring to.) Danny will never again make asinine comments, as he did to *Newsweek*, which asked if he modeled himself after one of the league's more respected owners, Art Modell: "What model is Art Modell? He owned the team 42 years and won one Super Bowl." Well, let's see how many you win, Danny. But most of all, Danny will act like an adult. If he does not follow any of these edicts, the czar will put him in a room with Gary Coleman and let the two slug it out.

12 Paul Tagliabue, the excellent commissioner, is to be given a ten-year contract worth $100 million. He deserves it. He is one of the biggest reasons the NFL is so stable. When his contract expires, the league will hire Condoleezza Rice—if she isn't already the president of the country.

13 When Jerry Rice leaves the game, his number 80 will be retired, and no player in any sport will ever be allowed to wear it again.

14 Preseason games test the czar's patience. They are more boring than a congressional vote on C-SPAN. But the czar also realizes that a few are needed. Thus, today's four preseason contests, an unnecessarily large number considering players now study and stay in shape year-round, will be reduced to two.

15 Instant replay will be a permanent part of the game. It is better to get the call right than have all of America see how the refs blew it as fans watch five different angles of a screwed-up call. But the czar wants the process sped up. There is no need for a decision to take three minutes or longer. The czar has microwaved dinner in a shorter amount of time. The replay official will have 30 seconds to review the replay and decide if a call should be reversed. If he fails to complete the task within that amount of time, a trap door will open and the official will fall into a pit of vipers.

16 No player shall weigh over 400 pounds. It's getting ridiculous. Some defensive linemen are getting so portly, they don't walk, they float into orbit.

17 Those loud, obnoxious, blaring scoreboards that sound like fighter jets shall be abolished. The czar is worried about his long-term hearing loss.

18 Stadiums will no longer be named after companies. They will be named after Hall-of-Famers. Joe Montana Stadium. Mean Joe Greene Park. Crazylegs Pavilion. In other words, the

Packers got it right when they named their stadium Lambeau Field after famous Packer coach Curly Lambeau.

19 Any kicker who plunks a kickoff out of bounds shall be banned from the sport on the spot. If a professional who kicks a football every day in practice can't put one inside such a large area, he ain't ever gonna be any good.

20 The old-boy coaching network is abolished. The czar hates when more-than-qualified black candidates are passed over for a not-so-qualified white one because an owner or general manager is not "comfortable" with a black candidate. And what does "comfortable" mean, anyway? Should black candidates wear robes and slippers to interviews?

21 There will only be grass football fields. Forever. They're easy on the knees and easy on the eyes. The NFL will also pay for all high school fields to be converted to grass.

22 Those Frisbee-grabbing dogs will always be a part of half-time shows during regular-season games. Nothing bumps them. Not Whitney Houston. Not Up With People. Not Lil Bow Wow. Dogs, baby!

23 Rookies entering the NFL will not have a chip on their shoulder. They are newly made millionaires. What is there to be so angry about? Relax, fellas. Cut the attitude. This shall be called the "Jeremy Shockey Rule."

24 Gene Upshaw, the union executive director, shall be recognized as one of the great leaders in all of sports. He has earned it.

25 Before Marshall Faulk waltzes into the Hall of Fame a few years from now, the czar orders him to smile more than once a season.

26 The 1,000-yard rushing statistic has become extremely over-rated. In a 16-game season that's just 62.5 yards a game. Most good running backs can hit that mark sleepwalking. The new standard for ground excellence is hereby 1,300 yards.

27 Albert Einstein once said that the greatest experience we can have is the mysterious. That would explain Ricky Williams, the bizarre dreadlocked one. The czar orders that no NFL player shall wear a wedding dress on a national magazine cover ever again.

28 When a wide receiver bravely crosses the middle, makes a catch, and gets pulverized, as happens 90 percent of the time in the NFL, upon getting up he shall get a kiss from the most beautiful woman in the stadium.

29 There shall never be a punt on fourth-and-1. Ever. Offenses must always go for it. Hey, these are all big boys who get big bucks. Earn those paychecks. And since punters will have more free time, during games they can escort fans to their seats.

30 Any idiot fan or knucklehead member of the media who uses the word "wimp" or the phrase "he lacks heart" when describing an NFL player shall be sentenced to five years of playing middle linebacker. Or fullback. Let's see how soft they think players are after a few of their own spinal contusions.

31 There will be no more sideline interviews during NFL broadcasts. With the exception of those by Armen Keteyian, a skilled reporter, they are a total waste of oxygen. Consider this scintillating thought from actress/model Jill Arrington, who masquerades as a football sideline reporter for CBS. Her comment was part of a rated-PG photo spread for a men's magazine. "There was this mannequin named Ike that took a real liking to me one game and asked me for a kiss," Her Jillness explained, referring to a prop some fans had brought into a football game she was working. "At the next game he showed up dressed in a tuxedo and asked me to marry him." Why wonder what defense a team is playing or question a coach's decision to go for it on fourth down when there is hard-hitting information like that available? Does the czar desire rose-petal-soft questions lobbed by soft "journalists"? Nope. Instead, there will be "The Wheel of Truth," and selected players must take a turn. Thus, the only job of a sideline reporter is to spin the wheel and be propositioned by mannequins. The wheel has six questions:

1. Which coach do you think is the most overpaid in the NFL? Explain.
2. Which teammate do you hate the most? Why?
3. Does Joe Theismann talk too much?
4. Boxers or briefs? Please elaborate.
5. How many guns are in your locker right now?
6. Who's cuter: your wife or your wife's sister?

32 The NFL higher-ups constantly cater to television. That's because TV paid the league $17.5 billion for broadcast rights. Big deal. After all, what's a few billions between friends? The lifeblood of the NFL is the print media, but we are treated like a foot fungus. Meanwhile, TV heads get to go into the locker room and film halftime speeches. TV heads get to go onto the field during games. TV heads get better access. Yes, the czar is whining and wants better treatment for his print sisters and brothers. Thus granted immediately, a print football writer shall receive the following during games. A pedicure. A massage from J. Lo, or for my women reporter friends, one from Denzel. Leather chairs that move on a conveyor belt from the press box to the locker room for interviews so the writer never has to leave his or her seat. Family pets are allowed in the press box—but no cats. They go on the field with the TV heads. The czar doesn't want any felines walking across his keyboard on deadline. And cats make the czar sneeze. One last thing. Every writer shall receive five packs of Bubble Yum chewing gum. Grape flavored.

33 Every fan shall have the opportunity to meet Giants co-owner Robert Tisch, one of the nicest people in sports.

34 The Hall of Fame selection process needs a wrench put to it. There are too many grudges and personal agendas that affect the selections and keep good candidates out. Discrimination happens because the voting is done in secret. The czar orders that every vote be published on NFL.com along with a 100-word explanation from each selector.

35 The pension plan for older, disabled former players shall be tripled. The league and union can afford it. That hundreds of ex-NFL warriors are now financially struggling and physically broken is football's greatest shame.

36 There will be a day set aside each season for recognition of the efforts put forth by assistant coaches. They work 15-hour days most of the year, earn a fraction of the salaries of players and head coaches, and are often recognized only when something on the unit they coach goes wrong.

37 After each season, players are required to watch classic football movies like *Everybody's All-American* and *Rudy* and *Brian's Song*. This would be done so players never forget that they play football first because they love it.

38 The czar believes chop blocking is one of the more gutless acts in sports. It ruins careers. Players who commit this disgusting maneuver shall be sentenced to paying for any injuries sustained by their victim and must apologize to him and his family.

39 Boomer Esiason and Chris Russo's *Inside the Huddle* football show shall be required listening for all football fans. Sometimes the two talk-show hosts are a tad obnoxious, but I now believe there is nothing better for a football addict like the czar than listening to Boomer and Chris talking football. They're entertaining, extremely knowledgeable, and have a bit of an attitude.

40 Opening week shall be a seven-day holiday for all Americans so there is plenty of time to digest just how lucky we are that football is here.

The 7^c Game

99 REASONS WHY FOOTBALL IS BETTER THAN BASEBALL

I like baseball. I always watch it when I really, really need to fall asleep. It's a great sport—compared to soccer. There is nothing more exciting than sitting through regular-season game 78 as the Tampa Bay Devil Rays, with its minor league payroll, lose 15–0 to the New York Yankees, who have more money than Canada.

Baseball is good for one thing. Passing time until football training camps open. How much better a sport is football than baseball? Let us count the ways, 99 times.

1 My mother hates baseball, and she is the smartest person I know.

2 A sport that has players constantly grabbing their crotches can't be all that sophisticated.

3 Donald Fehr.

4 A pulled hamstring sidelines a baseball player for six weeks. Jack Youngblood, a star defensive lineman from the 1970s, once played in the Super Bowl with a broken leg.

5 There's no tobacco spitting in football. What a disgusting habit.

6 While there is no crying in baseball, as Tom Hanks declared in the movie *A League of Their Own*, tough, hardened footballers have been known to shed a tear or two, and that's a good thing.

7 NFL head coaches don't wear those silly, form-fitting polyester uniforms like baseball managers do. Real leaders don't sport tights.

8 Footballs aren't juiced.

9 The NFL commissioner has power. Real power.

10 The NFL doesn't allow ties in its all-star games.

11 Cheerleaders.

12 Quarterbacks have three to five seconds to release the football, or they get hit. Simple. Pitchers take forever to deliver the baseball: rub the cap, scratch the rear end, stare at the catcher for a few seconds, spit, scratch again, spit, and then pitch. Enough already.

13 Statistics are part of the NFL, not all of it.

14 The NFL has a comprehensive testing program for steroids. Baseball crosses its fingers and hopes the majority of its veteran players aren't using.

15 Football's union realized long ago that in its dealings with management, cooperation does not mean capitulation.

16 Football requires tougher athletes with more guts.

17 Most football game officials are in excellent physical condition. Baseball's umpires need a salad or two. They're all shaped like John Candy.

18 *NFL Films.*

19 The NFL has better Joes: Montana, Gibbs, Morris, Klecko, Theismann, and Namath, to name a few.

20 Baseball tops out at 162 games. Have they ever heard the phrase "less is more"?

21 Baseball recently went to a wild-card system. Wonder where MLB got that idea?

22 Baseball players drink way too much beer. Look at those guts.

23 Actors who have played football players: Warren Beatty, Kathy Ireland, Tom Cruise, and Dennis Quaid. Actors who have played baseball players: Kevin Costner, Wesley Snipes, Tom Berenger, and Dennis Quaid. Winner: football.

24 Actor who has played a football coach: Denzel Washington. Actor who has played a baseball coach: Keanu Reeves. Winner by a mile: football.

25 Chicago Cubs outfielder Sammy Sosa drops too many fly balls to make so much money.

26 Baseball players don't hustle. Is it too much to ask Barry Bonds to run hard to first base after every ground ball?

27 "One Mississippi, two Mississippi, three Mississippi, four Mississippi, five Mississippi."

28 A good report card meant I could stay up late and watch the Washington Redskins on *Monday Night Football*. A bad report card meant tickets to a Baltimore Orioles game.

29 One offensive lineman consistently offers a more intellectual quote than ten baseball players.

30 A tiny, frozen, small market wonder like Green Bay can win it all.

31 A tiny, frozen small market like Milwaukee can't.

32 Serious revenue sharing.

33 What, exactly, does a baseball manager do?

34 The NFL's draft actually has a moment or two of drama.

35 Football, as far as we know, has never had its version of a Black Sox scandal, the World Series blowup that is often cited by sports historians as one of the worst events in the annals of professional sports.

36 Then there is the lovely case of Steve Howe. In 1994 the New York Yankees signed the pitcher despite his being given a "lifetime" ban two years earlier for his seventh drug suspension. Seven suspensions? What is Howe? A cat?

37 Jackie Robinson broke the color barrier in 1959, but it took the Boston Red Sox another 13 years to hire their first black player, Pumpsie Green.

38 Football has had its own problems in terms of hiring blacks to become head coaches. But there hasn't been anything in the recent history of the sport that approaches the ugliness of the words coming from the mouth of former baseball executive Al Campanis, who told Ted Koppel that black players lack the "necessities" to become managers.

39 Nothing in baseball comes close to the excitement of a perfectly executed blitz, a toes-just-inside-the-sideline catch, or 60 minutes of watching Michael Vick.

40 Professional football is a thinking person's game. It requires preparation and study. Baseball is "grab a mitt and a bat and let's play."

41 There's no tailgating in baseball. You haven't lived until you've hung out with the Packers faithful and their cold-weather barbecues behind the parking lot of Lambeau Field.

42 How many professional baseball players try professional football? Not many. Know why? Why would a baseball player give up his cushy job for a real one?

43 Football tests for ephedra.

44 Football tests for human growth hormone.

45 Baseball tests your patience. Games can last four or five hours, which is ridiculous. Some wars have been fought in less time.

46 Short of military and astronaut training, NFL summer camps are among the toughest physical feats to complete. Baseball's spring training consists of playing catch and playing golf.

47 A Lawrence Taylor pass rush.

48 A Jim Brown run.

49 A Mike Singletary crushing tackle.

50 Too many raindrops and a baseball game is canceled. Football contests are played in monsoons. And speaking of the weather, it's always amusing how baseball players talk of getting too cold when the temperature dips into the fifties. They put on their little parkas and fuzzy little sweaters and start a campfire around home plate. Could a baseball player have survived the Ice Bowl?

51 In baseball you need a calculator to figure out a simple play. A 6–4–3? Everyone knows first-and-10. Everyone knows "Montana to Rice—touchdown!"

52 The "Hail Mary."

53 Instant replay. The NFL wants to get the calls right. That's a good thing.

54 How's this for passion: Rickey Henderson, considered one of the greatest baseball players of all time, and Bobby Bonilla, both with the Mets, played cards in the clubhouse during a game six loss of the 1999 National League Championship Series. Talk about supreme indifference. Can you imagine Dan Marino, while the defense is on the field during a heated AFC title game, playing a few hands of gin rummy? One word: no.

55 End-zone celebrations. Most of the time they're funny and fun.

56 In the opening game of the 1996 American League Champi- onship Series at Yankee Stadium, a 12-year-old little snot named Jeffrey Maier reached over Tony Tarasco, Baltimore's right fielder, and grabbed Derek Jeter's fly ball, which gave the Yankees a game-tying home run. How's that for a well-run sport? A preteen affects the outcome of a vital postseason game.

57 Now this is a fan. Michael Pantazis leaped some 25 feet from a concrete wall during a Monday night Chicago–Green Bay game in an attempt to snag an extra point. He made national news. That's a football fan for you. Daring, passionate, and knows how to stay the hell out of the way of the game.

58 Speaking of fans, when a crazed, out-of-control one races onto a baseball field, baseball players allow security to han- dle the situation. Football players tackle the guy themselves.

59 Mike Ditka is a reason football is better than baseball because *Saturday Night Live* based an entire skit around his fiery and eclectic character. Baseball managers are too boring to make fun of.

60 A play clock. Football has it. It keeps the game moving and fluid.

61 Super Bowl commercials. They're more entertaining than some movies. Advertisers don't bother spending all that cash on a World Series contest. No one's watching.

62 Ted Turner and Jane Fonda attended Atlanta Braves games together and played kissy-face in the stands. Yuck.

63 There is no owner in baseball with the class of Wellington Mara.

64 There is no owner in baseball who knows as much about that sport as Art Modell knows about football.

65 If baseball ever had managers like Bill Parcells, always barking, always telling the players how they suck, half of the players would hit their shrinks' couches. But football guys hear that crap and keep on moving on.

66 Baseball managers don't even shake hands after games; football coaches do. Where's the sportsmanship? Where's the love?

67 One Halloween night Albert Belle chased some kids trick-or-treating away from his house. Now that's not very nice. If the kids had happened to stumble upon the house of, say, 340-pound former defensive lineman Tony Siragusa, he would have invited them in and told a few jokes. ("How many baseball players does it take to change a lightbulb?" Siragusa would quip. "Zero. Because the union doesn't allow its players to do such things without permission.") The kids would have gotten plenty of candy too, because Siragusa would have 32 boxes of Snickers stashed under his bed.

68 The Bill Cowher glare.

69 A recent Yankees-Oakland game lasted six hours. Think about all the things you can do in six hours. You could go to the moon in six hours.

70 Baseball has purists. Purists are whiners pining about the good old days before wild-card playoff games and the time when those damn colored folk had their own league. C'mon. Relax. You know why football doesn't have purists? Football fans enjoy the game for what it is, not for what it once was, or will be.

71 Football has surprise. Football has suspense. You don't know who will win the Super Bowl. Consider the last *three* champions prior to the 2002 season: New England in 2001, Baltimore in 2000, and St. Louis in 1999. None had winning records the previous year.

72 If one more B-list celebrity sings "Take Me out to the Ball Game" at a Chicago Cubs contest, I'm going to go to Wrigley Field and tear down all that ivy, after I disconnect the stadium's audio system.

73 The single-bar facemask.

74 The Lambeau Leap.

75 The Dawg Pound.

76 David Justice, the baseball player, was once married to Halle Berry, the beautiful Academy Award–winning actress. Now, how smart can a baseball player be when he breaks up with Ms. Berry?

77 ESPN reporter Andrea Kremer—the best thing to happen to football since the heated press box.

78 Football is a great sport for kids. A bunch of buddies get together, find a field or street corner, grab a football, and go long. No gloves. No bats. No bases.

79 Football is also a better date sport. You know. Two-hand touch.

80 Only football could produce a likable character like Hall of Fame quarterback and country boy Terry Bradshaw. Yeeeee-haawww!

81 The NFL has a superior minor league system. It's called college football.

82 The elements. Wind, snow, rain, frozen beer—all are what make a football contest more unpredictable and fun to watch.

83 Jim Kelly, the former Buffalo quarterback, invited a record 1,114 people to his Hall of Fame induction. No baseball player has that many friends.

84 Deion Sanders, the former two-sport star, once told me that baseball was a nice "vacation" from the rigors of football. No one ever describes playing football as a "vacation."

85 The Pro Bowl is in Hawaii.

86 A measly 5,167 people peppered the bleachers for a Friday night Florida Marlins–Milwaukee Brewers game last season. The WNBA gets better attendance.

87 Meanwhile, that same night, a pre-preseason scrimmage between the Houston Texans and Dallas Cowboys drew 27,536. *A scrimmage. Featuring an expansion team.*

88 Dogs are a superior species, and they love football. It's their kind of sport, with lots of running and chasing. Cats, more boring than a calculus class, are definitely baseball fans.

89 When a sport talks of contraction, you know it is on life support. Baseball seriously erred when it added four teams in the 1990s. That's too fast and too many. Even the NFL, which has expanded too much in my opinion, will probably put a team in Los Angeles and then not expand again for decades.

90 John Rocker.

91 "He Hate Me."

92 Steve Rushin of *Sports Illustrated* wrote: "Football is Paris. Baseball is Paris, Texas."

93 Fighting is a bad thing. We want to teach our children not to fight. But if you're gonna fight, then fight. Fifty players will leave the bench in a baseball brawl, and not one will throw a punch. But two football players will smash each other's faces in.

94 Sportsvision Inc. launched a website (www.lovetheline.com) so fans could express their great affection for the yellow electronic first-down marker the company developed for television football coverage. Thousands responded.

95 Football has quotes from players like Cleveland's Gerard Warren, a third-year player, who said, when asked if he felt like a seasoned veteran, "Maybe not a seasoned vet, but a marinating one."

96 Al Michaels.

97 Ernie Accorsi.

98 My wife covers football, and she's the second-smartest person I know (see reason number 1 for the first).

99 Most of all, football is better than baseball because football is back for another season.

Afterword

END ZONE

In researching a book about a Trappist monk—no, not Art Monk—named Thomas Merton, a poet and author of more than 70 books, historian and football fan James Harford came across one of Merton's journal entries. In *The Other Side of the Mountain,* written in the final year of his life, Merton described August 26, 1968, a rare evening spent with friends watching television in Louisville, Kentucky, about 30 miles from his monastery in Gethsemani, Kentucky. The passage, as Harford wrote, is an unusual and eloquent description of American professional football.

> *Finally, a crowning American ritual, sitting dead tired with a glass of bourbon in the lounge of the Franciscan Friary watching pro football on TV—at midnight!!*
>
> *The Packers beat the Dallas Cowboys—and it was, I must say, damn good football because it was preseason and many contracts depended on it.*
>
> *Football is one of the really valid and deep American rituals. It has a religious seriousness which American religion can never achieve. A comic, contemplative dynamism, a gratuity, a*

*movement from play to play, a definitiveness that responds to
some deep need, a religious need, a sense of meaning that is at
once final and provisional: a substratum of dependable regularity, continuity, and an ever renewed variety, openness to new pos-
sibilities, new chances. It happens. It is done. It is possible again.
It happens. Another play is decided, played out, "done" (replay
for the good ones so you can really see how it happened) and
that's enough, on to the next one—until the final gun blows them
out of the huddle and the last play never happens. They disperse.
Cosmic breakup. Final score, 31–27, is now football history. This
will last forever. It is secure in its having happened. And we saw
it happen. We existed.*

Peter King is not a monk but a longtime journalist for *Sports Illustrated*
and one of the best football writers of our time. In a September 2002
Internet column for the CNN/SI website, King put it best in explaining
why the NFL is so popular now. Professional football, more than any
other sport, sells hope.

> *Pete Rozelle preached parity. Paul Tagliabue, without say-
ing so, has made it his mantra. There's more drama, more hope
for the formerly hopeless, today than yesterday. In the first nine
seasons with free agency, 29 of 30 teams (excluding 1999 expansion entry Cleveland) made the playoffs; only prehistoric
Cincinnati hasn't. Of the 36 spots in the conference championship
games over those nine years, 22 different teams filled them. Sixteen different teams filled the same number of slots in the nine
years before free agency. The day of the dynasty is over, and,
unlike baseball, which has the Yankees to either love or hate, it's
highly unlikely any team will be a conference champ four or five
years in a row ever again. But who does that hurt? By autumn
2003, 17 of the league's 32 teams will have built new stadiums or
radically refurbished their own over the past decade. Ten years
after the Patriots had 23,000 season-ticket holders in a Division
1AA-quality stadium, New England will open a new, sold-out,
60,000-seat palace in Foxboro, Massachusetts, this fall—with*

48,000 hopefuls waiting to buy tickets on a paid season-ticket waiting list.

It's not all free agency. It's not all the salary cap. But the free market and the cap on spending have combined to produce hope annually. What this free-agency-with-cap system has done in the NFL is sell hope to the good, the mediocre, and the bad.

On Saturday afternoon, I visited Arizona coach Dave McGinnis at his hotel in the Maryland suburbs. We talked about how the circus was in town with the Steve Spurrier debut, and McGinnis appreciated it. "You know what your team is this week?" I told him. "The Washington Generals." That's how it felt, really. Spurrier coached the Globetrotters, and McGinnis had a team sneaking in for the payday. But you know what? The Cardinals were OK. They were more than OK, in fact. They scratched and clawed and there they were, with the ball in Jake Plummer's hands, down a touchdown and a two-point conversion at the Arizona 19 with just over a minute to go. They were in it. Plummer threw his first pick of the season to end the game, but they were in it. That's the thing about this league. Twenty-eight teams, give or take a couple, are in it every week. That's why this is such a great game right now.

Two scenes I witnessed, one at the beginning of last season and one at the very end, may even better explain football's popularity. It is July 2002 and thousands of Carolina Panthers fans crowd the practice field in Spartanburg, South Carolina, to watch their team. Before drills, a few players sign autographs and tousle kids' hair, and the team mascot, "Sir Purr," dressed in a black furry Panther suit, dances for the crowd. It is miserably hot, about 95 degrees and sticky, in the middle of the day, and it is a meaningless training camp practice of a team that the year before had one of the worst records in football. Yet there are fans as far as the eye can see, filled with optimism—and hope. And in a salary cap era, when most of the NFL's teams have a realistic chance at the postseason, that hope is not unrealistic. It is this fact that makes professional football such a superior sport to baseball, the former pastime.

Fast forward to Super Bowl XXXVII. Tampa Bay quarterback Brad Johnson, an NFL castoff for much of his career who bounced around from Minnesota to Washington to Tampa Bay, is smiling ear to ear after winning the championship over Oakland. The man many football fans just a few years ago couldn't have identified if his face had been on the back of a milk carton is now world-famous. He's on top of the sport, no longer invisible, a star on a team of stars. "This is an incredible feeling," Johnson says. "One time in your life to say that you are the best in the world. It doesn't last very long, but for one moment it's incredible.

"What a game," Johnson says. "What a game."

Answers to Wonderlic Personnel Test Questions

1   1—True

2   84 cents

3   One

4   3—Neither the same nor the opposite

5   300 feet

6   6 feet

7   September

8 .33

9 17

10 $560

11 3—Not certain

12 40 years old

Acknowledgments

This book could not have been written without the superb editing skills of Susan Thornton Hobby, who juggles kids and adverbs with the greatest of ease. Mauro DiPreta at HarperCollins gave me the opportunity to wax about the NFL, and for that I am appreciative. His assistant, Joelle Yudin, is kind and sharp. Thanks also to my agent, John Monteleone of Mountain Lion, always a supportive voice.

Jon Gruden, Michael Strahan, and Steven Thompson provided me with a better understanding of the NFL world, with both their actions on the field and their conversations off of it, and for that I am eternally grateful. Those chapters were written with the help of dozens of NFL players and team and league executives. I thank them all.

Condoleezza Rice allowed me to talk football with her at the White House. It doesn't get much better than that.

Mike Utley and his foundation helped me understand how life after a devastating football injury can still be vibrant and important. Dr. Maria Gonzalez read the Steven Thompson chapter with a critical eye. Larry Kennan, head of the NFL's coaching association, provided valuable insight into the health issues facing coaches. Attorney David Rudolf, sports psychologist Mitch Abrams, and Christine Hansen of the

Miles Foundation wrote excellent responses to my antiviolence plan. Gruden's agent, Bob LaMonte, is one of the most powerful men in professional football, but he has managed to stay remarkably grounded and was a tremendous help to me for the coaching section. Profootballtalk.com and Sportspages.com were invaluable.

Most of all, I would like to thank the many NFL coaches and players—and their wives—as well as team and league officials who answered my phone calls and e-mail messages at all hours of the night and dared to go to various lunch and dinner gatherings to endure my many nosy questions.